IN SEARCH OF THE BRICKS OF HISTORY

BASIL SAFFER

Published by
The General Shale Museum
P.O. Box 3547
Johnson City, Tennessee, 37602

Library of Congress Catalog Card Number: 94-75573
ISBN 0-9641277-0-9

Printed in the United States of America.

Cover photograph: 2000 year-old Dagoba (tomb),
Anuradhapura, Sri Lanka

To Judy
who kept a stiff upper lip whilst
her husband wandered the world.
Also, to
George C. Sells II,
who backed me all the way.

CONTENTS

"....and the bricks are alive at
this day to testify it."
Wm. Shakespeare

CHAPTER 1

AFGHANISTAN, AT LAST.

When I was nine years old, I surprised my mother by remarking that I wouldn't like to have the problems of King Amanullah of Afghanistan. Thanks to a children's newspaper that arrived every Thursday, my sisters, my brother and I had the advantage of having knowledge of world affairs from our first reading days. Those being the heady days of the fabulous British Empire, we were well aware of the glorious exploits of our troops who had been fighting the stubborn Afghans on India's Northwest Frontier for a century. One year after my comment on the poor state of affairs in Afghanistan, Amanullah abdicated. Some 46 years later, on a bracing April morning, I flew into Kabul airport to try to find two ancient bricks for the General Shale Museum of Ancient Brick and see for myself just what England's former enemies were really like.

Getting my visa from the small Afghan embassy in Washington had necessitated three visits and each time I had found just one person in the basement receiving area. I had written several letters to Kabul, with copies to the embassy, and sent some brochures on our museum along. Finally, I got three copies of a visa which the embassy minister stapled inside my passport. He assured me that my request to "rescue" two ancient bricks had been approved in Kabul and that I would have no problems on that score.

A couple of weeks before I left for Afghanistan, a former assistant of mine sent me an article which mentioned that during the previous year some two dozen American tourists had mysteriously disappeared whilst in Afghanistan. I was not unduly alarmed knowing that these disappearances were probably caused by the lost tourists disregarding the first rule of traveling in Moslem countries...keep away from the ladies. Still, one week prior to my departure, I was at the University Museum in Philadelphia when word was received that one of their expeditions in Afghanistan had been fired upon by bandits.

Another friend of mine, an archaeologist who had worked in Afghanistan for a number of years, told me to be very careful when talking to the Director of Archaeology over there. He said the man had been suspected of illegally selling many of the rare Afghan antiquities and not to mention his name to the Director because he was one of the persons who had brought up the accusations.

So there I was, awed by the sight of the majestic Hindu Kush mountains to the north, walking from the plane into the Kabul arrival hall. The place was shabby and uninviting. As I walked through the door, I found a group of men crowding the entrance. Each was calling out a name and was holding a piece of cardboard with a name printed on it. I had arranged for a private guide and a car to be at my disposal as soon as I arrived in Kabul. I espied my man immediately. He was a short rotund fellow, dressed in western clothes carrying the largest card, which bore my name. I pointed to him and he pushed through the throng, grabbed me by the arm and just said one word, "Visa." I handed him my passport and he pushed through another line that had been formed for the immigration authorities. It was impressive to see how much influence he had. He slapped my passport down in front of one of the officers and just nodded in my direction. The officer tore out one of the visas, stamped the passport, returned it to "my man" and waved me through.

My cicerone then introduced himself as the head guide of the government tourist bureau, having been a guide for over twenty years. I estimated his age at around forty. He pointed to a tall thin man also in western clothing with a peaked chauffeur's cap and told me that he was our driver. We went over to where the baggage was being dumped. I got to my single case which was immediately picked up by the driver. We were supposed to go through Customs but, here again, we were just waved through.

We got to our car where my guide held the open the door to the rear for me. His face fell when I told him that I always rode in the front, and I got in next to the driver. It was the poor guide, not I, who spent the next few days sliding around in the back of the car. I expressed the desire that we ought to go straight to my hotel. However, the guide said I was expected at the Foreign Ministry, so that's where we headed.

The ride was rapid and I didn't get much of an opportunity to look closely at the people on the streets, or the city itself which appeared to have grown up a mountain side. I was deposited at the door of the ministry and told to go up one flight of steps and turn left. This I did and found myself in a large open office with several desks occupied by obviously very busy clerks. At the far end of the office, in the center of the wall, was an oversize desk behind which was sitting a smiling, well dressed bearded gentleman. I walked up to him and he stood up, shook hands with me and, addressing me by name, asked me to be seated. He introduced himself as Mr. Hosseini. What surprised me was the fact that his English was absolutely perfect with a strong Cambridge accent. As he looked at the titles on about a dozen dossiers perched on the edge of the desk, he asked if I had a pleasant trip. Finally, he pulled out one of the red folders, opened it and looked at its contents. From where I was sitting I could easily recognize our museum's letterhead and one of our brochures. While he read, he asked me for my passport and relieved it of one of the two remaining visas.

As he continued perusing the documents, I brought up a subject I had long contemplated. I asked Mr. Hosseini if arrangements could be made for me to travel with the nomadic Kuchis for a couple of days. He looked at me and slowly shook his head saying, "That, Mr. Saffer, would be rather uncomfortable and dangerous." My reply was that I could stand discomfort and that surely, in a Moslem country, as a guest of the tribe I would be perfectly safe. No go! His excuse was that there were no Kuchis anywhere in the area and that I had more faith in his countrymen than he. So we got down to the matter of an export permit for the two bricks I hoped to get.

"Ah," said he, "that has to be issued by the Director of Archaeology and since tomorrow is The Prophet's birthday, a national holiday, you must go directly to the museum and talk to him now." "I thought," said I, "that had already been approved." "Sorry, old boy," came the reply, "but things have changed since we last wrote to you. Just run along and see the Director and talk to him about it."

I didn't like the turn in the conversation. I had asked about traveling with the Kuchis in one of my first letters and had hoped they would have made arrangements for me to join up with a group. (The Kuchis are, as I have written, nomads and they adhere to the strictest Islamic Code. If they could tolerate me, my safety was assured. They travel with the weather and the grazing, making something like a semicircular tour of Afghanistan.) Now, here was a setback in the export license. I remembered what my archaeologist friend had told me about the Director and it didn't make me feel at all comfortable.

I invited Mr. Hosseini to be my lunch guest at The Intercontinental at 1 p.m. He accepted very gracefully, and I scooted down the stairs and into the car. The driver already knew where we were supposed to be going. Incidentally, the driver spoke perfect English, also, but only when forced to.

As we raced towards the museum a few miles away, my guide started pointing out places of interest. We approached a large English style edifice which he told me was the Parliament building. I had one of my three cameras at the ready and, before the guide could stop me, I got a nice wide angle shot of the place. The guide told me that it was against the law to photograph Government buildings. That, however was my modus operandi all the time I was in the country. I would shoot first and then listen to his complaint.

I have always made it a rule never to discuss politics in foreign countries. It is none of my business. My job is to collect specimens for the museum and, at the same time, make picture studies of life in whichever country I'm in. This time, however, I did remark that the Parliament building looked quite deserted. My guide said that the building had never been occupied. That national elections to seat a parliament had never been held. According to him, all members could be appointed by the King. At the time I was there the King ruled with a cabinet of twelve men selected by the monarch! He pointed out the King's residence to me...a quick picture was snapped followed by a reminder that I mustn't do such things. The monarch was not in residence; he was in Italy for his annual medical exam from which he has still not returned!

Finally, we arrived at the museum which was a large old residence, the conversion of which was still being worked on. I entered and found myself in a long hallway. A few feet inside the entrance, one on the left and the other on the right, stood two carved stone phalluses. Each was about four feet high with faint designs etched into the surface. These were obviously trophies from centuries' old raids into Hindu India where the phallus was, and still is, worshipped. The walls of the wide balustraded staircase ahead of me had several antique Afghan rifles mounted on them. Along the two walls to my left were some large cases containing a few exquisite Islamic miniatures in front of which a dour faced fellow, neatly dressed in the western style, was glaring at me.

I realized that this was the Director and walked over and proceeded to introduce myself. He interrupted me saying, "I know who you are and what you want but I cannot help you." Somewhat taken aback, I said, "All I need is an export permit for one brick from Ghazni and another from Bamiyan, or from any other ancient sites you would rather I got them." "No!" he said sharply. "I will

3

not give you a permit for a single brick from any site. You have wasted your time coming here. The Foreign Ministry did not have the authority to make any decisions that relate to the Department of Archaeology."

"I regret if the Ministry 'trod on your toes'." I replied. "That was not my doing and the first letter I wrote to Kabul was to you. However, sir, if that is the way you feel there is nothing I can do about it. Or is there?" That was leaving the door open for him to accept an apology or even 'baksheesh'. He didn't bother to reply, so I asked him if he had any objection to my visiting the sites as a tourist. He shook his head. Then I asked if he would permit me to look at his displays and take some photographs. Again, no words only a positive nod of his head.

"Well, Director," I said, "thank you for your time. I'll just photograph these artifacts first so that when I lecture in the United States my audiences can get a good idea of your interests." I turned my back on him and took a shot of each of the stone phalluses, and then proceeded up the staircase.

He was seething, and so was I. I took a couple of shots of the guns on the stairway, came down and tried for some pictures of the miniatures. My stand, a lightweight unipod, was in the car but I managed to brace myself against a wall and clicked away. The Director was still in his original spot, staring at me. I complimented him on the outstanding gun display and the gorgeous miniatures, sincerely. Inside I had a faint hope that he would relent and help me. After all, what were two valueless bricks out of millions. No soap!

I started to leave and said, "Good morning, sir, Dr. 'X' warned me that even though I would be some nine thousand miles away from home I could expect little, or no, help from your department. You seem to have a worldwide reputation." With that I made my exit and got into the car and told my guide to get me to The Inter-Continental Hotel.

On the way to the hotel I had a better opportunity to see the Kabulis. There were the burly tribesmen with their unique turbans, heavy and having a long piece of material falling down behind to below the neck, and their rolled up blankets slung over the shoulder like a Scottish plaid. The material, though, was invariably quite drab and dirty. Every now and then I would see one of the men with a rifle slung across his back. There were quite a lot of sloppily dressed soldiers around, usually in pairs, unarmed and just wandering around in their coarse unpressed heavy khakis.

What fascinated me most were the wraithlike figures of some of the few women on the streets covered from head to toe in their chadris. When a girl attained the age of puberty, she had to start wearing this garb whenever she was permitted to leave her home. No man outside her family was permitted to see her face. The chadri had an inpenetrable thick mesh over the face which permitted the wearer to see out but hid her features from the world. The colors of these were, mostly, dark. However, occasionally I would see a lavender or a light brown chadri and catch sight of colored high heeled shoes as the wearers "floated" along the road or sidewalk. Some old women could be seen in Sari-like robes without any kind of veil. Every now and then, even with the occasional female passing, I would see a man move off the roadway to urinate against a wall. In response to my query, the guide told me that the women weren't supposed to be out of their homes and, therefore, could be ignored. I asked who, normally, did the marketing if the women were virtual prisoners in their houses and was told that the husband did it. Concerning his own wife, the guide said that he was "enlightened" and didn't believe in the chadri and she could come and go as she pleased. He told me that the driver was extremely orthodox and that his wife never left the home. As he told me this, the driver turned round and gave me a big grin.

We entered the hotel driveway and I was amazed to see barbed wire on all the walls and rifle-bearing guards strolling around. The hotel was just outside the city proper and was in a beautiful mountain setting surrounded by snow covered peaks and clear blue skies. Two porters insisted on helping me carry my single suitcase and my camera bag into the hotel! I told the guide to be back at 2:30 and then moved towards the reception desk.

It was a relatively new hotel and, except for the lack of hustle and bustle of patrons, was just like other Inter-Continentals in which I had stayed. A money changer's desk was placed across one corner of the lobby, and I could see only two businesses at the far end. One was a travel bureau whilst the other was a lightly stocked antique shop. The latter had a few Afghan rifles, a scattering of rugs, and some old swords on display. I had been forewarned about the trade in "antique" Afghan guns. It seems that there are small towns in the country that specialize in manufacturing supposedly 150 year-old firearms and that in order to convince the unsuspecting travelers that the guns were really antiques, an export license had to be obtained from the Department of Archaeology. Apart from the staff, there were only about ten men sitting in the lobby. They were spread around in pairs. Each was dressed in an ill-fitting business suit. After I had checked in and exchanged some travelers' checks for afs (Afghanis), the country's own currency, the bellhop escorting me to my room told me that they were all Russians. I further learned that, apart from myself, all the guests were either Russian or Chinese.

My room was comfortably furnished and had all the conveniences of a western hotel, including room and valet service tariffs. The only fault I found was the fact that the water pressure was so low that I could only get about two inches of water in the bathtub after letting the water run or, rather, drip for half an hour. I had been prepared to stay downtown in one of the old bug infested cheap hotels; but I had read that these were the haunts of "hippies" from all over Europe and the U.S. who gathered in Kabul, where hashish was plentiful and cheap. Other drugs were available, too. Just one year prior to my visit, the Afghan Government had started to expel these creatures. This had raised an outcry in the homelands of the "hippies" which didn't want them back. In order to force Afghanistan to keep them, the countries concerned had threatened to cut off foreign aid, citing "unfriendliness to our nationals" as the excuse. The result was the return of the pot-smoking community.

I managed to wash up, changed into my khakis, and went to greet my luncheon guest. Mr. Hosseini was just coming into the hotel as I reached the lobby. He was fine looking, tall, forties, with a smiling face. We shook hands and went into the dining room where the waiter asked if we wanted a drink. (Whenever I have taken a Moslem diplomat out for lunch in Washington, D.C. he has, with one exception, taken a drink or two.) So, before I gave my order,

I waited for Mr. Hosseini to answer. He asked for a scotch and soda, so I did likewise. I didn't bring up my problems immediately. I asked him how long he had lived in England. To my surprise, in his strong Cambridge accent, he said he had never been to England! He told me that he hadn't been any further away from home than Tehran where his father had been the Afghan Ambassador. As for his accent, he said that for several years his private tutor had been a Cambridge man. I was just one of many who had thought he had been educated in England.

While we sipped our drinks, a slight breeze wafted some heavily scented air around our heads. I sniffed and asked what it was that I could smell. Mr. Hosseini laughed and said, "Haven't you ever smoked hashish?" "No," I replied, "I'm surprised they permit it in this restaurant." It was then I learned how prevalent "grass" smoking was in Afghanistan. I had read "The Arabian Nights" which was full of stories in which people used various kinds of drugs, and we were next to Persia (Iran). Hosseini's wife, a royal princess, held a "hashish party" every Saturday night. He invited me to be their guest at that week's get-together. I told him I would have to see how my brick hunting worked out and would let him know in a couple of days.

That brought the conversation around to my strange situation. However, before continuing, we stopped talking long enough for my guest to order another drink and for both of us to order our meal. The menu wasn't extensive. I could have had a hamburger "...with fresh flown-in American beef," at a cost of $10, or one made with local beef for $1.00! There were a variety of pilaus...rice cooked with beef, lamb, chicken or vegetables. Lamb curry and beef stew were also on the menu. Mr. Hosseini ordered a pilau and I asked for the lamb curry.

My guest then told me, quite bluntly, that I was "fighting a losing battle." I asked him if there was a higher authority than the Director of Archaeology to whom I might appeal. I let him know that this episode would be reported to the press in the U.S. and would not make for good public relations and could affect tourism. This gave him food for thought. He then remarked that the Foreign Minister was helpless in the matter, and that I could try two other persons. One was Prince Ghazi, who was apparently the power in the country when the King was away. He had more authority, he said, than Prime Minister Daud. However, he suggested that before contacting the prince I should telephone a Mr. Sultani. This gentleman, I gathered, had the authority to issue export licenses and might oblige me, if I managed to get any brick. He gave me Sultani's telephone number and the prince's number, too.

Our meal arrived. My lamb curry was the blandest curry it has ever been my misfortune to eat. The lamb, itself, was exceedingly tough. This I had expected, having eaten meat in several countries where grazing was sparse. I remember ,during the war, watching sides of beef being loaded onto my ship in Lagos, Nigeria, and pointing out to a friend that the beef was so scrawny one could almost see through it. During my stay in Kabul, I stuck to the hotel's beef stew whenever I had dinner there. Afghan food, to me, was insipid. Lunch over, I asked Mr. Hosseini if he would come to my room so I could take his photograph. This done, I escorted him to the hotel front. We shook hands and he wished me luck on my expedition reminding me to call him about the Saturday night party. I could see my car with the guide and driver parked along the driveway and waved to them. Mr. Hosseini walked away, and out of my life. A few years later, after the revolution and the Russian invasion of Afghanistan, I checked with his embassy in Washington and found that he had been transferred to London, England. When I was over there, I looked him up in the phone book but didn't call him because I was fully "tied up" with family and museums.

Returning to my room, I telephoned Mr. Sultani who was quite sympathetic towards my predicament. He told me not to be concerned about the export license and that all I had to do was find my brick, return to Kabul, and that he would give me a license. Feeling much more confident, I got my windbreaker and camera bag and walked out to the car. The guide and I discussed plans for the rest of that day and the succeeding days. It was decided that for the rest of the day I would be driven all around Kabul visiting the animal market, the ancient wall, the tomb of the former king, Nadir Shah, and take time to wander around the city center. The next morning I planned to fly to Bamiyan, just 45 minutes away, to see the giant statues of Buddha and look for a single Buddhist brick dating back to about 500 A.D. The following day we would head for Ghazni, the ancient capital of the Ghaznavid Empire which once stretched all the way from Persia to Northern India. However, today was to be my indoctrination into Afghanistan life in the raw, so off we drove.

Kabul is six thousand feet above sea level and is best described as drab and smelly. The major part of the city consists of hundreds of small mud homes struggling to reach the top of the mountain. The center is the business section with movie houses, small hotels, chai houses (tea shops), clothing stores with an assortment of second hand European suits and coats and several bazaars, including the rambling Four Arcades Bazaar. In the bazaars may be purchased Afghan rugs, carpets, jewelry, embroidered goods and native dress. The air inside the bazaars is heavy with the smell of hashish and, when I was there, at least a third of the noisy throng was made up of long haired, leather- jacketed hippies. As we drove along the paved road we kept meeting, or passing, men or boys whose legs were the only part of them visible beneath tremendous loads of firewood....a scarce and valuable commodity.... or some with just a few pieces of board strapped to their back, asses with dirt-loaded panniers, and everywhere vintage automobiles recklessly controlled by drivers who seemed to be in doubt as to whether they were supposed to drive on the left or the right. Right, was correct. In addition, they kept sounding their horns almost continuously.

As we passed out of the business section, we drove along the bank of the Kabul River where I could see women washing their clothes in the muddy waters in which men were trying to get rid of the dust that seemed to be everywhere. We were heading east of the city towards a hill on which was the mausoleum of King Nadir Shah and from which I was promised an all-embracing view of Kabul. Nadir Shah was the man who was powerful enough to turn his country away from anarchy and try to bring it into the twentieth century, back in 1929. The marble edifice proved to be quite impressive and so was the view all around. From my vantage point I could see not only almost the whole of the old part of Kabul, but also the 500 year old mud walls that had once been part of the city's fortifications. In the distance I could see the ruins of the ancient citadel of Bala

7

Hissar at which a British military delegation had been fouly betrayed and massacred in 1879. My guide drew my attention to a large forbidding concrete building which, he said, was the prison. He told me that to get thrown in there was as good as a death sentence. All the guards were Judo experts and exceedingly brutal. He got off that subject very quickly. Just out of my sight, he told me, was the Noon Gun. This gun was fired every day at noon. (I had heard it go off earlier and had wondered what caused the noise. This gun was once part of the fortifications and sometimes had served a double purpose. It seems that for centuries condemned men had been strapped across its muzzle and blown apart at noon.)

Our next stop was the animal market. I got out of the car and asked my guide not to come with me. He was startled by my request and tried to go with me. His face wore a worried look as I just walked away from the car and onto the acreage on which the market was held. As I wandered around, I was surprised to note that there were some modern highrise apartment buildings just beyond. The market was a delight! There were all kinds of goats, oxen, sheep, horses and, of course, camels galore. Nobody took the slightest bit of notice of me as I wandered around and took several photographs. I came across a man who was selling sheep. He had a customer who was feeling and hefting the animals. I just stood and watched them as they went about their bargaining. Not a word passed between the buyer and the seller. After a few minutes, finally the buyer nodded at one of the animals and squatted on his haunches. The seller took the blanket off his shoulders and put it over his two hands. The customer put his hands underneath as well and I could tell from the movement of the blanket that they were "talking" with their fingers. After only a minute, the blanket was back on the seller's shoulders, money passed between the two men and the new owner picked up his sheep and slung it around his shoulders and stode away. The seller then looked at me and smiled. I said, "Salaam." To which he replied, "Salaam."

The camels were my next point of call. How they stank! They were a mangy looking crowd and somewhat rambunctious, as camels can get. I walked up to one of them and patted its side. Its owner watched me with a grin on his face and then came over and put my hand on the beast's head. I patted it and, at the same time, realized that I was asking for fleas so my display of affection for the "ship of the desert" was brief. The animals that I chose as "the best looking in the show" were the long silken-haired goats. They looked so much better than their shaggy common-or-garden cousins. The men with the horses seemed to me to be taller, more broad shouldered than the other "ranchers." Their steeds were sleek and muscular, as though reflecting the image of their owner. It was whilst I was looking at these handsome animals, with my untrained eye, that I got a sensation of being watched. I turned around expecting to see my guide. No, he was nowhere in sight; and search as hard as I could, I couldn't see anyone who was taking any notice of me.

Having spent quite some time in the animal market and needing time to reload my cameras, I walked away towards a narrow street which had small shops lining both sides with their owners standing in the doorway. It seemed that they were all antique shops. I may have got that impression from the fact

8

that everywhere I looked I saw old looking Asian silver necklaces, earrings and bangles hanging in windows and, what attracted me most, so many English style umbrella stands stuffed with all kinds of old swords. I examined some of them and found them to be undoubtedly British. Some even had very English names etched into the blades. The hilts were mostly covered with faded velvet wrapped around with silver wire, for better grasp. As I examined the swords and sabers, I couldn't help thinking of the many thousands of courageous British soldiers who had been killed whilst fighting the Afghans or massacred by them during their negotiated retreat in 1842. The British fought three wars with the Afghans in order to try and keep Russia from gaining a foothold in Afghanistan. Such a foothold would have given them easy access to India. If I had still been living in England, I might have purchased one of the weapons and tried to trace the family of its former owner and try to find his descendants. It was quite depressing handling the swords and remembering the tragedies of over a century past. The name of the street was "The Street of the Chickens," and I left it, in a somber mood, and walked to where my car should have been. It was where I had left it, with the guide standing outside talking to the driver. I told him I wanted to get a cup of tea and to take me to a "Chai House." He said there was one at the Gardens of Babur. Babur was the founder of the Moghul Empire and had asked that he be buried in the gardens he had caused to be built on a hill overlooking the Kabul River.

On the way there, we passed the American University; and just as we turned down a street, nearby, we drove past ten lovely young ladies dressed in the latest Western fashions, no chadris, sitting and talking on two park benches. I told the driver to stop. He ignored me. I turned to my guide and told him to get the car stopped. He said that I couldn't take photographs of the girls. (I had just finished reloading my cameras, so he knew what I had in mind.) I told him, sternly, to make the driver back the car up to where the girls were and that the guide should come with me and speak to the young ladies before I opened my mouth. The driver glared at me but did as I had requested. The guide and I got out, and I asked him to go up to the girls and tell them that I was from America and would like permission to take their photograph so I could show the people back home just how beautiful the Afghan girls were. I told him to tell them that they were the first girls I had seen without the chadri. Well, he did exactly as I asked. The girls looked at me and then went into a huddle. After a minute, they had agreed to let me take their picture. I walked up to them and took a shot of each bench. Then I said, "I would imagine that you all speak English, since you attend the American University." They all smiled at me. I took out my notebook and pen and asked the girl who appeared to be their leader if she would give me her name and address so I could send her enough copies of the picture so each of them could have one. She obliged me, and I thanked them for their courtesy and their beauty, which had certainly brightened my day. (I sent copies of the photographs to Afghanistan within days of returning home.) I decided not to try and shake hands and just said, "Goodbye," and got back into the car. As we drove off, the guide said that the girls had told him none of them had ever been photographed before.

As I mentioned earlier, Babur was the founder of the Mogul, or Mohgul, Empire. The name is a corruption of the word "Mongol," from whose famous warriors, Tamerlane and Ghengiz Khan, Babur was a direct descendent. Although a man of great artistic talent..a poet and writer..with an appreciation of nature's beauty, Babur was also a great warrior and tactician. His armies conquered the whole of northern India, as far south as Delhi. He died in 1530 and so loved Kabul that he had said that he wanted to be buried in one of the beautiful gardens he had designed. That is where we strolled after our cup of tea. I was impressed by the wonderful western vista that unfolded before my eyes as I entered the gardens. It overlooked the wide fertile valley and the mountains beyond. The flowers had not yet begun to bloom, for I was there at the very beginning of spring, but I could delight in the layout with shrubs and shade trees abounding. I saw the simple tomb of Babur. a low-lying white marble sarcophagus with a headstone of the same material, both inscribed with the flowing Arabic letters. Just about twenty feet away there was an open, but covered, shrine at which a man was on his knees, praying. His shoes were on the ground outside. I couldn't resist getting him in one of my pictures. There was a young boy, about 15 or 16 years old, with the ever present rolled blanket across his shoulders, slowly wending his way around the gardens and I walked up to him and asked him if he spoke English. He gave me a nice smile and nodded his head. I asked him if I could take his photograph. He hesitated and looked past me at the guide, who had walked up behind me. The guide spoke to him in their native Pushtu tongue and then told me it was alright. I got a fine head and shoulders shot, an enlargement of which still adorns my study wall, and got him to print his name and address in my book. (He, too, eventually got a copy.)

The light was starting to diminish and I asked that I be taken back to the hotel. Nowhere had I seen what looked like an ancient brick, lying around, but I was assured by the guide that I would, undoubtedly, find what I was looking for when I visited Bamiyan, the next day. He told me that the day after we would be visiting the ancient capital of Afghanistan, Ghazni, where there were many to be found. It was arranged that I would be driven to the airport, early the next morning, and would take a taxi back after I flew back from the Buddhist site of Bamiyan. The car would pick me up, again, the morning after, at seven a.m. for the trip to Ghazni. Back in the hotel, the first thing I did was to follow my practice of thinking back over the day's events and dictating comments elaborating on some of those I had taped as I went around. One comment I put on the tiny machine was to the effect that Prince Ghazi wasn't someone I would care to meet. You see, the Ghazis are members of a fanatical sect of Muslims whose two ambitions are to die in battle and to kill anyone, Muslim or non-Muslim, who does not worship Allah in their fashion. However, if push came to shove, I would make the sacrifice and call upon him. Another comment had to do with peoples' ages. It seemed that, in Afghanistan and most other Asian countries, until quite recently, family birth records were rarely kept. The result being that only those under twenty or so, knew exactly how old they were. Neither my guide nor my driver had any idea whether they were 30, 35, 40 or whatever! The most important of my comments, it turned out, was concerning the large number of soldiers I had seen wherever we went in Kabul. They were all over the place. Not only that, there were policemen stationed at almost every corner.

Dictation over, I washed up, and wandered into the restaurant for dinner. The menu was exactly the same as that presented at lunch. I ordered some tomato soup and the Afghan Beef Stew, deciding that even if the meat was too tough to handle I would get some nourishment from the vegetables and the nan (bread.) I asked for a pot of tea, with a jug of boiled milk. Actually, in Afghanistan, whenever I ordered tea, no matter where I was, the milk provided was freshly boiled. The stew was quite enjoyable, even if very bland. After my meal, I looked around the hotel lobby and found the same scene I had found on my arrival, earlier in the day. Pairs of men, in ill fitting business suits, deeply engaged in conversation. I discovered that there was a small shop in the basement that sold newspapers, film, postcards, candy, souvenirs and the usual over the counter drugs found in American hotel lobby shops. There was also a tiny post office. I then walked outside. Darkness had descended but the Hindu Kush mountains, to the North, could still be seen. The perimeter of the hotel grounds was brightly illuminated and the rifle bearing guards could be seen patrolling just inside the barbed wire. I hadn't any information that bandits, quite common further west, had been anywhere near Kabul. It had been a long day, so I got back to my room at which time I dialed Room Service and ordered some bottled water so I could brush my teeth. It arrived shortly.

I asked the uniformed waiter if I could take his picture. He was delighted and, after that was done, he turned my bed down, bade me a goodnight and departed. It was then, when I took my bath, that I made the discovery about the low pressure in the water system and had to make do in the two inches of water which trickled out during a thirty minute period. After my alarm clock was set for 6 a.m., I put my head on my pillow, crawled in after it and quickly fell asleep.

I was up and about before the alarm went off. After I had washed and shaved, I managed to get enough water into the washbasin to wash my previous day's khakis, which were then hung up to dry over the bath. Then I checked my cameras and walked out towards the hotel's restaurant. The lights were on but no waiters were about, so I went down to the shop in the basement. That was open and I asked the young clerk if that day's Kabul Times had been delivered. It had, and smiling he handed me a copy of the four paged, thin-papered, periodical. While waiting for my change, I looked at the front page. It carried a startling item in large headlines and bold subheads. It seemed that, the day before, Israeli commandos had landed in Beirut, Lebanon, and had shot and killed some six P.L.O. terrorist leaders and set fire to the two houses they had lived in. This done, the Israelis had managed to get away in their boat without sustaining any casualties. The clerk, handing me my change, told me to look inside the paper. I turned to the editorial page where, beneath the official expression of horror at the incident, there was a large black edged panel two columns by four inches. In this was the following appeal:

FROM THE PALESTINE LIBERATION ORGANIZATION

TO ALL OUR MOSLEM BRETHREN
THE ISRAELIS AND THE AMERICANS HAVE SLAUGHTERED
OUR MARTYRS IN BEIRUT. WE APPEAL TO YOU, ARAB
OR NON-ARAB, TO KILL AN AMERICAN WHEREVER YOU
CAN FIND ONE."

I turned to the Moslem clerk and said, "Well, I'm an American, do you want to kill me?" He laughed and replied, "The Palestine people are a big headache to many of the other Moslems. They are always wanting us to hurt ourselves by hurting our friends." That was reassuring, although I hadn't really felt I was in any danger. Everyone was too friendly.

Back upstairs, I found the restaurant manned and sat down to a breakfast of one hardboiled egg, tea, toast and marmalade. Then it was back to my room where I put on my windbreaker, got my camera case and an old "friend," my B.O.A.C. bag, which had carried many an ancient brick in several parts of the world for almost twenty years. Inside was my only tool, a skinny scoutknife used for "liberating" bricks from walls.

My car and "crew" were waiting for me down the hotel driveway and I walked over and was then driven to the airport. The day was nice and clear, although a little chilly. At the airport, when I bought my ticket, the clerk told me that the weather at Bamiyan was not the best. According to him, it was slightly overcast with some light rain. He suggested that I might want to wait for better weather. My reply was that I hadn't time to spend an extra day and that, in any case, a little rain wouldn't make me melt away like the snow. So, after about an hour's flight in a twin Otter Turbojet, I found myself at Bamiyan where it really was drizzling and the heads of the two giant Buddhas were hard to make out.

Bamiyan is an ancient Buddhist center with gigantic figures of Buddha carved into the cliff face. These carvings date back about fifteen hundred years. Between the 1st and 6th centuries it had been a place to which pilgrims from all over the Buddhist world came. Thousands of monks used to live in the many cave monasteries. There are still some monks in the caves to this day. The monks used to climb up to the heads of the figures, and visitors may still do likewise. The two fabulous figures are 175 and 115 feet high and some four hundred yards apart. Standing at the foot of the largest, in the company of an unwanted guide who had attached himself to me, I could see the damage wrought by Shah Aurangzeb in the mid 17th century. This destroyer of temple and art was the son of Shah Jehan, builder of the Taj Mahal.

The rain was beginning to get heavier, but I could still hear the rushing of a stream that would be heaven to a trout fisherman. My feet were wet and my trousers soaked through and there was a mist shrouding a large part of the cliffs. I knew that there were some Buddhist brick in the ruins of a couple of ancient forts built onto the cliffs. I asked the guide to lead me to one of them. He pointed somewhere in the distance and said that getting up to it would be impossible in the rain. He suggested that I return another day.

I pushed my way over to the second carving, wondering if Buddha had put a curse on me. All I wanted was one miserable piece of dried clay and I was being thwarted at every turn. The smaller figure, also, showed the signs of

Aurangzeb's attempt at destruction. As I looked upwards, all I got was a face full of now-pelting rain. Looking around I could still see just how beautiful the valley was. It nestled between the two mountain ranges of the Hindu Kush and Kohi-Baba, and was lush and fertile, and so peaceful. It was like a Shangri-La, the perfect place for peace loving Buddhists to live an undisturbed religious life. There was no point in trying to get any pictures. Shots into the pouring rain through wet lenses do not show anything. So, still with my unwanted guide, I returned to the airstrip, gave my companion 100 afs ($1.30), and waited fifteen minutes until I could reboard the same plane that brought me.

It was noon when I got back to the Inter-Continental. I changed my clothes and then hopped into the restaurant for more tomato soup and beef stew. After lunch, I took just one camera and walked out of the hotel, down the road a few yards, and turned into a long tree lined driveway. From the other side of Kabul I had seen a small, attractive building peeping from among tall trees on a western hill. It was called "Bagh-i-Bala", which translates into "The Garden on the Hill." It had been the summer palace of Amir Abdur Rahman, a late 19th century ruler who had been the first to unify the many factions and tribes in Afghanistan. My guide told me that it was now a very good restaurant. Since it was so close to the hotel, I had decided to look it over. As I strolled down the seemingly endless driveway, I came across some of the locals going towards or away from the palace. They were mostly teenage boys, some with bicycles. As they passed me, these young fellows would give me a big grin and always responded to my "Salaam."

After about 15 minutes, I got to the palace which overlooked a vast valley. Standing by the wall, looking at what T.E. Lawrence would have described as "a gracious view," I became surrounded by about twenty of the young gentle-men. Some wore the traditional Afghan dress; others were in western clothes. I "Salaamed" everyone who came close, and shook hands with them. They were obviously flattered. To further win them over, I started talking to them asking questions I knew they would be able to answer in very simple English. Questions such as: "Do you go to school?" "Do you like learning English?" "How old are you?" (Since they were so young they would know their age.) "Isn't this a beautiful view?" "Do you come here often?", and so on. I was a big hit! I took several photographs of these youngsters, making sure to get their names and addresses. Eventually, I walked around the outside of the palace. It was closed until dinnertime. It certainly was a handsome example of late 19th century Afghan architecture. I shot it from several angles.

As I walked back towards my hotel, I was accompanied by a cheerful group of these young Afghans who kept asking me to repeat my name and the name of the American city I lived in. I found a taxi outside the hotel and asked the driver to take me to the center of the old city. I reloaded my camera as we went. Arriving at the busiest crossing, I got out, put my back against a building and pointed my camera at a building directly opposite. To the casual onlooker I was just idling away my time and no one took the slightest bit of interest in me. Naturally, what I was doing was photographing just about everyone who crossed the street towards me. These were people going about their everyday business.

13

One was photographed peeling an orange as he walked. After a while, I crossed over to where a young man was selling cigarettes, candy and fruit from a pedal operated cart. Pointing to my camera, I asked him if he would let me take his picture. He didn't speak, but merely shrugged his shoulders and smiled right into my lens. I had already managed to get shots of some of the wood-carrying men, a trio of dirt-carrying donkeys, some hippies and a real find. There was a man striding down the sidewalk carrying a full animal skin of water. As I moved parallel to him to get him, too, he marched into a shop. I waited. He was out again in a couple of minutes. However, I could see his water skin was empty with only a slight drip coming from the downward facing neck. This shot I got! Parking myself against another wall, I reloaded the camera and started again. This time I managed to get a series of pictures of people doing business from street stalls, and their customers, too. Women in all shades of Chadri were "caught," as well as a couple of older women whose faces were uncovered. One of Afghanistan's industries is home loomed rugs. In order to make them look much used, and therefore more valuable, sellers use a variety of tricks. One is to lay them out on the sidewalk for everyone to tread on. Another, more often used in the villages, is to leave them in the roadway. I found several buildings that had rugs hanging out of windows, or hanging from the roof.

Time was getting on, but I thought I'd stay around another half an hour. I walked away from the city center, away from the shops and stalls, and came across a tall gray monument set in front of a dark, barren hill. It was unusual, to say the least. First of all, there were men of all ages all around and on top of it, resting! Secondly, the inscription, which was both in English and Pushtu, indicated that the monument had been erected in 1919 to commemorate the departure of the British who didn't leave until 1921! Photographs were taken from all angles. I had just taken my last shot and was looking up at one of the men draped across the top when I smelled an exceptionally strong odor that could only have come from a urinating horse. How wrong I was! I looked down and saw that I was standing in a steady stream of liquid which was emanating from an old man who was lying on the step above me. I beat a hasty retreat and got back into the city center where I was able to flag a taxi which got me back to the hotel.

Dinner that night was taken at Bagh-i-Bala. Before eating, I looked around at the antiques which included all kinds of ancient Afghan weapons. The menu was a mixture of European and Afghan cuisine. However, I asked if I could possibly have, besides the vegetable soup, two hard boiled eggs in an extra-hot curry sauce. No problem. It was a delicious meal which I topped off with a little cheese, bread, and a couple of cups of nice hot tea. The brisk walk back to the hotel helped the digestion, and I was ready to sit at the desk and listen to my day's tapes. I then dictated for several minutes, ran my bath ...again, only two inches deep,... and went to bed.

I was just dozing off when someone started banging on my door and shouting, in a high pitched voice. Remembering the P.L.O. item in the morning paper, I left the door on the chain as I looked to see who was making all the din. I found four giggling teenage Chinese, two boys and two girls, obviously "high".

They were surprised when they saw me because one of them said, in very good English, that they were looking for a friend's room and the number written on a scrap of paper was my room number. Having got that matter sorted out, I got back into bed and had a good night's sleep.

Another simple breakfast over, and I was speeding southwesterly towards Ghazni. The road was narrow, but well paved. We passed a number of nomad camps, none of them very large. Usually, only about three tents with four or five camels and a dozen kids who, as soon as they saw our car approaching, would run towards us waving their hands in a friendly greeting. I asked the guide about stopping so I could visit one of the encampments. He told me that he had strict orders not to go near any of the nomads. Too bad. Everyone except myself was scared of these people. There were men toiling in the barren looking fields. The ground certainly didn't look at all fertile and was covered with small stones. These men were scrabbling to clear enough spots to deposit whatever they were planting. Every hundred yards, or so, was to be seen a small cairn of stones which were boundary markers. Here and there, we could see what appeared to be mud forts with big heavy gates and slits, not windows, cut into the walls. The guide told me that the farmers let their cattle graze outside during the day, while they farmed the land. Come nightfall, everyone, and everything, was brought into the farmhouse which was well protected not only by the thick walls but also by the guns of the farmer's family. Yes, there were bandits around. I got the car to stop close to one of the farmhouses so I could get some photographs. Outside, there were dozens of small mounds. Each was between three and six feet long and had a rough piece of rock stuck into the earth at each end. While I was taking a photo of these mounds, my right foot went through the top of the ground up to my ankle. As I pulled it out, it released the unmistakable stench of a decaying corpse. Truly, at that time, I had one foot in the grave! (As we drove in Kabul and out on the highway, I was aware of the fact there were mounds with green flags beside the roadway and on the tops of hills. As we passed these mounds, the driver would make some quick gesture with his hand and mutter a few words. These were the graves of holy men who were buried on the same spot on which they had died. Our driver missed only one, that I could catch). At one place, the road was blocked by a balanced steel barrier. There was a policeman standing outside a small hut, and we stopped just in front of him. The guide asked me for a few afs, the toll, which I handed over. The barrier was swung open and on we went.

The landscape was barren. Once it had been fertile, but that was before the Mongol Ghengis Khan and his descendant, Tamerlane, had wreaked havoc with the country's well developed irrigation system. That was twice in less than a hundred years. As a point of interest, the cruelty of the Mongols is well known but Tamerlane was probably the worst of all. After one of his grandsons had been killed in battle, this famous, or infamous, man had thousands of the enemy, including women and children, slaughtered and their skulls piled up in the form of a pyramid. On we traveled. The day had turned rather chilly, and shortly all we could see was as barren and lonely looking territory as can be imagined. There was absolutely nothing now visible. Not a farmhouse or even a solitary bird. The wind began to rise and then we were driving through a mist of dust

15

which later became mixed with light snow flurries. Eventually, I saw an imposing tower, something like a mosque minaret, about a mile ahead of us. Then I found a second, similar tower located about 200 yards beyond the first but set on the other side of the road. I got the car stopped and got out. I wanted to photograph the first tower from a distance; and just as I focused on the tower, which I could now see had a cone shaped copper roof, an old man walking alongside an ass came into my picture. To the disgust of the guide and driver, I sat down on the hard rocky ground to wait for the man and his animal to draw alongside the tower so I would have a good size reference. Fifteen minutes later they were just where I wanted them; I got my shots and returned to the car.

We reached the tower, which was an amazing piece of brick construction. It was 125 feet high with six sides and carved Kufic inscriptions covering the whole. (Kufic was the earliest Arabic writing, originating in Babylonia.) To get a good impression of its height, I got down on my back to take my picture. A pigeon-like bird alighted on the top edge of the tower as I released the shutter. These towers were actually the remains of the minarets of a tremendous 12th century mosque. There were no entrances to either of the towers, nor were there platforms near the top from which the muezzins would have called The Faithful to prayer. Therefore, the towers, originally, must have been somewhat higher. They are recognized as the finest examples of Islamic architecture still existing. Several minutes later, we passed a couple of very short and narrow streets with a small cluster of mud brick dwellings with a couple of very short and narrow streets. No shops or stalls. Just the homes and a group of friendly youngsters with a couple of donkeys. For the record, I posed my guide in the street and then swapped places with him and let him take my photograph. At the bottom of the street I noticed a substantial looking building with a couple of the ever present policemen outside. It was a small museum containing some religious relics. I energized my flash and was about to take a shot of an attractive panel bearing a design in stylized Arabic letters when one of the officers shouted at me and pointed at my camera. I asked my guide what was wrong. He spoke to the interrupter and then told me that everything in the tiny museum was of great religious significance and couldn't be photographed. I had to shoot something and, as a student of brickwork, had noticed that the brickwork of the vaulted ceiling was intricately laid. So I pointed upwards and getting the o.k. nod, took my picture. Even my guide couldn't tell me what it was that was so sacred about the objects in the museum. That, though, was only the beginning.

Another couple of minutes' drive and we pulled up just beyond another small, domed building. As I got out of the car, I noticed a large number of old, flat, dust covered bricks lying where they had originally fallen when the building of which they had been a part had collapsed. I thought to myself, "Here are my 'babies'," I asked my guide what building we were walking towards, and what had the ruins been. He told me that we were going to visit the tomb of Mahmud the Great, founder of the famous Ghaznevid Empire. The ruins had been a seminary that Mahmud had built in the 12th century, using treasure "won" from India to cover the costs. One part of the booty had been a solid gold figure of an elephant encrusted with diamonds and rubies.

Here, it seemed that I, too, had struck it rich! The short pavement leading into the tomb was lined with several men squatting and discussing something of great importance...or so it seemed. They stopped talking as I walked past them and through the doorway. The first thing I noticed, on entering, was the heavy green velvet cover which, except for a few inches around the bottom, covered Mahmud's tomb. Behind this, two crossed lances rested in a large niche in the wall. A mullah stood watching me as I walked around. Surrounding the tomb was a velvet rope supported by brass stands and it seemed that someone had dropped a bundle of rags to one side. The "bundle" turned out to be a very sick woman who, I was told, had been praying there for three days. I asked permission to photograph the tomb and was so permitted. After shooting it with the velvet cover on, I asked if I could see it without it. There was no problem. The mullah displayed to me the beautiful creamy marble tomb with its elegantly carved Arabic inscription. It was so lovely that it made me gasp. However, I was told that I could only look at, and not photograph, the uncovered tomb. Out of respect for the dear departed and for the benefit of the mullah, and those watching from the doorway, I stood in silent contemplation for a couple of minutes. Then I walked over to the mullah, handed him 100 afs and "Salaamed" him. As I left, a couple of the men outside held out their hands into which I dropped a few afs. After getting a few yards away, I turned and looked at the drab grey building which housed such a gorgeous monument.

It is of consequence to note that I was only carrying my camera bag; the guide was holding my trusty B.O.A.C. flight bag. I walked past the spot where the ruined seminary had been built alongside the tomb and moved to what looked like an archaeological dig. That's what it was. The Italians, none of whom were there, were excavating the palace of Sultan Massoud III. This was interesting! Eagerly I approached the "dig", only to find myself surrounded by about a dozen police officers. I "Salaamed" the man who was obviously in charge. He was the first person in the country who did not respond! Instead he turned to my guide and in a few moments they were engaged in a very heated conversation. Of course, I couldn't understand a word of what they said so, after a couple of minutes, I started towards the main part of the "dig" only to find my progress halted by four of the stalwart guards who stood right in front of me. I turned towards where my guide and the head guard were still arguing. I called out, "What's the problem?" My guide came over and told me about the Italians having the sole excavation rights for the palace and that the zealous police guards weren't going to let me prowl around. He said that photography was forbidden. I understood the reason for the ban on photography. After all, the archaeologists didn't want anyone publishing pictures of the dig before they did. However, to stop me from looking around was nonsensical. Just a few feet from where I was standing, I glimpsed the largest burned clay brick I have ever seen. It was about three and a half feet long, three feet wide and some eight inches thick. There it was, the bottom of what had been a gigantic wall. I looked at the head guard and just pointed to this brick. He came over to me, took my arm and led me over to it. Still holding my arm, he put his other hand over the lenses of my cameras. I turned them inward so that the lenses rested against my chest. Kneeling down, I ran my fingers all over the vast brick. When I moved to one end, I looked ahead and got a glimpse of a large marble facade which disappeared as a couple of the guardians, purposely, blocked my view. Then, I took out my tape measure only to have the head guard take it out of my hand and try to stuff it back in my pocket.

At this, I moved away from Massoud's palace, shook hands with a couple of the guards and headed towards the ruins of the Emperor Mahmoud's ruined seminary. The guards had no interest there and didn't follow.

Together with the guide, who was still carrying my empty flight bag, I walked among the fallen brick with my eyes on the ground until I saw what I was after. Among the shattered bats lay a sand and soil encrusted specimen that was about 95 percent intact. I looked around and saw that most of the men outside the tomb, as well as a few others who had materialized from the small settlement, were watching me very carefully. They had no idea what I was about, and puzzlement was written on each face. I said to my guide, "I am going to walk over to the tomb and I want you to pick up the brick under my foot, put it in the bag and walk back to the car." "Oh no sir!" he exclaimed, "If I am caught, they will throw me into the big prison I showed you in Kabul." "Listen to me, very carefully," I replied. "I am going to walk away from you and everybody will be looking at me, not you. I have a trick which will make it impossible for these men not to watch me. When you see what happens, and you feel safe, pick up the brick. If you are successful, I'll give you 100 afs." With that, I walked over to the tomb entrance, put my largest camera up to my eye and pointed the lens to the empty sky. I pretended to focus on something, took a shot, and then pretended to follow whatever was supposed to be up there. I made a big show out of all this and, when I took the camera away from my eye, saw that each and everybody was looking into the heavens trying to find whatever object I had photographed. Glancing towards our car I saw the guide standing beside it wearing a big grin on his face and the flight bag being held a little lower than usual.

We had the brick! Smiling at everyone in general, I walked over to the car giving a "Salaam" to three or four people who came over to shake my hand. As we drove off I waved and everyone waved back. Some, though, kept looking at the sky in the direction where I had "seen" my subject. We were now on our way to the ancient capital of Ghazni, which was just a few minutes away. The skies, though, had begun to darken a little and there was a swirling combination of dust and snowflakes just ahead of us. I took out the ancient eight hundred year-old Ghaznevid brick, examined it closely and, lovingly, put it back in the flight bag and concentrated upon what lay ahead. Approaching Ghazni I was surprised to see a vast brooding bulbous fortification that dominated the whole town. I say, "surprised" because James Michener, who had placed part of his book "Caravans" in Ghazni, hadn't made the slightest mention of this, the most overwhelming feature of the place. Michener had been in Afghanistan several times and had even done what I had tried to do; namely, travel with the Kuchis. The fort had been built in 332 b.c. by the troops of Alexander the Great. It was made of mud brick and from the sight of the flag flying above a white painted building, which peeped over the fortress wall, I could tell that it was still in use by the military. Additionally, several small homes had been built into the walls of the fort. This type of reuse of ancient forts and palaces was not new to me. In Istanbul, Turkey, there were many homes built into the old Roman walls. As we drew closer, I had the car stop while I got some pictures of Alexander's fort which, shrouded by the whipped up sand, looked quite menacing. Two men, with their robes tightly wrapped around them to keep out the stinging grit, shouted at me and pointed to the fort. They both shook their fists at me, also. I asked my guide what they had said. His translation was, "Leave it alone."

We passed right below the ancient citadel and made a turn into a short street. As a matter of fact, it was just long enough to hold a lovely white-painted, well kept bungalow with a painted wooden fence around it. That seemed to be all the color visible. Everything else was drab, drab, drab, until we drove into what was obviously the main street of Ghazni. There we came across an open shop from which a squatting Afghan was selling all kinds of materials, in a nice selection of colors. The bolts of red cloth really stood out, even from across the street. Of course, we had to stop so I could get the shopkeeper's permission to photograph him and his "emporium." We drove around the town and took in the miserable dwellings which lined the back streets. As we turned back onto "main street", through the dust I could make out two Afghan buses parked at the far end. I got out of the car and walked down the street. These gaily painted buses can be seen all over the country, overloaded with passengers, some of whom carry animals with them. My shots of the two in Ghazni, because of the dust storm, don't do justice to these colorful vehicles. As I progressed down the road, I found it hard to believe that this dismal place, now so small, had once been the capital of an Empire that stretched for thousands of miles. At one point, I stopped walking and indulged in one of my regular operations when in ancient places. I stood leaning against the wall of a storehouse and closed my eyes and tried to visualize the many things that had happened in that place: the invasions by Cyrus and Darius in 600 b.c., the occupation by Alexander in 332 b.c., the prosperous Ghaznevid era, the invasions and destructions by Ghengiz Khan and Tamerlane, and the wars and occupation by the British. As usual, when going back though history, there was nothing of glory to be found. Only death, destruction and horrible misery.

I snapped out of my reverie and started back to the car. The guide got out and suggested we have lunch. Lunch? Where? He said there was a nice hotel down the street which he could recommend. This lunch hour was one to be remembered. To get into the hotel one had to enter through a narrow door let into the wall between some closed business places; go up a steep flight of stairs and down a long passage which had several guest rooms which had exceptionally heavy doors. Each door was secured by a heavy padlock and there were many signs that every room had been broken into several times. As I passed one of the rooms, the door opened and I could see that all that was inside was a truckle bed, a much scarred heavy wooden dresser and a low table. (No window and no chair). The person who was exiting the room was a burly man in the usual rural clothing with his blanket covering the lower part of his face. Obviously he knew it was blowing outside. At the end of the passageway we entered the restaurant, a dimly lit, low ceilinged room with an assortment of small tables, some with marble tops and iron legs..just like those that used to be found in American ice cream parlors. There were about ten tables scattered around, with a handful of guests occupying a few of them. The three of us, the guide, the driver and I, plopped down onto the ancient wooden chairs. As I looked around, two things impressed me: how filthy the windows were; and two gorgeous rugs hung on a far wall. Cleaning the windows would have almost doubled the light in the place.

A man, wearing a western jacket, along with the traditional local robes, appeared and greeted my guide and driver like old friends. He was introduced to me as the hotel owner. I shook hands with him and gave him my "Salaam." He seemed surprised to hear even such a simple greeting from a "Ferengeh," the Afghan word for a foreigner. The guide asked what I would like to eat and said that he was "treating." I told him to order hot tea with boiled milk, and a very well cooked shishkabob and some nan (bread) and that I was the host. The tea came very quickly; and whilst I was sipping it, I kept looking at the two Persian rugs hung on the wall. After a few minutes, my guide informed me that I wasn't looking at actual rugs but paintings! Apparently. several years previously, a penniless..or afless..visitor had offered to decorate the walls in exchange for food and lodgings. I walked over and examined the artist's work. It was truly amazing. Even from a few feet away they looked like real rugs. The detailing was superb. Even the fringes had been painted individually and made to look round. I photographed them, of course. Then I turned around and approached a handsome white-bearded Afghan and pointed to my camera. He put both his hands over his face and quickly turned his back to me. I had the same experience with two more tables, but two men sitting across the room beckoned me and let me "shoot" them. The shishkabob was on the table and I ate heartily of the tasty food. I went through the usual steps of focussing the camera on where the guide was sitting, changed places with him, and let him take my picture. (A couple of months earlier, I had given one of my lectures to a regional group of members of the National Secretaries' Association. When I started to take questions, one young woman said to me, "Mr. Saffer, you really don't look the adventurous kind of man." Dressed in a dark business suit, I'm sure I looked more at home in an office than I would have in the wilds of Pakistan. After that episode, I made a point of showing at least one slide of me "on location" at each lecture.)

The meal over, I asked how much I should pay the hotel owner and was told that 100 afs ($1.30) would cover the three meals. Having duly paid the reckoning and again shaken hands with the owner, I led the way out to the street. Except for three men walking with their heads down and robes tightly held, the dismal street was deserted. The ancient fortress could still be seen looming over the town as we drove out of Ghazni and headed back towards Kabul.

After half an hour, when we were way out of sight of any structure of any kind, I told the driver to stop and let me get out. My instructions to the guide were for him and the car to drive along the road for twenty minutes, then turn around and come and pick me up. He was baffled by these orders, but off they went. I walked up a low hill, and down so I couldn't be seen from the road. All I could see was a vast desert of dirt and small stones, with the ever-present Hindu Kush mountains to the north. I sat down on the damp ground, with dust and snow blowing around me and, again, let my imagination run wild. Here, on the very ground on which I was sitting, the Mongol hordes had made their bloody trek across Afghanistan. The sounds of galloping horses, yelling warriors, and the creaking of ancient wagons were in my ears. Looking eastward, I could "see" them approaching, their vast numbers seeming to swallow the entire countryside. They moved westward, disappearing into the distance, finally leaving me, a lonely figure, a mere speck, looking at the tracks they had left behind. I began to feel the cold, as I came back to the present. I thought, "What am I doing here, in this cold, God-forsaken place, nine thousand miles away from home, when I could be with my family in warm comfort." To try to keep warm, I walked back up the hill and strode around, keeping my eyes on the road waiting for the car. It appeared in just a few minutes, picked me up, and got me back to my hotel. It was very late in the afternoon and I was surprised to see about a dozen young men, waiters, and others of the hotel staff, dressed in very fancy Afghan vests, dancing in the driveway.

They had drums and tambourines, the sounds of which reverberated in the lovely mountain setting. They sang as they danced. Each, in turn, performed a solo. I forgot I was chilled through, and stood watching as the seemingly endless performance continued. One of the dancers was the young man from the basement shop. I learned from him that Afghan men love to dance and usually keep going, continuously, for several hours. The light was beginning to fade when I remembered that I had to call Mr. Sultani. I took my brick to my room and tried his number, without success. There was still one more day left, so I wasn't too concerned. I washed up, dictated those thoughts I had missed during the day, and took a nap. When I awoke, it was time for dinner. I had preferred the food at Bagh-i-Bala, but didn't feel like making the trip there, so it was Inter-Continental beef stew again.

The next morning was the start of my last full day in Afghanistan. I had succeeded in only part of my mission. One ancient brick, instead of two, although I still didn't have my export permit. Excellent photo opportunities and conditions, except at Bamiyan, which would make a fascinating lecture. The car was waiting for me when I left the hotel at 7:30. The first thing I told the guide was the fact that I still had to get in touch with Mr. Sultani. He assured me that we would have many opportunities to call him. However, he told me that he had a big surprise waiting for me later in the morning. First of all, though, he was going to show me the modern part of Kabul, including the various foreign embassy buildings. I let him know that the embassies could be left out. From our vantage point on Bagh-i-Bala hill, he pointed out some modern, though architecturally unimaginative, buildings which were part of the Russian University. The Russians were still, after centuries of futile effort, working at influencing the Afghan government. They had even built a beautiful mosque for the students. We drove down there. The streets were narrow but on either side were large European style homes, surrounded by high walls. I saw, and photographed, a group of youngsters dressed just like English school children, even to little blazers and school caps. There was one street which was unique. It was paved and cars were driving on it, as we did until I saw a tomb which had a protective circular wall around it. The whole took up almost half the width of the road. Cars had to go around it. This was the tomb of a holy man who had been shot dead, during the second Afghan war with the British. The man had been buried on the exact spot upon which he fell, even though, even then, it was a busy street. When I got in the car at the hotel, I could see that the driver was very upset about something. He didn't even wish me a "good morning." Then when I got out of the car to photograph the tomb, he objected, quite strenuously. The guide had to hold his arms so he couldn't drive off before I got out of the car.

We drove past so many modern homes that it became a bore. I asked the driver to take us over to the old part and get me up to the top of the hill by the ancient walls. It was in my mind not only to examine the wall and see the view but, maybe, to get a piece of the mud structure. However, when we got there, it turned out that there were dozens of little homes built right against the wall. I found some youngsters playing in an old burial ground where the mounds had long since disappeared, leaving only the head and foot markers. I looked at these kids in whose faces I could see the features of many ancient peoples. The Mongol characteristics seemed to predominate among the Persian and the few Arab faces surrounding me. An old man came over. I gave him the "Salaam" and held out my hand. Ruefully, he held up his right arm which was handless. Apparently, he'd had it lopped off for stealing, the standard orthodox Moslem punishment for that crime. This must have put the old man in a horrible predicament. You see, Moslems use their right hand for eating from communal bowls. The left hand is reserved for toilet activities. I had no questions to ask. I just reached out and shook his wrist.

I made the old man sit in a chair the children had brought for me, surrounded him with all the children, and took a photograph which showed the grave markers as well as the group. There being nothing much of interest up there, I got back into the car and we drove away.

The guide got the driver to stop at a place that had a telephone and I called Mr. Sultani. Again, no answer. On we went, with the guide pointing out some places of minor interest, until I noticed a fort built on the summit of a high hill. I managed to get the driver to turn into the long road leading to the fort but he stopped after going only a short way up. I got out and took a quick shot of the building, just as the guide told me not to. I thought I could hear voices in my right ear, but looking over, all I could see was a well-grassed steep hill which reached right up to the fort. There were, though, several cars parked on the hillside. Then I heard an unmistakable laugh. I looked at the grassy hill, again, and caught a slight movement in the ground. Bending down, I found myself looking into a long underground gallery which looked out onto the city. There were soldiers there! It then appeared that the entire hillside was a maze of such galleries, cunningly camouflaged. I beat a hasty retreat back into the car, realizing that I could be in very serious trouble if seen photographing in that vicinity. As I mentioned earlier, there were soldiers all over Kabul. I sensed that "something was brewing." How right I was! Two weeks after I left Afghanistan there was a revolution which was later followed by the Russian invasion. The Russians finally attained their objective of controlling the country. However, they found themselves with a "Viet Nam" on their hands.

Off we went to visit a small open air market. Vendors were doing business from rickety handcarts, selling some clothing and fruit and vegetables. There was a mudbrick bakery which had nan (bread) hanging from the ceiling! A man sat in the front and it wasn't difficult to get him to pose with a loaf. I saw two startling stalls, almost side by side. One had pieces of beef hanging out of the front; the other specialized in lamb, with flies all over. We were there for just a few minutes until the guide said it was time to watch the Buzkashi match. This was his surprise. Buzkashi is Afghanistan's national sport and involves anywhere from thirty to three hundred horsemen, probably the world's finest riders, in a very dangerous and spectacular contest. As we walked to the car, I was asked if I minded having the driver stop at his home to pick up his two young sons so they could see the match. Of course, I agreed. On the outskirts of the city we stopped by a brand new housing estate. It resembled an American subdivision having several parallel streets lined with neatly kept bungalows. Each of these was surrounded by a six foot fence. As the driver disappeared through a gate in one fence, the guide told me why our driver was in such poor spirits. Apparently, that morning he had thrown some dishes at his wife during a row about her having to wear the chadri. She said she'd had enough of living as a prisoner, permanently confined to the house and yard. It was her intention to run away! After hearing this last threat, he had beaten her.

The driver returned with his small sons and we drove another mile or so until we reached a large open space with a short stretch of "bleachers" on just one side. The Buzkashi field was about the size of one and a half football fields, in length and width. There was a wide ditch, a few feet deep, completely surrounding the field. Towards one end, there was a post in the ground. The name of the game means "Goat Dragging" and involves a headless goat which each team tries to "capture" from the opponents and drop into a circle around this post. The riders are rugged and fierce. They ride with an abandon that has to be seen to be believed. With whips between their teeth, they lean out of the saddle to scoop up the goat from the ground, at the same time fighting off members of the opposing team who are hitting them, and their steeds, while trying to snatch the carcass away. The big horses are specially bred for this game. They can be seen trying to bite one another as they gallop along! The game I saw had about twenty riders on each team. Tough looking men with the scars of many other Buzkashi games behind them. I could never differentiate one team from the other. Of course, they must have known one another or have been wearing some distinctive piece of cloth. The game seemed to be mostly in the center of the field, a struggling mass of men and animals. Then, suddenly, one man would break away from the pack and head for the post with everyone else in hot pursuit. He was usually caught and had to fight his way along, supported by his team mates. Suddenly, one of the horses and its rider jumped over the ditch and came tearing down towards where I was standing with a cluster of other spectators. Everyone scattered, except for me. I stood right in the path of the duo, determined to get a head on shot. I felt that the rider was good enough to veer away from me. He did, but only just in time. In a second or so, he was being chased by a dozen other riders and I couldn't tell who had the goat. The first rider didn't. It was my guess that he had whipped someone too hard and was going to have to pay for it.

My guide came up to me and told me, in no uncertain terms, that what I had done was foolhardy and that he was personally responsible for my safety. Yet, several of the other spectators who had scattered came up to me and shook my hand and patted me on the back. It's one of my most memorable photographs. Usually, in a Buzkashi game there are some fatalities and several injuries. Fortunately, this day there were only a few injuries. When the big games are played, with hundreds of participants, the deaths are many. It's a rough life for the players but they are all heroes and very well paid. The four of us got into the car and went back to the driver's house. As he lifted his youngsters onto the ground, I asked him if I could see his home. By this time he was back to his old, not too miserable self and readily agreed. We went through the gate where I found a neatly laid out vegetable garden. I put my camera, one with a silent shutter, to my eye and saw a young woman against the back of the house, without a chadri. Her husband shouted at her as she scuttled away and into the house. She was there long enough to get in my picture. I took my hands off my camera, as the driver turned around and asked him if I could take a picture of him with his sons. He was pleased and obligingly they stood there for me. Then he went into his house while the guide and I got back into the car. We waited a few minutes for the driver to return. He was wearing a big smile. He spoke to the guide who later told me that the man's wife had changed her mind and wasn't going to leave him. He, in turn, wasn't going to throw things at her.

It was past lunch time and I still hadn't got hold of Sultani. I got to the hotel where I sat in the lobby and paid off my guide. It is interesting to know that after I left Mr. Hosseini's office, I asked the Tourist Bureau about paying the guide and driver and he told me that I could pay by travelers' checks, cash, personal check or be billed. Anyway, I had an ample supply of travelers' checks and those are what I used. I asked the guide if he had an official bill. He said that he didn't use them but would write out two bills for me on hotel stationery. Why two bills? One for the guide and the other for the car rental. It seemed a bit fishy but I went along with him. The sum of the bills was very reasonable and was promptly paid, with the checks being made out to the guide. I thanked him for his outstanding job. He told me that I was the best person who had ever used his services. I gave him a few hundred afs for himself and some for the driver. We shook hands and parted. I went to my room and tried to get Mr. Sultani again. He answered! I said, "Mr. Sultani, this is Mr. Saffer. I hope you had a nice holiday." He replied, "Yes I did, thank you. What can I do for you?" "Mr. Sultani," said I, "I have an ancient brick and you promised to give me an export license." "You have brick?" he answered, "I'm sorry but I cannot help you." With that, he hung up on me. I washed off the dust and went to eat.

On the way to the dining room, I stopped at the small travel bureau at the end of the lobby to reconfirm my airline bookings. I was scheduled to fly from Kabul to Lahore, Pakistan, at eleven the following morning on Afghan Airlines. After a few days in Lahore, I was booked on an Alitalia flight to Rome for connection with a flight to Malta, where I had made plans to rest up for a week.

(I had already received permission to operate an amateur radio station there). The agent checked my ticket, made notes, and told me he would teletype Lahore and get me reconfirmed.

That matter out of the way, I went into the dining room, ordered a drink and my meal and tried to decide on a plan of action. Was I going to try and get the brick through Customs, pleading the fact that it came from an open ruin...if I were caught? Or, because of the tension I could feel inside Kabul with what now seemed like expectations of some sort of disturbance, was I going to "play it safe" and leave the Ghaznevid brick behind under my dresser? I had photographed it along with the previous day's edition of the Kabul Times, as proof of its existence as well as the date I got it. No! I was not going to give up that which I had traveled so far to get. The answer came in a flash.

The guide had told me that he was promoted to Head Guide because of his twenty years of service and that he was known all over Afghanistan and, indeed, even inside Pakistan. There was the solution. I told the waiter to hold up my meal for a few minutes, dashed to my room and telephoned the guide, at his home. I asked him if he would come over to the hotel in an hour or so. He readily agreed, although I didn't tell him what I had in mind.

Shortly after finishing my meal, I was strolling around the hotel driveway when he showed up, in his own car and with an unveiled woman beside him, his wife. He introduced her to me. She spoke English as well as her husband did and we chatted about the places I had visited during the past few days. I asked her to excuse us while I talked business with her husband, in my room.

First of all, I again complimented him on the fine job he had done for me. Then I asked if it was really true that he was well known even in Pakistan. He reassured me on that point. Then I asked him if he was on close terms with the Afghan Border Customs officers. For a couple of minutes he regaled me with the names of all the Customs and Immigration officers with whom he was on the closest of terms. Telling him that as a native-born Englishman I had always wanted to go through the Khyber Pass, I asked him if he and his driver would be able to pick me up at six o-clock the following morning and take me from Kabul, through the Kabul Gorge, into Pakistan and through the Khyber to Peshawar. For a price it was possible. He quoted me a fair fare and the deal was sealed and he departed.

By this time I had used up twenty rolls of film and thought it would be good if I packed them in my special boxes and mailed them back to my photofinishers, in the U.S. With a lot of frustration, I succeeded in getting ten rolls into each mailer which I took down to the hotel post office. The man in charge made me unpack both mailers and he carefully smelled each and every cassette. I asked him what he was trying to find and he told me that it was illegal to export hashish. Of course, he didn't find any and he let me wrestle, again, trying to get the cassettes back into the boxes. That being done, he put the required stamps on the boxes, canceled them, put a special Customs' stamp on and then tightly wrapped each mailer with very wide and heavy "Scotch" tape. There were, as mentioned, a total of twenty rolls. When the mailers arrived at the photofinishers there were only eighteen rolls! One had been removed from each box! That must have been the work of the U.S. Customs Service. The least they could have done was to have the two rolls they abstracted developed and sent on to me. One of the missing rolls had the shot of the driver's wife outside the house.

I got the hotel manager to get a couple of cheese sandwiches and some bottled water sent to my room and paid my bill. The sandwiches were very carefully wrapped and put into my flight bag, along with my ancient brick, and I turned in early.

CHAPTER 2

DASH TO KHYBER AND BEYOND

It was cold (40 degrees) and drizzling when we drove away from the hotel onto the nicely paved road which would lead us through the amazing Kabul Gorge, past Torkham, and into Pakistan and the Khyber Pass. For the first half an hour, nothing much was visible save the waning stars. During this time I ate my sandwiches and took a swig or two of my bottled water. Then, as the sun rose, I was able to get a good look at the ever-winding road and the sights along it. The road was steep and, even with the windows up, I could hear the sound of the Kabul River as it torrented down to its lowest point. The towering rocks were grey tinged with copper and soared so high that I couldn't even see the top of the mountain. A small group of nomads appeared, slowly edging up towards Kabul, including a man, three women, several children, and three heavily laden camels. I couldn't tell what two of them were carrying. However, the third was burdened with the nomads' heavy skin tents and poles, atop of which was a small round-faced boy securely fastened by a rope so he wouldn't fall off. As our car pulled over to the left side of the road, which had a grassy plot beside the racing river, I hopped out and walked over to the nomad, pointed to my camera, and waved a 100 af note. He smiled and pointed to himself and the camel carrying the boy, an indication that it was fine as long as I didn't take pictures of his women. I took several pictures, including one of the man who stopped the "caravan" long enough to pose for me. Posed photography is not my desired modus operandi, but when dealing with people whose religious tenets, normally, include a ban on any representation of the human form, unless shooting from afar, I always asked permission first. Usually, those who agreed to be photographed "struck a pose."

After I got back in the car, I was told that the nomads I had just met, typical of thousands who wintered in the southern border city of Jalalabad, could purchase goods that were not readily available in Kabul and other places in Afghanistan. When spring came, they would leave Jalalabad with its pleasant trees and grass covered plateau and go north spending several months peddling their wares from village to village and town to town.

At the end of the gorge, we pulled over so I could photograph the point where the river formed a vortex before continuing. The power of the water had worn a large "bowl" in the rock. The guide drew my attention to the mountain-side down which we had been rapidly driven. From that vantage point I could see where the road kept appearing right alongside the precipice, as well as the wrecks of two Afghan buses that had gone over the edge probably with most of their passengers still in them. Yes, traveling in Afghanistan was a perilous business. The road had now turned into a gentle slope and began to pass cultivated fields on both sides. The river had disappeared from view.

We came across two ancient-looking conical brick kilns at which, of course, we had to stop. I walked into the field and examined them closely. Heaven only knows how old they were, but it was obvious that they were still being used. To get a good all embracing shot, I stepped back several yards and, once again, found myself with a foot in a grave. Although my stomach was churning, because of the stench, I stayed put and got my picture. It took a long drink from my bottle of water to get my tummy settled down.

We approached the town of Jalalabad where the temperature was over 100 degrees, quite a difference from the miserable 40 degrees we had left behind in Kabul, that morning. However, we had come down some 4,200 feet with more to go. The town, I had heard, was really a very interesting place to see and well known as a good source of souvenirs, but I wanted to get past the Afghan border post before eleven o-clock. (That was the time when my failure to board my plane in Kabul just might have caused the authorities to wonder where I was). So on we went until we came to vast fields of beautiful poppies, in variegated colors, on both sides of the road. They were the biggest and healthiest looking poppies I had ever seen and I had to have the car stopped so I could get a close look at them. The guide told me we were in a "no man's land" separating Afghanistan from Pakistan, that it was claimed by neither country and what I was looking at were high grade opium poppies. I asked the driver to go into one of the fields for a photograph. With a big grin he obliged and, after I had taken my pictures, came out of the field holding a flower which he offered to me...a gift I declined.

Even though this was supposed to be neutral territory, the Afghan Customs and Immigration offices were "parked" there. Just a mile down the road from where we had stopped was the Customs Office, a place with which I certainly didn't want to become involved. I told the guide I didn't want any problems; indeed didn't even want to get out of the car. I reminded him of his boast that he was very close to the Customs and the Immigration officers, and handed him a 100 af note telling him to give it to whomever was manning the office. The poor chap looked uncomfortable. He ran his finger around the inside of his collar, looked down at the flight bag with its contraband brick, but still got out of the car. He disappeared behind a privet hedge, returned smiling in less than a minute, got into the car and told the driver to move on to the Immigration Office which was just twenty-five yards down the road. Here, again, I handed the guide 100 afs, as well as my passport with the last of my Afghan visas and sat back. No-one came near the car! My "messenger" returned in a couple of minutes, handed me my passport (properly stamped) and got us on our way. The reader must have gathered that in Afghanistan one drives on the right. Well, some twenty-five yards beyond the Afghan Immigration office, our driver suddenly swerved over to the left side of the road and I knew I had arrived in Pakistan.

A strange thing happened to both my guide and my driver the moment we crossed over. The guide made himself as inconspicuous as possible, even to putting one knee on the car floor, and the driver seemed to slide under the steering column. When I asked what was going on the guide told me that he couldn't get out of the car at the border stations because the Pakistani officers didn't like Afghans. He really looked very scared.

At the Immigration office I stepped out of the car and went inside. The officer on duty looked at my passport which had a stamped-in visa, put his own official stamp on the page, which indicated that I had entered Pakistan at Torkham, handed my passport back and said that he hoped I would have a nice holiday in Pakistan. Next, on to the Customs. This office was of especial interest to me because the moment I entered I could hear the sound of people playing table tennis. There was a uniformed officer sitting at a small desk facing the entrance, while along the wall two Americans, a long haired young man and a girl, both wearing black leather jackets, sat perspiring in the now 110 degree heat. I was still somewhat uneasy about my brick. Although Afghanistan and Pakistan and are contiguous countries, because of Afghanistan's reputation for having soil that harbors several plant diseases, there was a ban on certain agricultural products entering Pakistan. My brick, although of burned clay, still had some of the ancient dirt on it. (I should have washed it at the hotel). For the record, in case I had to dump the brick or it was confiscated, I had photographed it in my Kabul hotel room resting on the Kabul Times with the date showing.

I said "Good morning, sir," to the officer, who returned my greeting as he held out his hand for my passport. Taking this out of my shirt pocket, I held on to it and asked him who was playing table tennis. He pointed to an open doorway through which I could see a large barn with several other customs officials, two of whom were having an active game. Without asking permission, I walked through and stood watching the game. At one point, when one of the players made an excellent shot, I said loudly, "Jolly good shot!" Everyone looked at me, smiled and made room for me to sit and watch the game. After that match was over, one of the officers asked me if I played. Well, table tennis was "my game." I said I played a modest game and would like to play one of them. Someone gave me a paddle and off we went. It would have been bad form for me to show that I had played the game for fifty years, had a table in my basement, and could hold my own against my 19 year old son. So I made a good job of keeping even with my opponent, allowing him to win the game by three or four points. The onlookers were enthusiastic. They applauded every good shot that was made, especially by me. During my second game, one of the officers asked me if that was my car outside and, if so, would I give him a lift through the Khyber Pass to Peshawar. Naturally I agreed, and he went off to change into civilian clothes.

The "exhibition matches" lasted for several more games, until my rider appeared in "mufti" and indicated that he was ready to travel the twenty-six miles through the Pass. I was really glad at the prospect of having him along because just across the road from the Customs Office there was a brightly painted sign which was headed with the word "WARNING." It went on to state that persons driving through the Khyber Pass were advised that it was forbidden, and dangerous, to stop anywhere enroute. It ended with the advice that, if forced to stop, travelers should immediately look for a police officer! In other words, bandits abounded. Together, my passenger and I walked into the office and past the desk where the same officer on duty was sitting. He stood up and announced that he hadn't yet seen my passport nor examined my baggage for contraband. At this, my new companion turned round and told him that I was a friend of his who was giving him a lift into Peshawar, and that he knew I wasn't a smuggler. The other officer remonstrated, mildly, so I took out my passport and handed it to him so he could see I had passed through Immigration. He glanced at it very quickly, smiled at me and said that he still needed to examine my bags. An argument started between the two officers which I stopped by stating that I saw no reason why my bags shouldn't be looked at. The three of us walked outside, past the leather coated motorcyclists who were still sitting in the same place, and got to the car. Both the guide and the driver were so scrunched down that, at first, it appeared that the car was empty. I rapped on the front window and told the driver to give me the key to the trunk. The window was opened just wide enough for him to drop the keys out. We went to the back of the car and I opened the trunk and simply pointed to my solitary suitcase. My new friend said, "See, there's nothing there" and closed the lid. I shook hands with the Duty Officer and, despite the scared looks and grimaces of my guide and the driver, opened the door with the key and invited the passenger to step in. I got back into my front seat, and away we went. As we moved towards the Khyber, I asked the customs officer about the hippie couple sitting and sweating back at the office. He laughed and said that they had orders to discourage people like them from entering the country, even with a visa. It seems that they had both been searched and told that they would have to wait at Torkham until a mechanic arrived to check over their motorcycle. That, apparently, meant they would be held for another four hours at least.

The road sloped upwards to the Pass entrance where I could see dozens of concrete "dragon's teeth" ready to be moved into the roadway in the event of an invasion from the north. I asked who was expected. The officer said possibly the Pushtunistanis, a large and particularly troublesome Afghan tribe which wanted an independent state of its own. As we got to the Pass, the driver speeded up and I had to keep telling him to slow down so I could enjoy the thrill I had dreamed of as a boy. There were high, rocky cliffs, soaring a couple of thousand feet towards the sky. Every now and then I got a glimpse of one-man forts...simple stone circular walls...over the tops of which I would see the top of a rifle with its bayonet moving around as its owner walked to keep warm. Even though it was 110 degrees in the Pass, it was cold on top of the craggy cliffs. There was a waterfall cascading in the distance, and I asked the driver to stop. He said he wasn't allowed to. Patting the customs man on the back, I announced that he would see I didn't photograph anything I wasn't supposed to. So we stopped, the first of many such photography stops. We sped past a large sign, over a side road leading upwards, which said "HOME OF THE KHYBER RIFLES," a crack Pakistani regiment, and came to one of the hundred bends in the Khyber where, in the crook stood several memorial tablets. Each bore the insignia of a British regiment and the date of the fierce engagement that had taken place there. As I stood looking at these historic markers, some school children dressed in dark blazers, short pants, and English-type school caps walked by. It seemed strange to find these youngsters dawdling along in such a remote place, amid the perils of the Pass, and in their school uniforms they looked as though they might have just come from school in London. The boys didn't object to being photographed and I gave each some money. The driver was, again, asked to keep the speed down. The guide timidly told me that the reason for the haste was so they could get back to Kabul before nightfall. I nodded but told him that we had plenty of time and that I was paying them to show me the interesting places, not just to transport me. At another bend in the road the customs officer told the driver to stop and said I was missing a very important sight in the Khyber Pass. He walked me to the edge of the road and pointed out a second road that was far beneath us and which seemed to disappear around a bend in the distance. He told me that it was the camel road and unpaved to make it easier for those beasts of burden to keep their footing as well as being much cooler to their feet than paving.

After taking several photographs (including one of a one-man fort), I looked up at the thousands of boulders lining the route and realized that from their shelter the Afghan fighters had fired many a shot at the ill-fated British soldiers and, at times, their families. Thousands of Britishers had been slaughtered in the Khyber Pass, as well as a goodly number of Afghans. Every inch of the way had been a battleground. Even today, there is danger for everyone from some of the Pathan tribesmen, whose villages are at the top of the precipitous embankments, existing by pursuing a life of banditry. More regimental memorial markers were seen and photographed and then we approached a tremendous fort. It was vast, built with red brick and had ponderous solid gates that seemed impregnable. There was a large square box built on the far slope at the front. It was filled with black rocks with white rocks embedded and forming the words "FORT SHAGAI." My guide told me I shouldn't attempt to photograph this monster of a fortification, but it was so impressive that it put to shame anything I had ever seen in the movies about the fighting in the Khyber Pass. The customs officer also told me to forget a picture of the fort. Not to be denied, I rolled down my window, told the driver to put his foot on the accelerator, and set my shutter speed to a 500th of a second. I managed to get a shot showing two sides of the fort and another head-on shot. (When the slides were developed, I could make out the figure of a Pakistani soldier outside the fort on the front, waving a rifle at the car). We passed another fort, with mudwalls, and set back from the roadway with a screen of trees in front. This was "Fort Jamrud," one of the most famous forts in the Khyber Pass. A few minutes later, we passed through an impressive archway built in the 1960's as a formal entrance to the Pass. We were now in Peshawar.

The streets of Peshawar were crowded; and as we stopped to let the customs officer off, a young man came over to the car and handed us a handbill. The customs man told us that it was a message in support of the Prime Minister who was in Peshawar on a formal visit. I shook hands with our rider, who was profuse in his thanks, and watched him disappear into the crowd. Just then a squad of Pakistani soldiers marched by. They were smartly turned out and stood tall and erect like the Buckingham Palace guards. After the shabbily dressed and undisciplined Afghan troops I had seen, this was a real treat. Flags were flying all over the place and strings of bunting stretched across every street. I wanted to stop and walk around for a few minutes and, maybe, see Prime Minister Ali Bhutto, but it was impossible to find a spot in which to park the car, so we went straight to the airport weaving our way through the crowd which filled the streets. When we got there, I paid off my guide and driver who disappeared in a flash. I walked over to the Pakistan International Airlines' desk to see about my flight to Lahore. (Pakistan International Airlines handles all flights within the country as well as overseas' travel).

There were two young men behind the counter and they greeted me very warmly and asked how they could be of assistance. I told them I wanted to get on the next flight to Lahore which I knew was due to arrive in just over an hour. Both these fellows looked quite dismayed and one of them told me that it would be impossible for me to get on that flight since it was full and, just like home, overbooked. I told them that I had just spent a horrible week in Afghanistan and had been looking forward to getting back to Pakistan where I could get a good meal, and a plane to Lahore where a high ranking army officer was expecting me. The two young men held a brief conversation, in Urdu, and then told me to leave my case with them and go up to the restaurant and have my "good meal" while they tried to work something out for me. I thanked them and then remembered that I hadn't changed any travelers' checks into Pakistani rupees. When I asked them where the money changer's booth was located they told me that, since the Prime Minister was in town, it was a holiday and the money changer's booth was closed. So here was another quandry. Then one of the chaps told me to give him my plane ticket, a signed travelers' check, and to go and eat and wait in the restaurant. The Mulligatawny soup and the egg curry made a delicious meal. In fact, after the insipid Afghan food it was "a repast."

Having eaten, I sat watching the tarmac and soon saw an F227 coming in for a landing. I knew, instinctively, that it was the flight I wanted but I could only sit in the restaurant and wait. In a few minutes the young man to whom I had given the travelers' check came up to me. He handed me several rupees (at the official rate of exchange), my ticket, and told me to hurry down to his desk. I paid for my meal and dashed out. The airline clerk told me that they had a seat for me as far as Islamabad but I must promise them that I would get off there, even though the plane's final destination was Lahore. I agreed and my case was handed to me. I was told to go up a flight of stairs, past the security officer, and out to the plane. I tried to tip the young men but they wouldn't accept anything. So, up the stairs I went and stopped so the security officer could examine my bag but he just smiled and waved me through.

Aboard the plane the steward led me to the only vacant seat, which was beside one occupied by a tall Pakistani in a smart business suit. The door was shut and off we went. I sat back and considered my options. I had no idea how far it was from Islamabad to Lahore and toyed with the idea of renting a car and driving on. Then there was the attraction of taking a taxi from Islamabad, the new Pakistan capital, to the famous city of Rawalpindi with its exciting history. I turned to the man beside me and asked him how far it was, by road, from Islamabad to Lahore.

He looked surprised and said, "Why would you want to make such a grueling drive when this plane flies to Lahore?" I told him that there was no room for me after Islamabad and I was expected in Lahore that same day. He asked me the name of my friend in Lahore and when I told him Brigadier Riaz

Khan he said that he knew him. We chatted for a while and I told him what I was doing traveling around, and about my displeasure with the Afghan officials. The steward came around offering tea and biscuits, which both of us accepted. (I had to have a refill because a nice hot curry can make one quite thirsty).

I didn't ask my companion what he did. Really, I didn't get much of a chance because he was full of questions about the Museum of Ancient Brick and my travels collecting the unusual artifacts. Then, about fifteen minutes before we were due to land In Islamabad, he said, "Don't worry about getting to Lahore. You will be able to stay on this flight; but when we land, you must leave the plane with me and stay by my side."

The seat belt light went on and we made our descent and landed in Islamabad. While the other passengers were filing out, my companion asked me to let him go ahead of me. As we proceeded down the aisle, he kept his right hand on my arm so we wouldn't get separated. When we got to the doorway, I noticed an army officer and another man standing at the bottom of the steps. As my man stepped onto terra firma, he was greeted with a smart salute from the army officer and a hearty handshake from the other person. They spoke a few words in Urdu and then switched to English, for my benefit. It seemed that I had been traveling with someone of note and began to understand what it meant to "meet people in high places." He addressed himself to the non-military man and spoke thusly. "This gentleman is a friend of mine and he has to get to Lahore on this plane. Please make certain that there is a seat for him. The plane must not be permitted to take off without him."

I was asked for my ticket and baggage check by the person who turned out to be the airport manager. He was informed that we would be in the V.I.P. lounge having some refreshment. I followed my heaven-sent guide into the lounge where he asked me if I would care for a drink. Now this, too, was a Moslem country where alcohol is forbidden but kept available for foreign non-Moslem visitors. I said I would enjoy another cup of tea, a selection which pleased my host. We sat and talked and drank tea for about half an hour, being the object of many people's curiosity, until the airport manager appeared, handed me my ticket and claim check and said the plane was ready to take off as soon as I was on board. I turned to my host, thanked him for his great courtesy, and asked him if he would mind giving me his name and address so I could send him written thanks. As he wrote in my notebook, I asked what branch of the government he was in and his position. He hesitated and then let me know that he was Pakistan's Deputy Foreign Minister. On top of all this fine man had done, he insisted on walking out to the plane with me and shook hands and said goodbye only after I had identified the lone bag by the plane steps as mine, and was ready to board.

Now I was right on schedule. Before long I was checked into the Lahore Inter-Continental, had arranged for a car with a driver/guide for the next morning, and was luxuriating in the joy of a nice hot bath...with much more than two inches of water. I had planned to see the city and scout for brick for the museum for three days before contacting the Brigadier and his wife, because I knew they would insist on having me stay with them, instead of at the hotel. Also, I knew they would want to show me the outstanding features of historic Lahore and I would be tied down, unable to do my brick hunting. So I didn't call on my arrival.

I went down to dinner and afterwards strolled down the quiet leafy road on which the hotel was situated. It was a really peaceful and relaxing walk in the cool of the evening. Then, for a while, I watched the antics of several groups of Pakistani teenagers frolicking around the hotel swimming pool...teenagers are the same the world over. Then, to bed and the sleep of the much traveled innocent.

My driver/guide showed up promptly after breakfast the next morning. He was a well-spoken Moslem who happened to be an Anglophile. During our time together, he told me that he wished he could return to Bombay which he had been forced to leave at the 1947 Partition. He believed that life was much easier in India than in Pakistan. He didn't know, as I did, how much the place had changed and the heartbreaking poverty that could be seen throughout all India.

Lahore is the capital of the truncated Punjab. The larger part remained as part of India at Partition. I found this city rich in history, a city of opposites. For instance, there were the immaculate tree lined avenues with fine homes occupied by wealthy merchants and high grade civil servants. Then there were the grassless dusty acres in the shadow of the tremendous and almost impregnable Fort with a tent city occupied by listless people who were both underfed and underclothed. It is a city which, on one hand, curses the memory of the British Raj while part of the better-offs still try to emulate his way of life. It reveres and preserves, as a part of history, the office of author Rudyard Kipling while deprecating many of his writings on life on the Northwest frontier, through which I had just traveled. In the middle of the road, on a grassy railed-in mound between Kipling's old office and a museum, there was an ornate early 18th century cannon. Its real name is "Zam Zama" but is generally referred to as "Kim's Gun," after Kipling's exciting adventure story about a young lad named Kim.

We drove to the Fort which, because of the additions made by the Mogul emperor Akbar "The Great," is known as "The Royal Fort of Akbar." The main military gateway is built of massive masonry blocks with iron-reinforced wooden gates. There are several other towering gates, one of which is open to permit visitors to enter and see the handsome marble pavilions, the startling "Hall of Mirrors," and decorative pools which show that the royal residents didn't have to "rough it." The first thing I noticed, on going through the gateway, were several chipped places in the monstrous walls. To make sure one realized what had caused this damage, each had a metal sign, "BULLET HOLES."

Before I started my search for any possible brick in the Fort, I visited some of the exhibition rooms. One was entirely taken up by a large-scale model of the "Taj Mahal." Another had 19th century prints hung on three walls. They were hard to see, because the only light came from a 60 watt bulb hanging down from the ceiling on its power cord. When I saw the prints I also saw the reason for wanting to "keep them in the dark." They depicted the fighting between the British troops and the Sikhs who had over-run the Punjab and occupied it for 79 years. The Moslem leaders had called upon the British forces to get the Sikhs out. This they did. They also stayed around until 1947!

I visited a large display of weapons: swords, pistols, rifles and several small bore cannon barrels. I also saw a group of youths being taken in by a "shell game" run by an expert! Roaming around the courtyards I caught sight of some brick buildings. I was over there "like a shot" to examine them. The buildings needed some maintenance and several bricks were quite loose. However, I didn't do anything more than measure them for later reference. These bricks were a dull red and not very large. In fact, the size was about the same as the Ghaznevid brick resting in my hotel room. The dimensions were 8" x 5", length and width. The thickness was a mere 2-1/2". I knew that by going through the right channels one of these brick might end up in our museum. (It did). From the battlements of the Fort I saw, side by side, the red sandstone and white marble Badshai mosque and a much smaller, pristine white, Sikh temple. The Badshai mosque is said to be one of the largest in the world. My point of observation gave me the best overall view of a mosque that I had ever had before, or since.

The driver found a place for me to partake of my usual egg curry and then took me off to see the mosque of Wazir Khan, an extremely ornate structure with dozens of intricately designed tiled panels on the facade, sides and on the minaret. The inside was equally fancy, but I didn't spend much time there because there were no bricks in sight.

The next stop proved more to my liking. It was at the tomb and gardens of Shah Jehangir, father of Jehan who later built the Taj Mahal at Agra, India. We approached down handsome red sandstone walkways with manicured lawns alongside. I paid my respects to the Shah who had a silver embroidered cover on his tomb. His Empress, Noor Jehan, was entombed just a short distance away. Actually, the Moslems did not put the bodies in the tombs. The corpses were buried, seven feet down. Twenty-five yards from Jehangir's well kept tomb I saw another tomb which was in a dreadful state of disrepair. It was gray and dingy and what made it look even more sinister was the presence of several vultures perched on the dome, or soaring just above it. The contrast between Jehangir's tomb and this one was astonishing. I was even more astonished when my guide told me that this was the tomb of Jehangir's favorite Vizier. I walked over for a closer look. Perhaps there were some brick around. No luck. However, as I returned to the other tomb I noticed an old brick wall that could have used a little maintenance. The bricks were identical to those I had seen at the Fort, and were actually part of Jehangir's tomb building. Once again, I took photographs for later use. (Along with a brick from the Fort, the museum also got a second with a document certifying that it came from Jehangir's tomb).

I asked the driver to "roam" around the Fort area so I could get a closer look at the way of life of the "have nots." We slowly drove close to the tent city. Outside one of the tents I saw a half naked man who was busy picking vermin from a shirt. Yet, a few yards away, another man was sluicing himself down with water from a canvas bucket. This fellow turned and smiled at me. Obviously nothing was "biting him." I got out and walked past a whole row of tents and saw only one woman. She was making chapatti, a round flat unleavened bread which, along with rice, is their staple diet. After I had taken my photographs and had another look at the outside walls of the Fort which had a host of tiled panels depicting wild animals, we moved on to where there was a small outdoor market which showed very little activity. Bullock-drawn wagons carrying farm produce were there. There was also a man who was trying to get rid of a couple of ugly water buffalo, while another had a few scrawny chickens hanging upside down from a pole stuck in the ground. Also present was a miserable, slimy stream which was trying to ooze its way along as it emitted a malodorous vapor. It was time to move along, and we drove to a clean little place where we could get (what else?) tea. We had a couple of cups, taking advantage of the time to relax a little. We chatted about Lahore and Karachi. I told my companion that when I had first visited Karachi, many years before, its population was only 360,000 and, at the time of my last visit had swelled to two-and-a-half million. The driver said he'd managed to go to Karachi to visit some family members and thought it resembled Calcutta because of the dreadful overcrowding. He hadn't actually been to Calcutta but kept reading about it and had seen a lot of pictures of the streets with their jumbled masses of humanity sleeping on sidewalks, in the gutters, propped up on window ledges, and even right out in the roads. I had been in Calcutta and had seen all this and had often found it necessary to step over people who were sleeping right on the sidewalk in broad daylight.

After our tea, I had the driver take me down town to the Alitalia office so I could make sure that Kabul had really reconfirmed my flights through to Malta. Surprise! Not only was there no record of my name anywhere in that office, but it seemed that the teletype system betweem Kabul and Karachi had been "out" for nearly a week. On top of this, the manager told me that the flight on which I was supposed to be booked...and had a ticket for...no longer existed. In fact, it had been discontinued before I left The States! (It was a good job my now ex-travel agent was thousands of miles away.) I asked to be put on another flight leaving the same day as my original, only to be told that the only Alitalia flight on that date originated in Australia and was fully booked. Another pretty kettle of fish. I got the manager aside and invited him to join me in a cup of tea, or coffee, while we discussed my situation and how it could best be handled. In the same arcade, near his office, was a small cafe which served beverages, non-alcoholic, of course. Before I got around to my problem, I brought up the subject of Italy and the fact that it was one of my favorite countries. He was a Roman so I raved about all I had seen there, so many beautiful buildings and works of art. I even talked about the fantastic history of the Roman Empire. This approach worked even though, in all fairness, I might have achieved my objective without it. The man became very friendly and, eventually, it was he who changed the subject saying that the flight from Australia was overbooked and that was why he knew all the seats would be occupied. However, he told me to return the next morning when he would see what he could do for me. It was closing time and nothing could be done that day.

We parted company and the driver took me around the nicer parts of Lahore, very proudly pointing out the many colleges and schools. Just about everywhere he took me had an air of peace and prosperity which I knew was just on the surface. Politically, the country was at unrest and demonstrations against the government were a daily occurrence. It was very late in the afternoon when I got back to the hotel. I went down to the bar by the swimming pool and had still yet another cup of tea while I surveyed the people sitting inside. (In case the reader is wondering why I drank so much tea, the reason was that the temperature was hovering around 110 degrees and it was necessary to imbibe a lot of liquid to replace that lost by perspiration.) I was surprised to see only a couple of other Westerners. The rest of the guests were vacationing Pakistanis whose conversations were very low key, unusual for that part of the world.

Back at the Airline office, the next morning, the manager met me and asked for my ticket. He wrote out a new one but didn't give it to me until we were ensconced in the cafe drinking tea. He explained that he had put me on the plane I wanted but had left the reservation status blank. I told him that without "OK" written in I was still "up in the air." His reply was to tell me how to proceed when I got to Karachi. There was no problem getting to Karachi. Several passengers were due to board there, most of them residents of Karachi. What I had to do was get myself checked in very early and be the first in line for boarding. If there wasn't room for everybody, it would be no hardship for the local residents to have to wait until the following day to fly out. The absence of the "OK" was to protect him in case of any official questions about how I got onto the plane. The check-in clerk who would be on duty the night I left was a friend of his, and he'd already spoken to him and he had agreed to accept my ticket. I thanked him for going out of his way to help me and wanted to give him a gift, which he quickly and firmly refused.

After leaving the Alitalia man, I strolled around looking for gifts for my family and friends. I was not in any of the regular crowded bazaar areas but the merchants were still the hard sell types. I found the prices varied from shop to shop, naturally, but eventually found one where the merchant was not so aggressive and his prices quite reasonable. I bought several brass plates with embossed designs and enamel inlays, some slippers and a few hand carved miniature camels, complete with miniature burdens. The quality of merchandise in the shops was excellent, mostly because they were European and American imports, especially cameras.

There were gorgeous saris and embroidered vests in an array of rainbow hues from the most delicate pastels to strongest flamboyant. We passed a movie house which was showing an Indian movie, Patha Panchali ("The Weary Road"..I believe), which I had seen in New York a few years earlier. I told the driver to be sure to get me back to that cinema before he left me at the end of our day's touring.

Lahore has been called "the City of Gardens" because the Mogul love of glorious gardens is apparent everywhere. Even the great Royal Entrance to the Fort has gardens leading up to it. (This beauty is in direct contrast to what one sees on the other side of the Fort). There are the Jinnah Gardens, named after the founder and first president of Pakistan, and the world renowned Shalamar Gardens. It was to the latter that we drove on that nice hot day.

The Shalamar Gardens were laid out in the early 1640's and, although covering some 40 acres, were completed after exactly 17 months and four days of intensive labor. The place is breathtaking by its beauty and the pleasant scents of myriads of flowers and shrubs. The several pools boast almost five hundred fountains which jet ten feet into the air before arcing back to the water or gently splashing onto the numerous lily pads. Symmetry was the "watch-word" for the great Mogul emperors and here it was at its finest. The pink marble walkways led me through a maze of white marble gazebos and carefully crafted shelters. I photographed a sign which listed all the different plants, shrubs and trees planted in Shalamar. The list includes such trees as mango, cherry, plum, kokcha sultani, apple, pear, almond, quince, all kinds of oranges, cypress, poplar and still more. In Shah Jehan's day it took 128 gardeners to look after the gardens. I had to keep stepping around the many workmen who were busy repairing the walkways, and estimated that there must have been at least 100 fellows planting, pruning, mowing and repairing. I found some neglected brick walls at a point furthest from the entrance and was able to pick up a loose brick for close examination. It was exactly like the others I had seen in the fort and at Jehangir's tomb. I carefully put it down in its original spot and then took some pictures of the wall. The best photograph I got in the gardens was of a full-flowered mulberry framed by a delicate white arch with a cluster of large yellow chrysanthemums in the foreground. With the restful sound of the playing fountains and the chirping of happy birds in the trees, all was quiet and peaceful. I spent almost two hours wandering around and photographing the gardens. There were the usual beggars besieging the gateway. We had managed to elude them on the way in but as we left we were mobbed. In such cases, if you give something to one you have to be prepared to hand out to everyone. My way of handling this is to always carry a large number of coins, of small denomination, and start flipping them into the air in a direction away from my car. Then as these needy people, usually enjoying the game, try to pull the coins out of the air I quickly get in and drive off. At Shalamar I saw one young girl, possibly 14 or 15 years old, with a ring in a nostril and carrying a baby in her arms and offering small colored feathers for sale. She looked really pathetic and more miserable than some of the other young girls who were also begging. So much so that after I got in the car I beckoned to her, rolled the window down a crack and slipped a five rupee note (75 cents) through it into her grimy hand. She rewarded me with a wan smile and pushed one of her feathers through the same crack. We started to drive away and had to brake suddenly to avoid hitting a 300 pound man who was riding what appeared to be a child-size bicycle.

We went to part of the old city where we parked in a small business section so I could observe the citizens as they went about their daily life. There was a large pile of new bricks sitting on a scrubby grass median with lengths of used, and some new, lumber scattered further along. As I watched, a man with a donkey drawn cart drew up alongside the bricks and proceeded to load about fifty. Another man, obviously the seller, came out of a doorway and stood by the bricks. Leaving nothing to chance, he counted those loaded into the cart and was paid immediately. The purchaser then moved over to the lumber and selected several pieces. Before these were loaded, a little haggling went on which ended with more loading and more rupees changing hands. My driver/guide said that was the way most bricks and lumber were sold in that part of Lahore. Large scale builders, he informed me, would get bricks right at the kilns and lumber from large storage yards. There was a spice shop whose stock rested inside about a dozen large sacks just by where we were parked, and I walked over to enjoy the aroma. It was fascinating to watch two women, not together, take a scoop of such things as coriander, cumin, dried cinnamon leaves, ginger roots, turmeric, red peppers and peppercorns ...all fresh... have them put in quickly made cones of white paper, pay the reckoning and depart to do their daily chore of grinding the spices so the family would have fresh curry powder. The shop owner gave me a cardamom to smell and taste. The black seeds were inside a white pithy ball. I chewed a little of the outer shell and found it very pleasant and realized that the same taste was part of all the curry dishes I ate.

I left the driver and walked along the street. There were a goodly number of maniacally driven cars passing by with plenty of horn blowing. As we walked in, I looked some of the men in the eye and offered a "Salaam" which was usually returned. Some of them just stood and stared at me without saying a word. I asked one fellow where I would find somewhere to have some chai. He ignored me. Another, though, pointed across the street where a man was standing guarding a tremendous samovar which was resting on a large table surrounded by cups. I told him I wanted a cup of chai, but the milk had to be boiled. That was no problem for him and he told me that he only used freshly boiled milk, producing from behind the samovar a tiny pot of milk which he placed on top of the samovar's smoke vent. It boiled in a minute. The tea was strong, and already well sweetened. I really enjoyed it and went to tell my driver to go over and have a cup. He declined because it was now late afternoon and he wanted to get me to the cinema in the other part of the city.

When we got there, I thanked him for his excellent service and his very pleasant company and asked for a bill. This time, as opposed to my Afghan guide's suspicious bill(s), I was handed an official company bill which had been prepared beforehand in the office. As I paid him, I added a handsome tip to the total. He thanked me and remarked that perhaps, one day, he would meet me in Bombay.

I checked on the show time and realized that there was plenty of time for me to find a nice restaurant and have a leisurely dinner. Apart from the cup of tea, I hadn't eaten anything since breakfast. There was a handsome hotel nearby and I walked into its dining room and ordered some Mulligatawny soup and my usual curry. I told the waiter I wasn't in any hurry and didn't want to be rushed. Every spoonful of soup was like a drop of nectar; each mouthful of curry was ambrosia. Yes, it was an outstanding meal and I walked to the cinema feeling well fed and at peace with the world.

The movie was in Hindi and, to my surprise, had English subtitles like the movie I had seen in New York. "Patha Panchali" is a down to earth movie which deals with the extreme poverty of an Indian village. I was somewhat surprised that such a depressing movie would be shown in an area which was, itself, surrounded by terrible poverty. It was even more enjoyable than when I saw it in the U.S. When it was over, with a little difficulty I found a taxi which took me back to my hotel where I had tea brought to my room, dictated for a while, looked up the Brigadier's phone number, had my bath and turned in.

The Lahore climate must have been good for me since I didn't wake up until after 8 a.m. I dawdled over my breakfast and read the morning paper. At ten o-clock, I dialed the Brigadier's number. A soft and pleasant female voice answered and said "Hello. Who is this, please?" I replied, "I'm Mr. Saffer from the States. Is the Brigadier in?"

"Yes, one moment please," the voice said. There was a pause of a few seconds until another voice came on the line. This time it was a demanding man's voice. "Who is this?" it asked. "You are from the States and your name is Mr. Saffer? Mr. Saffer...are you Jeff's dad?"

"I certainly am," I said. "Welcome to Lahore, Mr. Saffer. Where are you now? We'll come and pick you up." In an apologetic voice I informed him that I was at the Inter-Continental Hotel. "What are you doing at the hotel? When did you get in? You know that you must stay with us all the time you are in Lahore."

I told him I had been there just three days and didn't want to bother him and his wife until I had finished some work. Very sharply the Brigadier told me I was in the wrong and should have contacted them as soon as I got to town. He announced that he and a servant would be down to pick me up in a few minutes.

I hurriedly started to pack but stopped when I realized that my new host would probably try to pay my hotel bill. So I got down to the lobby as fast as I could and settled with the hotel. Not a moment too soon, either. Just as I turned away from the cashier's spot, a stocky man dressed in a Hawaiian shirt and accompanied by a servant came into the lobby. He came straight up to me, shook my hand and then went over to the cashier. When he found I had already paid my bill he was annoyed, and told me so. We went up to my room to get my things. Several items were still unpacked so the servant picked up some of my articles of clothing, while the Brigadier grabbed my suitcase.

Off we went. I was told that I must call him Riaz, and that since it was too early for lunch he would take me to his club for a drink. Because we were not suitably dressed, we had to go into one of the club's smaller bars. Riaz ordered a Scotch. Since the temperature was already over 100 degrees, I decided to settle for lemonade. I didn't want to pass out on him. As we worked on our drinks, he asked about his youngest son and thanked me for opening my home to him. I gave him the latest on that son and what little I knew about his other two sons, also in the U.S. Talking with him, it was easy to tell that he was used to issuing commands and not being questioned.

We drove to the outskirts of Lahore to the military compound and pulled into the driveway of a smart new bungalow. As we passed the entrance I noticed that he had a brass nameplate with the letters "M.C." after his name. So I was with a war hero who had been awarded the British Military Cross. His wife, a very lovely lady in a fine sari, welcomed me at the door. She said that I was very welcome in their home and that Wisam, my son's room-mate, was always writing nice things about my son and his parents. I was shown into my room. It was nicely furnished with twin beds, a lovely dresser with pictures, a chair and a complete toilet set: military brushes, combs and a hand mirror. On the wall was a framed citation describing how the Brigadier, then a captain in the British army, had won his medal in WW2. Just off the bedroom there was a full bathroom, loaded with fine Turkish towels. Riaz showed me more of his immaculate home. Spread on the floor at the entrance to a formal dining room was the largest Bengal tiger skin I had ever seen.

Riaz told me that I was looking at his first tiger, shot when he was only 15. It was, he said, the second largest Bengal tiger ever shot anywhere on the Indian continent. There were two more bedrooms and a den whose walls were covered with a museum-worthy display of all kinds of weapons. Swords, daggers and guns ranging from the antique to the most modern. The informal eating room, or breakfast room, was an extension of the kitchen which had a modern American electric range. Unfortunately, the range and a large American refrigerator couldn't be used because there wasn't a 220 volt line feeding the house. Riaz said that he hoped to have it put in shortly. Meanwhile, all the cooking was done on a propane gas range.

The family name was "Khan" (actually the tribal name of those peoples who inhabited the eastern side of the Khyber Pass), and Mrs. Khan reappeared dressed in a different colored sari from the one I had seen her in when I arrived. She announced that lunch was ready. Riaz jokingly said, "She means Tiffin." That is the Hindi word for lunch, and all the time I was with the Khans Riaz would use Hindi words that most English-born people are familiar with. For "Chai" he would use the English corruption, "Char." He referred to my wife as my "Begum," a lady of high rank, and called his car the "Gharry" which is actually an animal drawn conveyance. It was a novel experience being with such a jolly man who continually pulled my leg. I went to my room and washed up and returned to find a beautiful slender young girl standing by the table. I had forgotten that Wisam had a sister, as well as three brothers. She was only about 14 but had the grace and deportment of someone much older. Her Sari matched her mother's.

We sat around the table and helped ourselves to plain rice over which we spooned a curry sauce. The bowl of rice had just two small cubes of meat in it, probably to add a little flavor, and I had never seen it cooked this way before. The servant kept us supplied with fresh hot chapattis which I could see him making on a flat piece of iron placed over one of the burners on the gas range. I learned a lot about the Khans during "tiffin." Riaz had been the Pakistani Military Attache in Washington and before that had served in the same capacity at the embassy in Buenos Aires. Both the Brigadier and Mrs. Khan were "died in the wool" Anglophiles and Ameriphiles. Mrs. Khan talked at length about how she missed her wonderful Washington friends and the endless diplomatic functions. I felt that she would return to the U.S. at the drop of a turban. Naturally, she regretted the fact that all her three sons seemed destined to be permanent residents of the U.S. The eldest had married an American girl and was already settled.

Riaz related an incident that had all the features of a classical fable. Just before they left the U.S., he took each of his sons aside, in turn according to age. Each was asked, "What one thing can I do for you before I go back to

Pakistan?" The eldest who was working in a stockbroker's office asked for a finely tailored business suit. The second son asked for a brand new, powerful, sports car. Wisam, the youngest and only 16 and already at the University of Maryland, asked that his father leave enough money in the bank account so that he, Wisam, could continue his education.

Lunch over, I stood up and said I would like to walk around the compound whereupon Riaz said, " Nonsense! It is 110 outside and far too hot for you to be walking around. It is time to take a nap; you can see the compound later when it is cooler." I murmured something about having been in hotter places and him having heard the saying: "Mad dogs and Englishmen go out in the noonday sun." He hadn't reached the exalted rank of Brigadier General or won his military cross by being easily contradicted, so it was off to bed for me. When I got to my room I found that the covers had been turned down and the bed was ready for me to slip into. I stripped to my underwear, got into the bed and fell fast asleep.

I was awakened by a couple of taps on my door. I invited the visitor to come in and was surprised to find it was the servant who wheeled in a tea trolley which he placed right beside my bed. After he had padded out of the room, I looked at the tray and found a pot of tea (covered with a padded "tea cosy"), a plate of imported biscuits, a container of hot water, milk and two cups and saucers. When I saw the second cup and saucer I thought that Riaz was probably coming to join me. After a few minutes I realized that the second set was for me. In the event that I wanted a second drink I would have a clean cup and saucer. The tea was delicious and I did have two cups.

I thought a shower would be refreshing and started towards my bathroom. On the way I had a closer look at Riaz's M.C. citation. He had been a tank battalion commander and had been ordered to delay a Japanese advance long enough for reinforcements to be brought up. All his tanks had been knocked out in the engagement. Just about all his men were dead and Riaz had hopped from one tank to the other, barely escaping with his life each time. Finally, there was only one smashed tank left that was in a position where its large gun and its machine gun could be brought to bear on the enemy. Riaz climbed aboard and, the sole survivor of the action, started firing both guns which kept the enemy from advancing up a hill. This final act managed to cause the required delay. This hero was my host!

After my shower I went looking for Riaz. I heard voices in the hallway and found the daughter engaged in a conversation, in Urdu, with a pleasant young man. They were sitting on a small bench and the moment they saw me they stood up and spoke in English. The daughter, who was now wearing a different sari, introduced the young man to me as her cousin. We shook hands and I asked where her father was and was told he was outside watering the lawn. Lawn? All was hard clay and dust and the only grass I had seen outside the bungalow was a scraggy patch of ground where a few blades of grass had managed to force their way through to the sunlight in very few places. At any rate I found Riaz doing just as his daughter had said, watering his "lawn." He asked me if I'd had a nice nap and I told him it had been very nice indeed and that I hoped that he'd had a nice nap also. "Nap? Me?" he said, "I don't take afternoon naps. I went to the club and played squash."

Mrs. Khan came out, in the third sari I had seen her in that day, and I got the Khan family assembled outside the bungalow so I could get some pictures to show his sons. I had already photographed the inside, including the tiger skin. As I took the first shot, through my lens I could see that the smoke from Riaz's ever present cigar had formed a pall in front of his face. I told him he'd disappeared in a puff of smoke!

The cousin had already gone, and Riaz loaded us into his car and took us on a tour of his city...the pleasant part only. As we traveled I learned that Riaz's father had been the only native born Indian to have ever been appointed District Commissioner under the British and that Mrs. Khan's father had been a District Police Commissioner. (I was definitely in high powered company.)

Once again, I had the places of learning pointed out to me, as well as a fine stadium where exhibitions of tent-pegging and polo were held and where a British style military tattoo was staged. We went on to Riaz's club where I saw the cricket pitches and the fine polo grounds there. Riaz, apparently, had his own string of polo ponies and was a prominent player. I remembered reading that polo had originated in Persia where, at one period, they used the heads of enemies instead of a ball. Riaz hadn't heard that one, but thought it quite plausible.

After nearly two hours of sight seeing, when it was getting dark, we were taken to an exclusive open air restaurant where the manager told Riaz that all the tables that were unoccupied were reserved and that Riaz knew that reservations were a must. I couldn't understand a single word but gathered from the rising voices and the pointings to the empty tables that trouble was brewing...for the manager. Riaz turned to me and apologized for the manager's "rudeness to an important foreign visitor." The man, of course, understood English and started moving his feet about and clasping and unclasping his hands. I felt sorry for him, especially so when Riaz turned back to him and starting "barking" his extreme displeasure. This did the trick and we were shown to a table right in the center of the garden. Menus were handed out but I didn't get a chance to look at mine. Riaz took it away from me and told me to order anything I wanted and it would be prepared for me. I asked for a cup of tea, to be followed by a vegetable curry.

The tea came very quickly with Riaz making sure that the milk had been freshly boiled. He stated that he didn't want me going home with, as he put it, "a sick belly." We chatted about the U.S., their sons, and how they missed Wisam most of all because his sister was growing up and hadn't seen him for over three years. His parents expressed the hope that he would finish at Maryland and then return to Lahore and enter Medical School. I told them of my adventures in Afghanistan, without mentioning the unusual military activity and the disguised hill fort. (After all, despite the shoddy treatment I had experienced at the hands of the Afghan officials, I was not a spy.) I related how I had found some interesting Mogul brick in Lahore and hoped that the Department of Archaeology would oblige me by shipping a couple to me at a later date. Riaz said I should have just picked them up and carried them away.

43

The meal arrived and the blend of aromas from the different dishes each of us had ordered was mouth watering. Subconsciously, I reached for my knife and fork. They weren't there! I quickly realized that knives and forks were only for foreigners and picked up a chapatti, tore off a small piece and proceeded to eat my curry "a la Pakistan," forming the chapatti into a small vee shape and picking up my food in that. Riaz had been talking to his wife and hadn't seen what I was doing. It was the daughter who drew his attention to the fact that I was eating in the local manner. Riaz "got hot" again. He shouted for the manager who got another dressing down, this time in English, for not supplying the visitor with cutlery. I interposed that I was quite comfortable without them, but the poor man had to dash off and return with a knife and fork. However, I ignored them and completed eating my meal in the way I had started. After dinner we returned to the Compound and had a cup of tea and some chitchat before I retired for the night.

The next morning, Riaz drove me downtown to a bustling, busy bazaar. There was no room to park, so Riaz made his own parking place. He left his car resting on the sidewalk with just two wheels resting in the road. We went from shop to shop with Riaz saying, "If you see anything you want, just tell me. I want to buy presents for your son, your wife and your daughter and for my daughter-in-law."

In this street bazaar I could see the garments being made on the spot. In one shop, where Riaz bought some Pakistani shirts, worn outside the pants, there were little boys busily plying needles as they produced some amazing embroidery. I was fascinated but had to move on after the purchase had been made. We passed shoe stores where the shoemakers were busy making shoes. (It reminded me of the man who made a pair for me in India several years earlier. He had drawn an outline of each of my feet, handed me an American shoe catalog telling me to pick out the style I wanted and producing well-fitting shoes in a matter of hours.) We went into a sari shop where he purchased a table runner for my wife and long Pakistani robes for my daughter and his daughter-in-law.

After a delightful hour in this street of wonders, Riaz told me that it was over 110 degrees and that I should be taking in some liquid. With that we drove back to his home where tea was served. While I was sipping my "brew", Riaz handed me a dagger. It had an ivory handle with a silver top and chain. The sheath was wood covered with tooled black leather. At several places there were small round holes in the leather through which peeped inset gold and silver. I drew the dagger from its sheath. I hadn't seen such a wicked looking weapon before. It was razor-sharp and had a quarter inch flat piece running the whole length of the blade. Riaz said it was called a "Pehj" and was quite capable of penetrating chain mail. I gingerly put it back in the scabbard and returned it to its owner. However, it turned out that I was the new owner. This was Riaz's gift to me. I remonstrated with him and told him that I couldn't take part of his fine collection. It was no use. The vicious looking dagger was mine. (On returning to the States, I showed it to a Customs Officer and told him that even looking at the blade made me bleed.)

We left the house for a sightseeing ride out in the countryside. The land looked quite fertile and full of growing crops. After some 30 miles we came to a large artificial lake. I was told it was a special reservoir, some 350 years old, which had been built as a pleasure spot for Jehangir. There was a causeway which led to a three-story monument named "Hiran Minar." There were several rowboats on the lake and I would have liked to have walked to the monument but Riaz said that it was out of bounds. So all I could do was enjoy the peaceful scene from the car.

Back home for lunch and another nap! I was getting so much rest I was beginning to feel like a loafer, even though I had just about exhausted Lahore's more interesting treasures. That afternoon, I was able to take a short stroll around the compound where I saw the homes of other officers, although none of them looked as nice as my host's. It was really arid out there and the dust rose up to greet me at every footstep.

I asked Riaz if it would be possible for me to visit one of the other bazaars downtown. Since we were going out for dinner, this was fine. Lahore has several bazaars and we went to one just inside the old city walls where the din was decidedly deafening. Yet here was the best "flavor" of the city I had yet "tasted." Whatever one wanted in the way of clothing, furniture, carpets and souvenirs was available. We roamed from store to store looking at such things as camel skin lamps. These are hand painted camel bladders, blown up, varnished, and fixed in the round position and then mounted on a wooden base over the lamp socket. There were all types of gold and silver ornaments (bangles, brooches, rings, etc.), large embroidered shawls, pieces of carved ivory, wooden tables inlaid with mother of pearl, and decorated brass plates in every shape and size. Having collected so many interesting souvenirs on other trips abroad throughout many years, I knew there was no room left in my home for any more. Yet the "just looking" was enjoyable.

We ate dinner at a nice restaurant where I was supplied with a set of cutlery, which I didn't use, and went back to the compound. I had a nightcap with Riaz and turned in for my last night in Lahore.

The next day was full of "mopping up" visits. I went to the Lahore museum, right across the road from Kipling's office and "Zam Zama," which has a wonderful collection of Moslem miniature paintings as well as statuary, weapon collections and, what interested me most of all, items collected from the various archaeological sites. These included bricks from sites from which I had already obtained bricks for our museum. There was one bronze that was outstanding. It represented a fasting Buddha with every rib shown. Riaz insisted on returning me to Jehangir's tomb so he could see the brick I intended to write for. He actually had one in his hand when I told him that nothing would make me take it without permission. He reminded me of my Afghan brick, but I told him that even though the circumstances of its removal from Ghazni to my room in his home was unusual, I did have written permission to enter the country and get two bricks. Reluctantly, he replaced it and we continued on our way. I was shown the "Pakistan Day Memorial" which reminded me of a miniature Eiffel Tower and, at my request, we went to the Fort. When I was there, a couple of days earlier, I had tried to get a photograph of the model of the Taj Mahal but had failed because of the constant stream of people walking between my camera and the model. I wanted to try again. In we went, and because Riaz held the people back I got my shot. We wandered up to the top of the Fort and I decided to get a picture of the old harem entrance, which I had missed before.

Now I was getting restless and concerned about my flight from Karachi to Italy and Malta. Again, I had lunch at the Khan's and tried to relax for an hour or so. Then it was time to go to the airport to get the plane to Karachi. I said my goodbyes and thanked the Khan's for their generous hospitality and boarded my plane at 4:30 p.m.

It was only a two hour flight to Karachi and it was still daylight there. I checked with the Alitalia agent and, lo and behold, the clerk took my suitcase telling me that I should pick it up when I came back close to flight time, midnight. In the meantime, since I was going to have a long wait, he said I would be taken to one of their Rest Houses. I said I wanted to take a walk first, but it seemed that to get to the rest house I had to go immediately. So I got into a taxi, provided by Alitalia, and set off. The Rest House was in the center of the city and turned out to be a very old grey stone building that had an air of decay. Inside it was really dingy with a fetid atmosphere. The man at the reception desk came out to greet me. He addressed me by name and said that an Alitalia taxi would pick me up to return me to the airport at 11 p.m. I was escorted to a room on the second floor. It contained a camp cot, a straight chair and table on which stood an old fashioned ewer of water and a basin. The odor in the room wasn't merely stale, it was positively horrible. I had to get out quickly, so I asked the clerk to please have a towel and some soap placed in the room and then walked out into the streets of Karachi. Having been there a number of times before, I knew what to expect: the street vendors, which included public letter writers, astrologers, ear cleaners and barbers, doing business from carpets laid on the sidewalk. The light was fading rapidly, which was a pity because I hadn't been able to get photographs of these people on my last visit. At that time, the country was under Martial Law and there was no telling what official buildings might have shown up in my shots. So, once again, I was foiled and walked back to the Rest House.

I got to my room, lay on my sagging cot and closed my eyes. However, closing my eyes didn't close my nostrils which inhaled a now too familiar stench..decaying flesh. The first time I had this experience was when, as a schoolboy at camp, I climbed down a steep hill in North Yorkshire and came across the carcass of a sheep which had fallen over the edge. There was a large hole in its stomach which was home to thousands of nasty fat flies. I hadn't had a similar experience until I got to Afghanistan where I kept stepping into new graves. It flashed across my mind that a body had been immured in one of the walls of my room. I stepped into the hallway, moved to the next room, and gently opened the door expecting to find a corpse in there. The room was empty! I was getting nauseated and went straight downstairs, found the clerk and asked him to get me some tea. That, at least took the foul taste out of my mouth. I then asked him to get me a taxi so I could go back to the airport early. In any case, I would have had to leave before the Alitalia taxi came so I could follow the company's Lahore manager's instructions to be first at the gate.

At the airport there wasn't anyone behind the Alitalia desk, in fact the whole terminal seemed strangely short of bodies. (Wrong word!) I could see my suitcase standing, lonely, off to one side. I found a bell on the desk and hit it a couple of times and waited. A man came through the door, not the same one who had taken my bag earlier, and announced that it was too early to check in for the next plane. I pointed to my bag and told him that it was mine.

At this point he said, "We didn't expect you so early, sir, please let me have your ticket." He took the ticket, tagged my bag, which he handed over to me because the Customs might want to examine it, gave me a tag for my flight bag, filled out a boarding pass and stapled the suitcase stub to the inside of a folder and handed everything back to me, and reminded me that I had to be at the head of the line when the plane came in from Australia. I still had quite a few rupees left, having cashed several travelers checks at the hotel, and I offered some to the clerk telling him that I wasn't allowed to take them out of the country.

He declined, courteously, and told me to give whatever I had left to the Customs Officer who would be at the gate. He said that the officer would really appreciate some financial help. I still had about an hour and a half until the plane came in, if it was on time, so I looked for a place to get a sandwich and some tea.

Half an hour before the plane was due, I was standing, a line of one, at the gate chatting with the Customs Officer. According to him, several people would get off this regular flight to stretch their legs and to be able to brag about being in Pakistan. Further, some of them would wander away only to find, when they reboarded, that their seats had been taken by others who were starting off from that airport. I asked him what happened next. His words were, "What you would call 'a bloody mess'! There will be many more passengers than seats and some of them will be asked to leave the plane and travel tomorrow." He looked down at my bags and asked me if I had any National Treasures in them. I laughed and replied that all I had were items of clothing, cameras, too many gifts from Pakistan and a broken brick from Afghanistan. He grinned and said, "That is fine, sir, are you sure you bought enough Pakistani souvenirs?" With that he chalked on my bags one of the undecipherable marks used world-wide by Customs Officers. I was still a line of one, so I told him that I had some Pakistani rupees left and knew I wasn't permitted to take out more than 80 and would appreciate it if he would take charge of what I had and put it to some good use. He accepted the gift, shook hands with me, and quietly said, "Don't get off the plane, sir."

People started to line up behind me and I struck up a conversation with the man next to me. He was an Italian and had just finished a nice holiday in Kashmir and swore that it was the most beautiful place in the world. Suddenly the door leading to the planes was opened and a goodly mass of humanity came swarming through. They were talking, or shouting, in a number of languages ...Australian, Italian, German and, of course, Urdu. They spread out all over the lobby and entered the few shops that had opened just for them. A line of porters had formed behind the barrier through which we had to pass; and the first one looked for the customs' mark on my suitcase, picked it up and went towards the plane. By this time there were more potential passengers than I could count, but I was the first to go out. As we walked out towards the DC10 I gave the porter a five rupee note which I had reserved for the occasion. He saluted me and went to put my bag into the belly of the plane.

I went up the steps to the plane and handed my boarding pass to a sweet young thing who greeted me with a smiling "Buona Sera." Despite the exodus, there were still plenty of people left on the plane and all the vacant seats had "Occupado" signs on them. All, except one, that is. It was a window seat and I had to squeeze between two well fed Italian ladies who were excitedly trying to tell me something. Having arrived at my seat, I plopped down into its welcoming well-upholstered leather and promptly closed my eyes. Within half an hour there was a lot of yelling and screaming from several passengers who, by leaving the plane, had lost their seats. The entire aisle was jammed with these unfortunates. The lady next to me jabbed me in the ribs and again tried to tell me something. I couldn't have cared less. The seat I was in hadn't had a reserved sign on it, so it was fair game.

The situation in the aisle was getting nasty. People were trying to pull others from their seats to the accompaniment of much screaming. The aisle was so jammed that the stewardesses couldn't get through. Eventually, after another half an hour the captain's voice was heard on the intercom. In three languages, he announced that the plane was overloaded and couldn't take off until the aisles and toilets were clear. To assist him he had asked the police to come aboard and forcibly remove anyone who refused to go willingly. So the police came, and apart from the loud conversation between the occupants of different rows of seats, the plane was ready for takeoff. I closed my eyes again, this time falling into a nice sleep.

It was the captain's voice that awakened me. He said that because of a strike by the refueling personnel in Rome, we would be landing at Taranto. In the meantime, breakfast was being served. After refueling at Taranto, it was only half an hour's low level flight to Rome.

The first thing I did when I entered Leonardo da Vinci airport was to find out about my flight to Malta. There was a young man behind the Alitalia counter and I asked him if the plane would be flying that day. He said, "Of course it will, why do you think it will not?" I mentioned the fact that they were experiencing a strike. To this he answered, "That was nothing, we have strikes all the time."

He spoke nothing but the truth. That airport was, at that time, the draftiest in the world and I didn't relish sitting there for several hours. I walked upstairs to the large restaurant to have another breakfast. I pushed through the doors and found the entire staff engaged in a meeting. One waiter came up to me and told me they were not serving that morning because they were on strike!

Since I had nearly five hours before my plane, I decided to take a taxi into Rome and spend a couple of useful hours there. But they wouldn't let me leave the airport. I had not been inoculated for typhoid recently; and since I had come from Pakistan, going into the city was forbidden. I tried to tell the officers that they were mixed up. There was no typhoid in Pakistan and they were confusing it with Bangladesh, which used to be East Pakistan, where there was certainly typhoid in the air. So I was stuck there reading, walking, and drinking innumerable cups of Caffe Latte at a stand-up bar for the next several hours.

48

Eventually, I was able to check in and joined the crowd which was excitedly waiting to board the bus which took us out to the plane to Malta.

CHAPTER 3

TURKISH DELIGHT AND DILEMMA

In the year 1352 B.C. the eighteen year old pharaoh Tutankhamen, twelfth ruler of the eighteenth dynasty of Egypt, died. That's how I came to be having lunch with the Turkish Cultural Attache in Washington, D.C., discussing ancient bricks.

The ill-fated youth had left behind a pretty young widow, Ankhesamun, who was constantly pressured to remarry, quickly. Whoever became the successful suitor also became the ruler of Egypt, and the most forceful of the would-be pharaohs was an ancient courtier called Ay, old enough to be Ankhesamun's grandfather. In desperation the young queen sent urgent messages, on clay tablets, to the ruler of the Hittites pleading with him to be so kind as to send one of his six sons down to Egypt to be her husband. The Hittite king, Supiluliumash, was somewhat suspicious of the request and decided to check with his old friend the king of Babylon. This worthy gentleman replied that the request was "kosher" and that a Hittite prince could do worse than become the ruler of Egypt. So one of the sons was, eventually, sent off to become a husband and ruler. However, the tablet mail was horribly slow and by the time he had started on his journey, Ankhesamun had fallen into the clutches of Ay who had the Hittite prince waylaid and slaughtered while on his trip.

This tragic story came to light when archaeologists unearthed a large cache of clay tablets at Tel-el-Amarna near the Nile. The tale was reinforced when German archaeologists, excavating in Turkey many years later, found more tablets in the remains of a library in the ruins of the Hittite capital of Hattusas. The library, of course, had been built of brick. My objective then was to get permission to go up into the hills beyond the Turkish capital of Ankara and dig out one of the ancient library bricks.

The man from the Turkish embassy told me that I would have to get permission not only from his government but also from the German Institute in Istanbul. Because of the many decades of excavating by the Germans, they had been granted the sole right to work at the ancient site of the Hittite capital. I wrote to the Director of the German Institute, Professor Dr. Rudolph Naumann, and asked for his permission and assistance in dealing with the Turkish Department of Archaeology. The result was a nice letter giving me the Institute's blessing and a promise to clear the way for me with the Turkish authorities. The professor told me to let him know when I would be arriving in Istanbul so that he could arrange to meet me. Just a few weeks later he was on hand to have dinner with me at my hotel the night I arrived in Istanbul.

Professor Naumann was a pleasant, dignified and very friendly person. After we had eaten a nice Turkish dinner and talked about the Museum of Ancient Brick and my efforts to try to show, as completely as possible, the history of the brickmaker's art he produced a map of Hattusas and a book of pictures which would be of help to me. He showed me the exact position of the remains of the old library. It seemed that there was just part of one wall still remaining. It contained less than 100 brick and these, apparently, had originally been just sundried mud brick. Then, when the city was put to flame during an invasion by the Assyrians, the extreme heat of the conflagration turned the sundried brick into fired brick. Before we parted company, the professor handed me a letter addressed to the Director of Archaeology in Ankara stating his approval of my "expedition." He asked me if we had any Byzantine bricks in our museum. We hadn't. So he said he thought one of the Government museums might let me have a couple dating back to the fifth century and that, if so, he would meet me at the airport on my return from Ankara bringing the Byzantine brick with him. It was a very fruitful evening indeed.

I was an ancient F27 that flew me to Ankara, mostly above the clouds. For the first forty five minutes I saw nothing below. Then we dived to a scary fifteen hundred feet at which time all was nice and clear below. It was an eye-wearying sight of endless desolation, with a great number of barren hills growing up from an unfriendly ground, with a background of distant mountains. However, here and there, I was able to pick out signs (only visible from the air) of the sites of long forgotten settlements. As we approached our destination, the land flattened out and we made a nice bumpy landing at the airport. Ankara, the capital since 1923, is at an elevation of just over twenty eight hundred feet and is, today, a modern city built on European lines. It has a long history and was once known as Angora. Today it has wide streets, universities, an opera house and grand public buildings. The weather was not very nice when I arrived there; in fact it was positively chilly. It took forty minutes to get from the airport to downtown Ankara and during the drive I passed several trenches that had been dug, and worked on, by archaeologists. I went straight to my hotel and checked in. I was amused by the method they used to prevent guests from taking room keys out of the hotel, accidentally. Each key was attached to a ring which, in turn, was attached to a heavy 3 1/2" wooden cube..impossible to put in one's pocket. I didn't take time to eat but went straight to the Department of Archaeology where the "fun" began.

I was greeted by the Deputy Director who showed me into the Director's office. This worthy gentleman didn't even stand up; he extended his hand across his desk and shook hands with me without uttering a word. The Deputy, who spoke perfect English, placed a chair for me which put me in a position between the Director and the Deputy. I turned to the Director and addressed him in English where-upon the Deputy informed me that his boss didn't speak English and that he would translate for both of us. Undaunted, I turned back to the Director and addressed him in French. Still no acknowledgment that he understood. Then I tried my poor Italian on him, only to be interrupted and told that the only language spoken by the Director was Turkish. This, I knew, was not the truth. Every archaeologist I have met has been at least bilingual. Many are tri-lingual. Still, I went along with the charade to see what would materialize. I handed over the letter from Dr. Naumann which, after being read by the Deputy, was passed to the Director. He looked at it. I knew, then, positively that the man understood English. I sat back while the other two had a conversation in Turkish, a language of which I knew not word one. After they had been at it for only a couple of minutes, the Deputy turned to me and said "Mr. Saffer, the director regrets that he cannot give you his permission to go up to Boghazkoy and Hattusas." (Boghazkoy is a small and ancient settlement just a short distance from the mountain aerie of Hattusas.)

"Why?" I replied. "I had the assurance from your Ambassador in the United States that I could go there and remove one brick, providing The German Institute approved; and Dr. Naumann has given that approval."

"The Director" he said "has information that it is snowing very hard in the mountains and that the mud is so deep you wouldn't be able to walk."

I turned and looked straight at the Director and told him that I had come so far that I wasn't about to let a little snow and mud deter me. I further told him that he was breaking the word of his government to mine which, that year, was going to give Turkey three hundred million dollars in Foreign Aid. I added that if I went home empty handed I would contact my Senator and ask him to bring the matter to the attention of the Committee on Foreign Aid. That did the trick! I was right about his knowing English, because without waiting for any comment from his Deputy, he spoke a few words to him, stood up and offered me his hand and said, "Please be very careful and put on your warmest clothing."

The Deputy, red faced, asked me to follow him while he prepared the necessary documents and gave me some instructions. These were as follows: I should travel to a town called Sungurlu where I must present the papers to the Governor. The Governor would arrange for someone to accompany me to the "dig." After getting my brick, I had to stop in Boghazkoy where the head guard of the "dig" would certify that I had removed no more than one brick from the ancient capital. That wasn't the end! I then had to go back into Sungurlu and get a written report from the Governor and return to the Department of Antiquities in Ankara with my brick and all the paperwork. The brick would remain in Ankara until it had been photographed, weighed, measured and entered into the records of the Hattusas excavations. Talk about red tape, this was it! I had spent well over an hour inside the Department before I came out and went to hire a car, for the next day, and have a very late lunch.

Lunch was no problem. I ordered Donnerkabob, which consisted of roasted thinly-sliced lamb, and an order of stuffed grape leaves. The Donnerkabob had been recommended by the Turkish Cultural Attache in D.C. I had imagined it would be served like Shishkabob. However, it did come with seared onion and peppers. The problem, after my tussle with the Department of Archaeology, was hiring a car. The man who drove me from the airport to the hotel had an Avis sign on his car, so I asked the hotel concierge how to get to the Avis rental office. He told me that it would be very expensive to rent a car and that I shouldn't make any commitment until I had checked back with him. At the Avis office they were horrified because I wanted to rent a car and drive it myself. The rate they quoted me was quite high and I so stated. Then they quoted me a much lower rate if I let one of their people do the driving! In Istanbul I had noticed that just about all the cabs were 20 year old American cars and wondered what they did for spare parts. The lower rate by having a Turkish driver, in Ankara, gave me the answer--spare parts were hard to come by and careful driving, their style, was the rule. Back at the hotel I told the concierge how much I had been quoted and he told me he would have a car and driver for me, the next morning, at half the price. Having settled that matter, I wandered around Ankara. I went into a bazaar and found that things hadn't changed from bazaars I had been in twenty years before, except for the types of merchandise, but with each booth offering the same items as his neighbor. There were the same noisy crowds and the same "odd" characters. Nothing tempted me and I went back into the streets which, on this damp drizzly day, made the city look just like any European city. The one thing that really impressed me was the thousands of sparrows, in the trees down many of the streets, making a heck of a noise. The people on the street, for the most part, were in European clothes. Here and there, I would see a man wearing a fez or the traditional Turkish baggy pantaloons. A few women wearing yashmaks, veils, made their appearance. There was very little to impress upon me that I was in Asia.

Yet, I was close to the home of the Hittites who were responsible for the introduction of the horse to the Egyptians and the Babylonians. The Hittites who swept down from their mountain fastness to conquer as far afield as Carchemish-on-the-Euphrates. Kemal Attaturk had made this the capital so it would be European in style and Turkey's big ambition was to become a part of the European community, even though ninety seven percent of the country lies in Asia.

I had asked for the car to pick me up at six a.m. so I thought I'd better go back to my room, do some dictating, check my cameras and my brick removing tool and have something to eat sent up after my bath. And that's exactly what I did, falling asleep as soon as I got into bed.

I was driven out of Ankara promptly at six a.m. on another wet and chilly day, the temperature dropping as we moved up into the hills towards Sungurlu. As daylight came, I could better see the countryside through which we were passing. There were very few indications of it being inhabited, although we did skip through one very small village. Here and there I would see a cluster of two or three homes with some farmland nearby. But that wasn't very often. I should mention that my driver couldn't understand more than three or four words of English! He had been given written instructions as to where to take me by the concierge at the hotel.

The road we were traveling on was badly paved, where it was paved. Mostly it was just gravel. Seeing a collection of small homes ahead, I tapped my driver on the shoulder and indicated that I wanted him to stop there. As we got closer I could see a small store with a rusting Coca-Cola sign nailed to its wall. I hadn't had any breakfast and thought that, here, I might get something bottled to slake my thirst. I was able to get a bottle of not-too-cold "Coke," while several residents from the homes came over to find out who I was. My driver must have given them a good "line" because everyone came up to me and shook my hand. I took the opportunity to examine the construction of the homes. They were all built of mud bricks with tin roofs. As I focussed my camera on one of them, everybody in the house came and stood in the doorway. There was the father and about five young boys, no girls. I had to shake hands with each of them before they would let me get back into the car, but not a single word passed between us.

Another hour passed before we made it to Sungurlu and the Town Hall. I went inside, with all my documents, and found my way into the most important looking office. It was the right one. Behind a large desk sat a large, beaming man dressed in a sturdy suit and with a small Turkish flag standing at one corner of the desk. He must have had a telephone call telling him about my forthcoming arrival. Here, again, there was a language barrier. There was no response to my greeting in any of three languages but he did stand up and give me a hearty handshake. I handed over my papers and sat in a chair while he looked over them. After he had finished, he just sat there and smiled at me. (I found out later in the day that this was not the Governor, nor the Assistant Governor. He was the "Acting Assistant to the Assistant Governor." His superiors were both out of town.)

I thought I'd better let him know that I had a car outside, so I drew a sketch of a car and pointed out of the window. He sat there and just nodded his head. Finally, he picked up his telephone and made a call in the middle of which he turned to me and said, "Chai?" I felt more like coffee than tea so I responded by saying the one word, "Coffee." He said "coffee" into the phone and then hung up. For several more minutes we looked and smiled at one another. I had my camera case and I took out a camera and indicated that I would like to take this official's picture. He nodded, in assent, leaned over the desk and let me take a shot. Then he reached out and brought the Turkish flag close to him and indicated that I should take another photograph. This was done just as a second person entered the office. He was tall and dressed in a nice dark business suit. He shook hands with me and drew up a chair and sat beside me. No response from this chap, either, to my multilingual greeting other than a smile. Then in came the coffee which had been well worth waiting for. (I love heavy, sweet Turkish coffee.)

After we had had our coffee, I was invited to go into an adjacent office to take another photograph with the official standing beneath a picture of Kemal Attaturk. Then it was back to the first office and another round of silence. Finally, after about forty five minutes, in came a slightly built young man who addressed me in French. The conversation lasted less than half a minute! He was a schoolteacher and had come to tell me that the man in the dark suit was the Director of Education for Sungurlu and would be accompanying me to Boghazkoy and Hattusas. Having said his piece, he shook hands with me and left. All that waiting when a couple of gestures would have conveyed all the necessary information and let us get on our way quickly.

There I was, sitting in the car, with two Turks with whom I couldn't converse. It was sleeting now, and before long we got some snow making it a long, slippery and slimy slide all the way, 50 kilometers, to the village of Boghazkoy. "Hattusas" and "Boghakoyy" are really the same place but are used, today, to differentiate between the present inhabited town and the long-deserted mountain stronghold. At Boghazkoy we stopped at a small building to pick up the guard who was going to act as a guide. He was a very tall, heavily built man with a good sense of humor, laughing at almost everything uttered by the Director of Education. We were now four, all going to get one brick from an ancient wall. I had handed my map to the guard who indicated that he knew just where to go. So on we drove, up and up and up, until the car could no longer make it up the grade. We got out and continued walking, slipping and scrambling, until I found myself overlooking a vast expanse where, here and there, could be seen many low stone walls, all that remained of the ancient Hittite buildings. The old citadels were easily picked out and it would appear that they should have been impregnable. With all the barrenness around me and the bone chilling sleet and snow coming down on us, I couldn't understand how the Hittites had managed to exist there. The red tile roofs of Boghazkoy, far below, made a nice colorful break in the monotony of the landscape. In the distance I could see the famous wall that had surrounded the city, and decided that I would have to make time to get right up to it with it's three thousand five hundred year old "Lion Gates" and Assyrian type wall carvings.

Finally, we reached "my" wall. There wasn't much left, but what remained was a beautiful red. I examined the various sections to decide where I could get my brick without doing any other damage to the wall. Eventually, I found a spot which required the removal of only a fragment to permit me to go to work. The fragment removed, I slowly scraped and chipped around the back and the ends of the brick. I then slipped my knife into the mud mortar and started to bring it out a scrap at a time. After I had finally loosened the brick, it took another half an hour to carefully work it out of the wall. I managed to get my hand under it, diagonally, so that I could give it maximum support as I slid it out. My three companions just stood and patiently watched me without any conversation. The brick was carefully carried to where we had left the car and placed in the trunk. We then, all of us, walked up to and along the ancient wall to the "Lion Gate." The lions stood about six feet high and were carved from solid rock. One of them had its face intact while the other had part of it destroyed. Really impressive, though. The wall was about fifteen feet thick and, at one point, had a tunnel going through it to the outside. The tunnel permitted those who lived outside the city walls to get inside when raiders appeared. After all were safely inside, heavy boulders were rolled into it making it virtually impossible for anyone to break through.

I took several photographs of Hattusas including a wide angle shot of the tunnel. Using that type of lens gave the impression that the tunnel was about thirty feet thick. Another long walk by the wall brought us to the massive carvings which were also recorded on film.

We climbed back into the car and did some more slithering until we got back to Boghazkoy where I had to let the people show me the little hotel that they were working on. We went into the kitchen where I was asked if I wanted some "chai." Of course, in that part of the world you don't refuse hospitality, but being concerned about not getting boiled milk I again asked for coffee. I was sitting with my three traveling companions, waiting for the coffee, when a procession of very short men came in. I had to shake hands with each of them. Then, a couple of minutes later four more men came in and I had to shake hands, not only with them but also with the previous contingent. My hand was getting sore from all the hand shaking! It seemed that the last four were connected with the archaeological site and I had to go into another room and stand by while my guide and the Director of Education signed a sheaf of documents. Then back to the kitchen just as the coffee was ready. I drank it quickly because I still had to report back at Sungurlu.

The drive back to Sungurlu was miserable. Not only because of the condition of the road but also because I had a sore throat, a headache and a cold that had developed overnight. On top of this, there was no heat in the car and my hands were scraped and sore. So, again we slithered along the roadway and skidded into a ditch. That brought a little life into the party. I couldn't get out of the car without help because of the angle of tilt. The others had to hold the door open and almost lift me out. They were amazed at the first thing I did when I got my feet on the ground...I started taking photographs. It so happened that we had passed a large truck loaded with manganese ore a few miles down the road, and eventually it caught up with us and with the help of a cable and six men we were back on the road. At Sungurlu, I reported back at the "Town Hall" where the papers were examined and I was given a new document to deliver to the Director of Archaeology in Ankara. While this was being done, a young man walked into the office and announced that he spoke English. Well, he did, terribly and kept asking me how good his English was and I kept lying and telling him it was very good. Then he told me that it ought to be since he had spent two months at George Washington University, in D.C. He said he was an engineer and proudly told me that he was responsible for building the road between Ankara and Sungurlu. I had no comment to make.

The same fellow invited me to have lunch with him, the Director of Education, and the Acting Assistant, etc. I tried to decline saying that I had to be back in Ankara before the office closed but he was most insistent. Off we went to a little restaurant, which was a novel experience. The first thing we did was to go into the kitchen to see what was being cooked that day. I saw some rather scrawny chickens being cooked and the cook throwing meat on a grill, after rolling each piece in his hands. I opted for the latter, as did the others. Then we went upstairs and sat at a table. Someone brought us a bottle of wine which we enjoyed until our meal came. Along with the meat we had a communal salad bowl and a communal yoghurt bowl. There was only one spoon but I bravely went along and ate a little of everything as the spoon was passed around. My English speaking host thought I hadn't eaten enough and wanted me to try the chicken. I declined, showing him my watch, and argued with him as to who was going to pay the bill. He insisted that I was his guest but the Director of Education beat us both to it and paid the reckoning. Just as I was leaving the restaurant, in came a couple of other fellows one of whom addressed me in elementary French. I managed to learn from him that all the people in the town of Boghazkoy were direct descendants of the Ancient Hittites.

Outside, the road builder asked me if I would mind taking his picture, along with two of his friends. Then it was "Goodbye" time and I shook hands with at least a dozen people, most of whom I hadn't seen before. Then, someone came forward and asked if I would give someone a ride into Ankara. Of course, I agreed and a young man hopped into the car. I found out two very interesting things about him. First of all, he spoke excellent French and then that he was studying archaeology. At last, I had someone to talk to, even though my throat was sore.

Unfortunately, by the time we got back to Ankara it was long past office hours and I was lucky to find anyone at all in the Department of Archaeology. A man took the brick from me, which I had wrapped in some newspapers I had been given at Bogazkhoy. This man spoke English and told me that the brick would, eventually, be sent to me in Tennessee.

One interesting event I should mention happened while I was in Sungurlu. It must have been about noon, Saturday, when I heard the sound of children singing. Just outside the school the kids were singing while soldiers, lined up outside the "Town Hall," stood at attention. A band was playing and everybody on the street stood at attention while the Turkish flag was raised up a pole. The flag was to remain flying until Sunday night.

After depositing the brick at the Department of Archaeology, I tramped into my hotel tracking in mud, wearing a muddy coat and with muddy hands and face. The look on the bellboy's face when I asked him to have my boots cleaned was one of amazement. The first thing I did when I got in my room was to take an antihistamine and have a luxurious hot bath. Before I went down to dinner, I called the Turkish Airline in Ankara to reconfirm my flight back to Istanbul the next morning and my Pan Am flight one day later. The airline clerk told me that he had no record of my name and that the plane to Istanbul was full up! I argued with him and went so far as to call Istanbul. The person I spoke to there told me that he couldn't answer for the flight from Ankara but I should take a chance and be on hand when the plane was supposed to take off. My Pan Am flight was o.k. I had my dinner, dictated, went to bed and showed up at the airport early the next morning. There was no difficulty getting a seat on the plane because there were only ten passengers! Breakfast was served during the flight. A very interesting meal, indeed. It consisted of nice oily black olives, goatsmilk cheese, bread and coffee. It may sound rather unusual for a breakfast but my cold symptoms seemed to have subsided and I really enjoyed that novel meal.

Arriving in Istanbul, I went straight to my hotel and checked in, giving me the whole day to "get into" the history of that famous city. On the way in I had noticed two things about the ancient taxicabs. One was the way they were driven. It seemed as though the drivers were "playing chicken," swerving away from each other at the last second. Then, it seemed that it was impossible to get one of them to stop for a pick-up. People would stand right in the road and wave at every cab that passed, with only an occasional one stopping. I later found out the way the system operated. The cabs, with a window down, would slow up slightly, just enough to hear the would-be passenger yell out his destination. If the cab, with the other occupants, was headed that way it would let the person in. If not, it just accelerated and went on. That was one of the reasons I had the hotel get me a car with a driver/guide, my favorite way to get about. Before I left the hotel, I called Professor Naumann who said he had two bricks for me and that I should look for him in the airport the next morning.

The outstanding attraction in Istanbul is "Topkapi", a palace fortress which, until Suleyman the Magnificent became Sultan, was merely a fort and a place to "store" part of the harem. After that it became the principal palace which housed and protected the usually bloated body of the Sultan. Many Turkish miniatures and other depictions of most Sultans show them as being grossly overweight. It was believed that the more a Sultan weighed the better ruler he was. "Topkapi," which overlooks the beautiful Bosphorus, is now home to fabulous and priceless treasures, as well as the keeper of horrible stories of despotism and fratricide. I spent hours just wandering from room to room, each more fascinating than the last. The most popular exhibit is the Treasury with what is probably the largest collection of gems and gold items in the world. It includes an 84 carat diamond, and jewel lovers from all over the globe have traveled to Istanbul just to gaze lovingly, and longingly, at this one gem. In the same room I saw the "Kandjar." This is a dagger with a watch in the hilt and three large emeralds set into its sheath. It was this weapon which was made famous by the movie "Topkapi." There are solid gold Koran covers and drinking vessels thickly encrusted with rubies, emeralds and diamonds. I was amused when I came to a case with a gold casket containing the head of John the Baptist, a bone from his arm and some of his finger bones. What was amusing? Well, in the year 1204 when members of the fourth Crusade captured Constantinople (the old name for Istanbul), they divided up the sacred relics and sent them back home to the leaders' sponsors. So Baldwin of Flanders sent a head of John the Baptist to Amiens and another head of John the Baptist to Soissions, both places in France.

I went into the Sanctuary, a place much revered by Moslems by virtue of the Mantle of the Prophet which has been piously preserved, along with one of his chipped teeth, a flask used in the ritual washing of his corpse, a hair of his head, and imprints of his feet. With my guide, I visited the Audience Room with a fountain playing in the center. There was a delightful marble fountain in the private garden by the harem. I had read of two special fountains in Topkapi and set off to find them. They were there alright. In front of each was a pillar. With a wave of a hand a Sultan would have his guards drag some unfortunate person who, for usually no reason, had offended him out to one of these fountains. Here, the offender's head was severed from his body and impaled on the pillar while the executioner washed his bloody scimitar. Lunch was taken in one of the many fine restaurants after which I walked around and was amazed at the dozens of shops displaying French pastries with whipped cream, marinated artichokes and roasted pigeons. Seeing these items made me feel hungry again. My driver took me over to the Blue Mosque, the only mosque with six minarets outside Mecca. It isn't blue colored on the outside, just a sun reflecting white. It gets its name from the blue cast of the stained glass windows and the blue tiles decorating the inside walls. Then we "hit" the Dolmabahce Palace with its rare flowers blooming in marble vases set out in the gardens and pebbled walkways lined with white-painted lamps. It has a large reflecting pool that duplicates the myriad colors of great conifers and magnolias. Inside there are a large number of rooms such as "The Hall of Entry," "The Sultan's Bath,""The Sultan's Mother's Room," etc.

I stopped at the impressive monument showing Attaturk surrounded by some of his soldiers, in Taksim Square, and then went on to the Spice Bazaar. Built in 1660 it had all the oriental charm and mystique I could have wished for. There were many little shops still selling mostly spices and scores more offering mouth-watering cheeses, lamb and beef. In another bazaar, the "Grand Bazaar" which reminded me of a rabbit warren, I bought some items to take home. I got a set of shishkabob skewers with brass handles in a Turkish motif, some pointed Turkish slippers, a copper coffee server and, for my son, a replica of the famous dagger I had seen in Topkapi.

Then I had a once-in-a-lifetime experience. I noticed an elderly man in an odd military uniform. He was wearing a big fur hat and had a sheathed dagger hung around him on a silver chain. There was a pistol in a holster by his side and a name patch on his right breast which said "CAPTAIN OSMAN." I asked one of the merchants who he was and found that he was one of the few remaining officers who fought with Kemal Attaturk. He was a pensioner and received some money from the state; but whenever he wanted to buy something, the vendors wouldn't accept any payment from him. A true-to-life hero! Naturally, I wanted to take his photograph and asked someone to get his permission for me. They told me that he had never allowed anyone to photograph him and always got annoyed when anyone tried to get a snapshot. So I asked the store owner to go up to him and tell him that I had heard of Kemal Attaturk and his brave soldiers ever since I was a child and would appreciate it if he would let me shake his hand and would have some chai with me. The old warrior listened to my messenger's words, turned in my direction, smiled at me and held out his hand. All the store owners came up and stared in amazement at the two of us together. One person brought out two chairs and a small table while another produced two glasses of sweetened tea. This man acted as an interpreter for me. While we sipped our hot tea, I asked Captain Osman if his fellow countrymen knew just how much they owed to brave men like him? I got a smile and he nodded his head. I then asked if he kept his pistol in good order. His answer to this was to take it out and hand it to me, while everyone gasped. The gun looked as though it had been freshly cleaned and oiled and I handed it back to him quickly. Someone in the back said that he hadn't been able to get ammunition for that pistol for many years. I pointed to his dagger which he took out of its sheath and handed over to me. It was a handsome piece of craftsmanship and, also, very sharp. After I gave it back to him, Captain Osman pointed to my camera and then to his face. Again, a gasp from the small crowd around us. He stood up, took his pistol out and posed with it across his chest. I got a couple of good pictures and then turned to see who I should pay for the tea. At this, the captain put his hand over mine and said something which was translated into, "You are a fine man and you are my guest." We shook hands again and parted company. I was sure that he wasn't permitted to pay for the chai.

After leaving this second bazaar, the driver showed me the tremendous number of ruined Roman walls which could be found down almost every road. He pointed out the five defense walls built by the Romans with the remains of old Roman Palaces built into some of them. Then he drove me into the old Asian part of Istanbul where I could see unpainted dry wooden homes with typical Islamic arched entrances. He pointed to the large number of wires that had been thrown from upper story windows across the power lines. He explained that electricity was so expensive that these people couldn't afford it.

So they stole it. Unfortunately, it seemed that each year hundreds of Turks came to a shocking end because of this practice.

I watched two old men sitting at a small table outside a food store playing some kind of board game. The guide asked if I could take their photograph at which one of the men who had seen me shooting the dilapidated residences shouted at me and waved me away. The translation was, "Why does everyone want to take pictures of the poor part of the city? Go away and find something that is beautiful." Off we went until we came across half a dozen Gypsy women trying to board a bus. I managed to get my picture just as someone else started shouting at me. This time the translation was, "Have you nothing else to do than show the shame of Turkey?" Apparently, the Gypsies were rather disliked.

I'd had enough for the day and we started back to the hotel, but on the way I got two "hippies" to stand in front of an old Roman wall while I took a shot of "the old" and "the new." I also got a picture of two young men walking hand in hand. This did not necessarily mean that it was a romantic liaison. It was a common enough sight in that part of the world and showed unashamed close friendship. Something else I kept seeing was quite a few men and women in the old traditional Turkish dress. Now Kemal Attaturk, in an effort to break the influence of the clergy, had outlawed the old dress. However, after so many years it was no longer a crime to wear those clothes because only the very old people, relics of the past, bothered to put them on.

After we got back to the hotel, I paid off the driver/guide who had done an excellent job for me and went to get my room key. There was a message from Professor Naumann to the effect that he wouldn't be able to get to the airport before I took off the next day. He said I should write to him and make other arrangements to get the two Byzantine bricks.

I flew out the next morning and eventually got back to Tennessee. Taking the Professor at his word, I wrote to him and said that whenever I came across an acquaintance who was going to visit Istanbul I would ask him to contact Professor Naumann and pick up the bricks. During the next year I made that request to two friends, both of whom returned with the same message that I would have to go and get them myself! As to the brick I had removed from the wall in Hattusas, it turned up in my office one afternoon. It had been airmailed in a battered cardboard carton three times the size of the brick, without any padding, still wrapped in my newspapers. A thick piece of cord was wrapped once around the carton. I opened the container and found to my dismay that the brick was smashed. There was one large portion, about half the brick, with some of the ancient plaster still in place. The rest lay in hundreds of tiny fragments! As I expected, the brick had lost its bright red coloring due to becoming more exposed in a different atmosphere. I wasn't too badly put out. After all, I did have the large and interesting piece for the museum, while I would be able to give the fragments away as ancient souvenirs to helpful people.

For another year I pondered on how I was going to get back to Istanbul to get the Byzantine bricks from Professor Naumann. Then, my wife and I decided to take a nice European vacation visiting France, Italy and England. When planning the trip I included a two day trip from Rome to Istanbul and I wrote to the good Professor and gave him the date of our arrival. Once again, he was on hand to meet us at the hotel. He apologized for not being able to give the bricks to my friends but that I could pick them up at his office the next morning. In the meantime, he wanted us to be his guests for dinner at a special restaurant right on the edge of the Bosphorus, the strait that connected the Sea of Marmara with the Black Sea. We ate an excellent meal, suggested by the Professor, with the waters gently lapping against the restaurant wall, just by our open window. The night was warm and the skies were clear and we were then taken for a drive along the edge of the Sea of Marmara before being returned to our hotel.

The next morning my wife and I had breakfast in our room, by a window overlooking a vista that included both the old and the new Istanbul. Then we took a taxi to the offices of the German Institute where the Professor ushered us into his office and handed me a big ... very big ... surprise. How I had goofed! When first told that the bricks were 4th century, I had thought that since Constantinople (now Istanbul) was then the Eastern capital of the Roman Empire, the construction would have been according to Roman standards. Therefore, my wife and I had brought flight bags just big enough for Roman size brick. They weren't! I had forgotten that the Romans hadn't tried to eradicate all Grecian influence and permitted the people to live in their own manner. The Byzantine bricks were very large. Each was 12" square and weighed almost twenty pounds. They were beautiful, though, and had the Greek brickmaker's stamp on each. Looking in his book, which listed all the known brickstamps and the name of each maker, he failed to find "our" marks. At any rate, we had a weighty problem on our hands.

We returned to the hotel and sat looking at the bricks, wondering how we were going to get them onto our plane when we left. The Professor had told me that they were a gift from a Government museum which had to remain nameless, so I wasn't trying to take out something that had been stolen. Still, as one left Istanbul you passed a large sign that stated that passengers were reminded that removing unauthorized antiquities from the country was punishable by severe penalties. I sat and looked at the bricks considering how I was going to handle the situation. My wife told me that I should be realistic and realize that, for once, I would have to give up. I left her for half an hour while I found a place that sold hacksaw blades. If I couldn't get the bricks home, I would at least get the brick stamps there. However, brick is very, very hard and is usually cut by a diamond coated rotary blade. After thirty minutes sawing with my blade, one end of which was wrapped in a towel to protect my hand, I had made only a single half inch cut. I gave up on that.

Then I had a brainwave. Leaving my wife in the hotel, I made my way to an airline company's office on the hotel grounds. Inside was a pleasant looking young man who greeted me in English. We chatted about the city and the weather before I asked him, "Who is the chief cargo officer for your company out at the airport?" Having learned his name, I then said, "That sounds familiar. How long has he been in charge there?" He told me twelve years. I remarked that I would look him up next time I was at the terminal.

Returning to the hotel room, I called the cargo officer and told him that I had been told in the U.S. that if I had any airline problems I should get in touch with him and since he'd had twelve year's experience out there he would be able to help me. I asked him if he would have lunch with my wife and me that day. He said he was tied up but that he would be pleased to see us at one p.m., so we went down to the lobby and managed to hire a car with a driver who could act as our guide. He was a pharmacist who wasn't making much money at his job and who drove to augment his income. First of all, he took us to the same restaurant at which I'd had lunch on my previous visit. Again, the Turkish food was very tasty. It was noon and the place was filled with Turkish businessmen having their lunch. Since we were the only foreigners in sight, there was a lot of staring at us and I could imagine them asking one another why we would be eating in a strictly oriental restaurant. Often, when someone is in a room with a lot of people who are speaking in a strange tongue he seems to get the feeling that he is being talked about. Usually, this isn't so. The people are probably talking about everyday matters, weather, business, clothes, food, etc. In the restaurant, however, there was no doubt we were the center of attraction because the patrons were turning around in their chairs to look at us.

Lunch over, just as we found our car, two of the famous Istanbul porters passed by. These men, bent almost double, their heads no more than three feet above the sidewalk, were loaded down with several heavy crates. Porters like these are a very common sight. On my previous visit I had seen one of them carrying a refrigerator on his back.

We had a pleasant drive out to the airport, along with an interesting commentary on the places of interest on the way. Our driver was well steeped in the history of his country and able to impart his knowledge in an easy to understand manner. Arrived at the airport, my wife and I went upstairs in the cargo building and found the office we were looking for. It was like a madhouse! Crates and packages strewn all over the place with a crew of clerks yelling at one another as they checked cargo against manifests. I asked for the man I had spoken to on the phone, and we were led into a nicely furnished office which had a well stocked bar standing open.

The manager, for that's who he was, asked us to be seated and then enquired how he could help. In a few words I explained about the Byzantine bricks and not knowing how to get them out of the country. I stressed the fact that I hadn't bought them or removed them from any structures. He smiled when I told him that I had been told that he was the man to get the job done. He invited us to have a drink, an invitation which I accepted. With a drink in his hand he went to the door of his office and called to someone. In came a uniformed Customs Officer! Seeing the startled look on my face he told me it was alright and that he and the Officer were old friends. He closed the door. The Customs Officer helped himself to a drink and flopped into a chair. The manager told me that each airline had a Customs Officer assigned to it and that they had their desks right inside the airline offices. This, he informed us, kept the cargo moving since it could be inspected on the spot. Then he asked me if I spoke German. I answered negatively. I said I spoke French and a little Italian. At that, he switched from English to French and said that the Customs man spoke German and French. He told the officer about my problem and asked for his suggestions. Then ensued a strange conversation with three of us speaking in French, while every now and then the other two exchanged a few words in Turkish. Eventually, the Customs Officer turned to me and asked me a number of questions. He wanted to know the exact size of the bricks, how much they weighed, did I have a spare suitcase, and had I bought a small Turkish rug yet. I gave him the size and weight of the two brick and said that I would buy a suitcase and a rug. He told me not only what size rug to buy, but also what quality! On his hands and knees he then demonstrated how the bricks should be wrapped in the rug. Meanwhile, my wife was sitting patiently on a comfortable ottoman listening to the "goings on." She understood the French conversation and looked puzzled when I was told the exact length of rug we were to buy. Finally, it was all arranged. Two mornings later, an hour before our flight took off, I was to bring the case, with the bricks and rug inside, up to that office and the Customs Officer would handle everything so the case would get on the same plane. Very good! I thanked both the Customs man and the Manager for their understanding and help, shook hands with them, remembered to take my wife and left.

It was too late to do much sightseeing so we had to settle for a visit to the Cistern Basilica, an underground reservoir with 336 marble columns and the capacity to hold enough drinking water to sustain the city during a long siege. I told the driver that the next day I wanted to go to Topkapi and, to save time, handed him a piece of paper on which was a list of the numbers of the rooms I wanted to visit and the numbers of the cases I especially needed to see. The reason for this was that I had been working on a lecture on Istanbul and needed to take pictures that I had omitted on my previous visit there, or reshoot others. We would want to go to the Grand Bazaar with hundreds of stalls in a labyrinth of passages and alleys, the same bazaar in which I had met Captain Osman, show my wife the Galata Bridge which links old Istanbul with the European city and drive out along the Bosphorus to see an old fort and the legendary Leander Tower.

We were dropped at the hotel where we had tea in our room before going out into the city to find a suitcase and a rug. It wasn't hard to find a cheap, but sturdy, suitcase. When it came to the rug we had a problem. Nearly every shop sold Turkish rugs, in all qualities and sizes. The problem was that the prices were horribly inflated and I won't waste my time haggling with the sellers. There was a shop in the hotel lobby that carried a good selection of rugs and I felt that whatever I got there would, at least, be of good quality. So we went back to the hotel shop where we found a rug that fitted the specifications given to me by the Customs Officer. I had it put on my hotel bill and took it up to the room. Together, my wife and I wrapped the two bricks in the rug (actually we had to layer them) and put the bundle in the suitcase. It was heavy! Very heavy! After getting this matter taken care of, we went back to more closely examine the shops in the hotel lobby and, although my wife wanted to see something of Istanbul's nightlife, I decide we would eat dinner at the hotel. That city's night spots are decidedly "shady" and, as far as I was concerned, no place to take a lady.

Once again, we breakfasted in our room with its superb view and went down to meet our driver at nine o-clock. Our first stop was at the Galata bridge where the driver parked down a side street and waited for us to visit the bridge and the fishermen who sold their catch from a platform at the bottom of some steps at the start of the bridge. What a colorful display! The Turkish fish vendors with blue striped aprons and woolen hats were pleased to see us. Without even asking, they produced two glasses of tea for us. Their catch was elaborately displayed with the different kinds of fish carefully arranged in symmetrical groups. We sipped our tea from the fishy tasting glasses and admired a large pelican which was tied to a pole. Its name, according to a roughly slapped on painted sign, was "Yser." One of the fishermen proudly held up an extremely large fish by its tail while I put my camera to work. We got a fishy handshake from these friendly folk and crossed over to the car.

At Topkapi we "did the rounds" with my spouse oohing and aahing at the fantastic collection of Chinese and European porcelains. We were looking at the world's finest porcelain display. The gems and gold Koran covers and boxes in the Treasury she found hard to believe were genuine. In the center of the room was the throne of the Shah Ismail, another unbelievably ornate treasure. It was made mainly of gold plate with a generous encrustation of pearls, rubies and emeralds. However, to my mind more attractive was the throne of Ahmet the First. This one was so much more delicate with tasteful inlays of mother-of-pearl and which stood on four gentle legs. I had to go into the armory to rephotograph a large suit of old Turkish armor which had belonged to an extremely tall warrior and a special collection of medieval swords and spears.

In what used to be the quarters of the Sultans' pages were the robes of long-departed rulers, in cases lining the walls. In the center of the room were the robes of two of the rulers who were murdered. One was strangled to death and the other was stabbed. The latter's enormous robe displayed the stains left by his blood as it ebbed from his body. I led the way to the two execution fountains where my wife was disturbed by the sight of tar-like streaks that could be seen reaching from the top down two feet on one of the pillars that was triangular with all-over carved serrations. They looked like old heavy blood deposits. I told her that's what the substance probably was and related how the Sultans were addicted to head removals.

I asked the driver/guide to lead us to the palace kitchen where I photographed two gigantic iron pots, capable of holding a ton of food, enormous soup ladles and several unusually shaped coffee pots. I had read that these kitchens were staffed by 1100 cooks and assistants! The sight of the kitchens made us realize that since there wasn't anything cooking there we should look for our own place for lunch. First, though, I showed my wife the sacred sanctuary with its relics of the Prophet. I pointed out the chest with his black wool mantle, over fourteen hundred years old and which the Turks had stolen from Egypt. Again, I saw the small silver box containing his chipped tooth, his foot prints and his swords. On my last visit I had been in a bit of a rush and had missed several objects in the Sanctuary. These included a pot that belonged to Abraham, Moses' staff, and Joseph's turban. Over a black marble archway we saw just how much beauty there is in the Arabic alphabet. The letters, in bright gold, which spelled out the Moslem creed, were gorgeously enlarged and decorated. All the script surrounding it was cunningly contrived and exaggerated. (There is a very good, religious reason for the use of lettering for designs, but that is a subject in itself.)

The three of us had lunch in a strictly Turkish restaurant, two of us over-eating because of the guide's vivid descriptions of the various dishes. We had to sample more than we could handle! The drive to the Basilica of Saint Sofia gave our tummies time to settle down before we entered that ancient and beautiful building. Originally, on that site, the Roman Emperor Constantine built a church in 325. This later burned down, as was its replacement built by Constantine's son. Along came the Emperor Justinian who decided to build a church that, for beauty and durability, would be the finest in the world. Over a hundred master masons and ten thousand laborers worked continuously for five years before it was completed and Justinian uttered his famous words, "O Solomon, I have surpassed thee!" It remained a Christian Basilica until it was ransacked by members of the Fourth Crusade, themselves Christians, in 1204. They robbed it of all its precious metal candelabra, chandeliers and religious ornaments. They even took away gold window frames and unique ornamental doors. All this as booty. The Basilica was a shambles and remained so for 250 years until the Turks captured Constantinople in 1453 and converted the ancient sanctuary into a mosque. It remained a mosque until Kemal Attaturk, as part of his plan to diminish the power of the clergy, declared the beautiful edifice to be a national museum.

One could spend a couple of hours examining just a few of the remarkable features of Hagia Sophia, as it is known to the Turks, and still have seen very little. The guide pointed out to my wife and me the salient features such as the exquisitely carved pulpit, two massive marble vases by the doorway leading to the upper galleries in which in the southern gallery there were two doors, one of which he said led to Heaven and the other to Hell. We looked at intricate mosaics until our eyes blurred. The most impressive feature of the building was the vast dome which was reinforced by a framework of iron frame during the last century. Descending, we looked at more mosaics all with Christian motifs, a matter which our Moslem guide didn't have an answer for. He said he thought the Moslems, on turning the church into a mosque, would have replaced these mosaics with traditional Moslem tilework with flower and lettered motifs. I was able to enlighten him on the subject. Throughout history whenever conquerors have occupied a city, or a town, whose people had a religion other than their own, they built their own houses of worship on the same spot so that, just in case the alien religion did have something of merit, the influence of their gods would be added to that of their own divinities. In other words, "they were taking no chances."

We had two other places to see before going back to the hotel. The first was "Leander's Tower" built on a tiny island in the middle of the Sea of Marmara. It wasn't very impressive but it was supposed to have a place in Greek mythology. In that tower, adjoining which an Athenian conqueror had built a Customs Office which was in continuous use for almost 1300 years, a Sultan had imprisoned his daughter, Hero, to try to nullify a prediction that she would die of a snake bite. It so happened that the unfortunate beauty had a lover, Leander, who would swim out to visit her every night. In order to guide her lover, Hero lit a lamp. One stormy night, the winds blew out the light and poor Leander lost his way and drowned. When she found out what had happened,

Hero threw herself into the sea and she, too, drowned. It is a romantic tale but when we looked at the Tower we weren't too impressed. First of all, the old wooden tower had been burned down and replaced by the present masonry structure in the middle of the 18th century and, secondly, Leander must have been a poor swimmer since the Tower was only a very short distance from shore. Still, we had seen another of "the sights."

Our last stop was at the old fortress of Rumeli Hisari, built in 1450 a.d., and where we arrived just as darkness was beginning to descend. It was situated on the European side of the Bosphorus and opposite its sister fortress Anadolu Hisari, on the Asian side. I had once, from the Asian side, been able to see why it had been included in a list of the world's most beautiful examples of military architecture. To give the tourist the "flavor" of its past, carved wooden figures of janisssaries, dressed in armored clothing and wearing visored hats were situated by the ancient cannons directed out to the sea. (Janissaries were captured slaves and Christian youths who had converted to Islam and served the Sultans as the cream of their bodyguards and fighting troops). The guide told us the reason for the two forts, built less than a hundred years apart. The shores at that point are only 660 meters apart and the cannons of those days had a range of just over half that. So, the combined artillery made certain that no ships could ever get through the straits without permission. As I said, the light was failing and the only other illumination was from some low powered lamps pointed at the figures of the janissaries. But by using the guide's shoulder as a rest, I was able to get some pictures. The day had ended and as we headed back to our hotel I asked the driver to pick us up at eight o-clock the following morning.

There was a night club on the top floor of the hotel and a placard in the lobby announced that one of the performers was a famous Egyptian "Belly Dancer." Believe it or not, it was my wife who suggested that we have dinner there, seeing that it was our last night in Turkey. The meal was excellent and the dancer made her midriff vibrate so much that as she passed our table the dishes shook. I had seen "Belly Dancers" before, but this one outdid all the rest.

In the morning, the car was waiting for us, and I instructed the driver on what the procedure would be when we got to the airport. First of all he would drop my wife and our suitcases at the passenger entrance, help her inside and then return to drive me over to the cargo building. My wife was a little uneasy about all this, especially so when I told her that if I hadn't made my appearance by the time the plane to London was boarded, on arrival there she should contact the American Embassy and tell them that her husband was being "held" in Istanbul.

I dragged my suitcase, with its precious cargo, into the building and up the flight of steps. It so happened that I suffered from a chronic back ailment and, even though wearing a brace, had to lift the case up one step at a time. When I got to the door of "my" airline's office, I just dumped the case on the floor outside and then went in. The Customs Officer came forward to meet me and asked to see my ticket. He made a note of it on a slip of paper and called to one of his helpers. This poor man then had to pick up my suitcase, go down the stairs with it and get it on my plane. Meanwhile, I was invited to take a seat in the

Cargo Manager's office until the hauler returned and advised us that the case was on board. I waited for twenty minutes and the man still hadn't come back. I was getting a little concerned. Meanwhile, I was given a cup of nice, thick, sweet, Turkish coffee. After about half an hour the man returned dragging my suitcase with him. He waved his hands in the air and shouted at the Customs Officer. This fellow then told me that the Customs man in charge of the plane was trying to be difficult and wanted to know what was in the case. I told him that besides the bricks there was the rug, some of my warm weather clothing and a spare car seat, which I used when riding in a car or a plane. (I always carried a spare in case I left one behind somewhere.) Off went the "porter" again, and we waited and drank some more coffee. Another half an hour and the suitcase man, visibly worn out, came back with his load. This time it seemed that the man at the plane wanted to know how much I had paid for the rug! I told the Customs Officer that I had paid $50 for it, and the suitcase went on another trek only to be brought back again. The Customs Officer became very angry and said that his "cohort" was trying to make things difficult for him and insisted on seeing the bill for the rug. The bricks were never mentioned by the "difficult one." Since I had charged the rug to my room account, the only receipt was my all-embracing hotel bill which was in the possession of my wife.

The now-distraught Customs Officer told me to catch my plane; and if he couldn't get the suitcase on the same flight, he would see that it DID leave on a flight to the U.S. I said goodbye to the manager and thanked him for his help and courtesy. He told me not to worry about the bricks and to look for my suitcase at the London terminal. If it wasn't there, then he would see that it was routed to my office in Tennessee. The Customs Officer came to the door with me and I asked him to step outside into the hall. I thanked him for his advice and hard work and said I knew that he would get my bricks out of the country. I took out my wallet and told him that I wished to give him a present. He demurred, but not too strenuously, and I handed him a twenty dollar bill. He took it gracefully and pointing to my wallet suggested that I give him another bill of the same denomination. Twenty dollars was a large sum to the residents of Turkey, so I told him I needed money for England and handed him a ten. He accepted this and we shook hands as he reassured me about getting the ancient bricks either in London or in the U.S. All this had been rather trying, but as I walked down the stairs and through to the passenger lounge, I felt that I would see my "treasures" again.

I reached the terminal just as they announced that they were boarding our flight. I saw my wife, looking very worried, sitting on a settee in front of the airline counter. I called to her and took a photograph just as she turned around with a look of relief. Together, we checked in and boarded our London flight.

At Heathrow, we searched in vain for the special suitcase. It showed up at my office two months later, with a broken handle but the two Byzantine brick safely inside. One of them is now on display in the Museum of Ancient Brick in Johnson City, Tennessee, alongside the piece of brick from Hattusas, while the other is in the Masonry Craft Museum in Annapolis, Maryland.

CHAPTER 4

EGYPTIAN BUSINESS AND BAKSHEESH

Some years ago, a small exhibition of items from the Pharaoh Tutankhamen's tomb was mounted in Richmond, Virginia. I hied myself thither one Sunday afternoon so I would have all day Monday to spend at the display. Unfortunately, when I got to the museum I found that it was closed every Monday, a feature of many non governmental museums both here and abroad. Shortly after my return to my home in Bristol, Tennessee, I found that the Egyptian gentleman escorting the exhibition was going to give a slide lecture on King "Tut" at Virginia Intermont College in Bristol, Virginia. Naturally, I showed up and sat through the presentation. The lecturer was a Mr. Chafik Farid, a tall cadaverous looking man whose English was very poor indeed. It was so poor that many members of the audience left after only a few minutes. I hung on in the hope that I might get to meet Mr.Farid and talk to him about getting two Egyptian bricks for our museum.

The lecture over, I had no difficulty in getting to Mr. Farid and trying to tell him of my desire. I was pretty sure that he couldn't really understand what I was after, and all I got in the way of a reply was "Must write Egypt."

The following day I drafted a letter for the signature of our company president. It was addressed to President Nasser of Egypt and requested, in the name of Cultural Exchange, that two ancient brick be made available to our museum. The letter specified one brick from the Pharaonic period and another from the time of the Roman occupation. The letter was air-mailed and I started an "Egyptian Brick" file. For many months a copy of that letter was all that rested therein. Then, out of the blue, we got a letter from the Egyptian Minister of Culture stating that President Nasser had passed our letter to him for attention and that we would be hearing further. As Curator of the museum, I acknowledged the minister's letter and expressed our thanks and anticipation. Further we did hear, but nothing to do with brick. My name had been put on the Egyptian propaganda mailing list and I was bombarded, monthly, with vitriolic anti-Israeli pamphlets. The propaganda was filed in the waste basket, but I kept writing to "The Land of the Pharaohs" for a report on the status of our request for the historic bricks. Not a single letter was answered. Eventually, after two years, I decided that if I wanted to find out anything I would have to drop into Cairo and do some "poking around" government offices. I made my plans which included staying at the rebuilt Shepheard's Hotel. The original, which had been "THE" place to stay for a century of famous travelers and archaeologists, had been burned down by the Egyptians as a protest against the British during the Suez Crisis. Still, I thought a few ghosts might be hanging around the place so my reservation was made.

I arrived at Shepheard's at two a.m. and walked to the massive reception desk. A clerk asked me what I wanted. I told him

I had a reservation and gave him my name. He didn't even bother to look at any papers but simply said, "You do not have a reservation at this hotel."

I handed him my reservation confirmation slip and said that he was in error. He didn't even look at what I handed him but merely repeated his earlier statement about no reservation. I asked him about "any old room." He didn't have anything at all, so he told me. I then asked him if he had a bath I could sleep in. He didn't. Then he told me that a special meeting of the Foreign Ministers of the members of The United Arab Republic was being held in Cairo and that there wasn't a room to be had anywhere in the city. Then I remembered I was in EGYPT and took out a pound note and slipped it to him with a request that he look over his room list to see if, possibly, there was one small room that wasn't occupied. Without any hesitation, he asked for my passport and gave me a registration form to fill out. With a nice smile, the clerk handed me a key with a caution that I probably wouldn't be able to stay at the hotel any longer than one night. However, if I would check with him after eight p.m. that same night, he would try and find a nice room for me. I read him loud and clear.

I went up in the elevator with a bellhop to show me the way. On the way to my room I noticed a man sitting in a straight chair at the junction of two corridors. From the way he looked me up and down I guessed he was an Egyptian Secret Service man. At any rate, a minute later I found myself in a very comfortable and large room. It had all modern facilities, something I had not expected as I walked from the elevator to the room on a well worn strip carpet. I went through my regular routine and asked the bellhop to try and get me some tea as I showed him I had some Egyptian piastres. He returned within a few minutes carrying a tray on which sat a pot of tea, a small jug of boiled milk, a plate of biscuits and, of course, a cup and saucer and sugar.

I poured my tea and studied my Arabic dictionary while I drank it. The Arabic alphabet hadn't presented me with any difficulty and I had learned it in a very short time. However, my vocabulary was sadly lacking. Many of the words I knew were those I had learned as a seafarer during several visits to Port Said, Suez and Alexandria. They were words that were not used in polite conversation. For about half an hour I tried to memorize several words. First by using an English transliteration and then by writing them in Arabic. Then it was time for bed and I set my alarm for seven thirty which would give me four and a half hours' sleep.

I put on khakis and a seersucker jacket and, after breakfast, asked the hotel doorman to point me in the direction of Kasr-el-Dubbara where the American Research Center in Egypt, with which I had been corresponding, had its office. It was a lovely day and I was able to take in the street sights and sounds as I strolled along. When I felt I should be close to the A.R.C.E., I started looking at the street signs, all in Arabic, and very quickly found my street. Inside the A.R.C.E. I was greeted by a lady who asked me if I was Mr. Saffer. After replying in the affirmative I was handed a letter from my contact in Cairo, Nick Millet. The letter apologized for not being on hand to greet me and invited me to go into Nubia where he was busy excavating and mentioned that there were two modern bricks from Kharga Oasis, in Nubia, waiting for me in the office. The lady who handed me the letter asked me if I would be going up the Nile to visit the "dig." I told her I would have to see how things worked out and that the first thing I had to do was to find Chafik Farid at the department of Archaeology. It so happened that there were two other people in the office. One was an archaeologist, Dr. Scanlon, the other was a very pretty young lady from Washington D.C. I had been introduced to them both when I first went into the office.

When the P.Y.L. from D.C. heard me mention Chafik Farid she asked if I would mind if she came along with me since she had heard a lot about him and wanted to see him because he had a lot of authority over who dug and where, in Egypt. I said I would be glad of the company and we set off. On the way she said she hoped I would go up to Nubia because she was headed that way herself. As an inducement she said, "It will be exciting, and I have a bottle of Scotch which will help us keep warm during our nights in the desert." I replied that my purpose was to find out about some ancient brick and that I doubted whether or not I had enough time to do my job, say "Hello" to the Great Pyramids and the Sphinx, spend time in the Cairo museum, and still be able to go with her.

We arrived at the Department of Archaeology and entering found ourselves in a narrow hallway.. I saw an open door on my right and peeped in. Inside were half a dozen Egyptians who seemed to be shouting simultaneously at someone who was sitting behind the only desk in the room. I was about to back out when the man behind the desk stood up and the shouting stopped. The man was Chafik Farid and when he saw me he pointed to me and said in a loud voice, "The brick man!" I was flabbergasted. After all, he had only seen me for a few minutes in a strange location and respectably dressed. With one exception, the men around him disappeared and I walked over to shake his hand and introduce the P.Y.L. from D.C.

I asked Mr. Farid how he was and told him I was still looking for two ancient bricks. "So," he said "here they are." He reached underneath his desk and produced two bricks which he placed on his desk. I examined them and found that they were exactly what I had requested, a Pharaonic brick and a Roman era specimen. Each was plainly labeled, showing that the Pharaonic specimen was about 3,000 years old and came from a place called Bubastis and the other, 2,000 years old and from Atribis. Mr. Farid pointed out that the Pharaonic brick was a rare specimen on account of it being a fired brick, since the Ancient Egyptians rarely fired brick. The brick had been wrapped in newspaper and I rewrapped them and put them under my arm but my Egyptian friend took them away from me. Apparently I needed a document of release from the Director of Antiquities. I suggested that we find him at once. Mr. Farid told me that he was out of town. I then suggested that the Deputy Director be approached. Reluctantly, he led us down the hallway into some other offices where he apparently discussed the situation with another man. Finally, Chafik Farid turned to me and said that the Director was the only person who had the authority to let me take the brick with me. Asked when he would be back in Cairo, I was told nobody knew. I asked how I could contact President Nasser. That request was like a bombshell! Both Mr. Farid and the other fellow looked startled and protested that I shouldn't bother the President and that I should make arrangements for a shipping container and return the next day in the hope that the Director would have returned.

I wasn't too concerned since, at least, the bricks had been brought in from their ancient sites. As we walked out of the Department of Archaeology, the lone man we had left in Farid's office came up and spoke to me. He said if I wanted a perfect guide to show me the pyramids at Sakkara and at Giza he knew just the person. Of course, he was that person and after he explained that he was the Chief Inspector of Hieroglyphics, I hired him on the spot. The P.Y.L. again invited her to join her in a visit to Nubia. The end result was that the Inspector and I walked her back to the American Research Bureau office where we shook hands and parted.

My guide explained just where we would be going, but asked that it not be made public that he was "moonlighting." He said that all government servants were very poorly paid, something I could well believe because Egypt is not a wealthy country. He stopped a taxi, made a deal with him and we were off, stopping only to pick up a lunch we could eat as we drove. We had four kinds of cheese, some bread, pickles and cokes...an excellent, satisfying meal for that hot day.

We drove past a large brick plant which was producing sun dried mud brick and then, just a short while later, came across some men making their own brick in the ancient manner. They had a large watery hole which was filled with black gooey clay which they were breaking down by treading. Then, in the distance, I got my first glimpse of Ancient Egypt.

Beyond the foreground green of grass and palm trees was the beginning of the desert with the famous Step Pyramid of Sakkara. From afar it appeared to be constructed of brick, however, close up I could see that it was made of hundreds of thousands of small rough hewn, though same sized, pieces of rock. This was supposed to be the last resting place of King Zoser, a Third Dynasty ruler who lived almost five thousand years ago. The Pyramid has six steps, although that wasn't its original design. First built as a mastaba, a long low tomb, Imhotep the king's treasurer decided to add the extra steps to further honor his master. At one point there was a wooden cover which prevented visitors from falling down a hole cut by tomb robbers, centuries ago. My guide told me that Zoser's mummy had never been found and that there was a valid theory that even though this pyramid had been built in his memory, he had actually been laid to rest elsewhere.

Close to the pyramid was a temple in which the soul of the departed king was able to worship. What I saw was the reconstruction. A long, low wall surrounded the complex and it was behind this ancient wall that I handed my guide the agreed amount, in modern Egyptian currency. During a walk down the remains of the causeway leading from the pyramid, my companion told me that he was going to let me go inside a newly discovered tomb. It was a mastaba and sealed from entry by a locked door, but my man had a key. Just inside there was a piece of sacking hanging on the wall. I pulled it aside and saw more of Ancient Egypt in the form of brightly colored hieroglyphics surrounding about a hundred incised figures representing Egyptian soldiers with their captured

71

enemies. The colors; black, white, a little red, and the deep flesh tones which seem to dominate Egyptian art, looked so fresh that I asked if the wall decoration had been touched up. I received an emphatic "NO!" He pointed out that the prisoners were uncircumcised and that naked figures were almost unknown in wall paintings. The only other thing to be seen there was the empty sarcophagus; the mummy, that of Nefer-Ki an early third dynasty figure had been removed to Cairo for examination. Back outside, there was much evidence of ancient mud brick walls, dating back almost five thousand years, and broken clay mummy containers with the reed mats that had been used to wrap them before being placed inside.

The nasty Egyptian flies, old biting enemies of mine, were working on me, and my arms were itching badly. Years before, during my seafaring days,they used to get me on the softest portion of my soles when I took naps in my cabin at Port Said or Alexandria, which made walking rather uncomfortable. We got back in the taxi and drove to another of Egypt's famous places, the Serapium. At one period, Apis, a live bull was worshiped and given all the respect due to any other "deity" until the day it died. Then it was mummified and laid to rest in the Serapium. A steep shaft led into the tomb with over a thousand feet of galleries with separate burial chambers. The sacred bulls' sarcophogi were of red and black granite, each nearly ten feet high, 13 feet long and six and a half feet wide. Each had been cut from a single block. It was awe inspiring to realize just how much work had gone into building this resting place for Apis. I didn't spend much time in there, although it was nice and cool. I got my photos and left to visit Memphis, the ancient Egyptian capital.

At Memphis there was a tremendous fallen statue of Ramses the Second around which had been built a large glass and steel building. I got onto the upper level and looked down on this famous carved figure of a very vain pharaoh. He had statues of himself built all over the country. Just outside the building just mentioned there was a sphinx with Ramses' face. I had my photograph taken with this 3,000 year old chap. When I tried to take one of my guide, he put his hands over his face and moved away. I didn't ask him if his refusal was on religious grounds or because he was scared someone of high authority might get to see that he was doing some extra-curricular activity. We were headed towards Giza, the home of the Great Pyramids, one of which, that of Cheops (Kufu), is counted as one of the Seven Wonders of the World. While at Sakkara, I took some pictures of several pyramids built out in the Libyan desert and then turned right around and was able to see the Great Pyramids, way off.

At Giza we drove past a tremendous necropolis whose "inhabitants" went back thousands of years, but it was the three tremendous pyramids ahead that held my attention. For the next couple of hours I became just another tourist even to taking a ride on a camel. The beast's owner produced a kaffiyeh, a head cover made by diagonally folding a square piece of white cloth, and the agel. This is the cord that holds the kaffiyeh in place. I was reluctant to put it on but the camel owner said that it was very clean and was washed every day. So, with my headcover and sunglasses I climbed aboard. For a minute the beast was led and then I was turned loose. It was like, well, riding a camel...a unique ride. As we swayed along I decided that enough was enough and tried to turn the camel's head around. No luck. I tried to remember what Peter O'Toole used to say when he wanted his camel to get down, in "Lawrence of Arabia." There were two sounds. One was "hut," the other was a guttural sound similar to the clearing of one's throat. I tried "hut" and the animal took off like a shot with me hanging onto the rope reins for dear life with my knees trying to press hard on the saddle as we swayed along. Fortunately, it started to turn and we started to go back to square one where my guide and the camel's owner were laughing themselves silly. The owner shouted something, and the animal slowed down to an amble and took me back to where its owner got it to kneel down and let me get off. I'd had the guide take a photo of me on my camel before I started my ride. It was a good job because I wasn't about to stay on the thing another second.

I had taken my ride in front of the Great Sphinx, which was situated between the pyramids of Chephren and Cheops, and decided to visit with that before going into the Great Pyramid. There were a couple of dozen people standing outside an iron rail that had been put around the monument. It seemed that some restoration work was going on and it was possible that a piece of masonry could fall and seriously hurt someone.

So, there were all these people complaining because they couldn't touch the Sphinx, and there was I waiting for my guide to take out his keys and unlock the gate. I was really getting my money's worth. The Great Sphinx, and known as such because there are thousands of other sphinxes all over Egypt, is 240 feet long and has the face of its builder, Chephren. The Sphinx had to have the body of the strongest animal in the world, the lion, and the face of the wisest man in the world. Since the Great Sphinx was Chephren's, naturally, it has his face. (Or what is left of it. Mameluke gunners and some of Napoleon's troops at different times used the face for target practice).

I noticed that the left forepaw of the Sphinx had been completely rebuilt. This led me to ask my guide if the masonry was solid or if there was the possibility of a small chamber being inside the paw. The answer was that it was absolutely solid. My reason for asking such an apparently stupid question was that I had read a book by a modern "prophet" in which he had stated, unequivocally, that "One day, the left front of the Great Sphinx would be opened up to disclose a secret chamber which would contain an amazing revelation."   As I walked around the vast monument, my guide pointed to a cartouche (the seal of a Pharaoh) and told me that it was that of Chephren. According to him, later Egyptian rulers had tried to efface all references to Chephren on the Sphinx and had their own cartouches chiseled into it. It was the common practice in Ancient Egypt for rulers to either destroy the monuments erected by their predecessors or, more often, replace their cartouches with their own. This saved the expense of erecting extra monuments to themselves, as well as getting rid of any residual divinity of those who had gone before. Even Ramses the Second was guilty of this practice, despite the hundreds of originals he had erected.

From the Great Sphinx we made our way to the Great Pyramid of Cheops, the largest of the pyramids. It was 470 feet high and constructed of two million tremendous limestone blocks each weighing about two-and-a-half tons and requiring a gang of fifty men to move each one. It is possible to climb to the top of this pyramid, and I intended to do just that after I had been inside it. There was a third, and smaller, pyramid which was part of the Great Pyramids. This one belonged to the Pharaoh Mycerinus. However, my interest was focused on that of Cheops. Because of my companion's familiar face and status, we didn't have to pay the usual fee to get inside. We walked up a steep ramp beside what seemed to be a bottomless pit. The lighting was very poor, but this only added to the sense of wonder and mystery that I felt while we moved ahead in the tomb.

The signs of ancient tomb robbers were pointed out to me. Incidentally, all the royal burial places found before the discovery of that of Tutankhamen had been broken into and looted. In almost every case the mummy had disappeared, but in 1881 an ex-tomb robber led an official from Cairo to a cache of 40 mummies, some of them Royal, hidden in an almost inaccessible cave. All had been unwrapped and several had been broken, with desiccated limbs lying all over the place. Tomb robbing was a family business that was passed down from generation to generation! Cheops' pyramid had been broken into and everything in the burial chamber, including his mummified corpse, had been long gone. All I saw was his dismal chamber with the empty granite sarcophagus. Even this sarcophagus, when first discovered, was partially broken and filled with rubble. Clinging to a handrail, we went down into the bowels of the pyramid, and below, into a subterranean room that had been the burial chamber of Cheops' wife. Here, too, there was nothing except the empty sarcophagus, and all was dimly lit and dank. There was no glory of Ancient Egypt to be found within the pyramid.

Outside again, in the sunlight, it wasn't as warm as it had been earlier, but I started to clamber up this Wonder of the World. It was hard work, and it seemed to get a little colder by the yard. My badly bitten arms were sore and aching so, after getting about halfway up, I took some photographs and started down. Back on the ground, I surveyed the area and its massive structures which had fascinated man since early writers, such as Herodotus, had first described it. About twenty years previously, a young Japanese girl who was afflicted with a fatal disease had asked that she be buried close to the pyramids at Giza. This kind of request is often received by the Egyptian government and always turned down. However, in this particular case, permission was granted; and when she died, the Japanese girl was interred in the pyramid area. I believe the burial site had to be unmarked.

My fine guide wanted to get the taxi driver to take us over to the ancient necropolis we had passed on the way to the pyramids. However, I could see that the sun was getting ready to set; and I had been on the go since breakfast, so I asked the driver to return me to my hotel. The other chap asked that he be dropped off about half a mile from the Department of Archaeology and offered me his services for the following day. I thanked him for the splendid job he had done for me and told him that on the morrow I was going back to see Chafik Farid and then to see the manager of British Airways. After that, I told him, I would just wander around both new and old Cairo on my own.

74

When I walked into my hotel, I looked for the clerk who held the fate of my accommodations in his greedy hands. (To be fair, I must mention that "Baksheesh" is the way of life in Egypt and other Middle Eastern countries, and visitors must be prepared to "shell out" good sized tips whenever they want something done for them.) Well, my fellow wasn't in sight so I went up to my room to wash up before going out to find a place for dinner. In the same elevator was the same man who had been sitting in the hallway during the previous night. I greeted him with a "salaam aleykoom" to which he gave the traditional response of "aleykoom salaam." Translated it means "peace be unto you" and "unto you peace, also." The boy running the elevator laughed and told me that I shouldn't talk to a police spy. I had figured him out earlier, but to be friendly I asked him if he was a secret service man. He responded by just smiling at me, but the elevator boy reached out and pulled the man's jacket open to reveal a nasty looking large pistol stuck in his belt. As we got off together, I told him that with him guarding my floor I would sleep feeling very secure.

Having got the desert dust off and bathed my still swelling arms and applied some lotion to them and to half a dozen mosquito bites I had sustained during the day, I waltzed out of Shepheard's for dinner. I wandered away from the hotel area but stayed in the new part of the city because I felt like having a good and hefty meal in comfortable surroundings where I could take my time and relax. I looked into three eating establishments before I found what I was looking for. Although there was a fine restaurant in the hotel, I decided that the waiters would neglect me in favor of the many high military and naval officers who were to be seen all over the hotel lobby. I lingered over my steak and chips and sticky regional dessert and read the English newspaper I had picked up at the hotel.

It was quite dark when I got back to the hotel. The man I wanted to see was there so I walked over to the desk to find out where I stood, or rather where I was going to lie down. He looked around at the other people behind the desk and quickly told me to go up to my room and wait for him to call me. Almost an hour passed before he called to tell me that he could talk to me and that I should come down. By this time, I had begun to feel confident that the room was mine for as long as I wanted it. I put a pound note in one of the hotel's envelopes and went down, waving to the "police spy" as I walked to the elevator. At the desk I shook hands with the clerk and slipped the envelope to him while he told me that he had been able to arrange it so I could stay there one more night. I reminded him that I had two more nights and he said he would "work for me" but couldn't promise anything. There it was. I was correct in my assumption that the room had been reserved for me as shown on my reservation confirmation and that it was just going to cost me an extra pound a night. I studied a little more Arabic, had a nice hot bath and slept like an innocent babe.

I was awakened early in the morning not by my alarm but by the sound of a military band playing right beneath my window. I didn't think I deserved such a signal honor and looked out to see ranks of Egyptian soldiers being inspected by a group of officials, which I expected was composed of the Foreign Ministers who had come to Cairo for their meeting.

I had my breakfast and headed for the Department of Archaeology where I found Chafik Farid sitting behind his desk reading a newspaper. He greeted me warmly and invited me to have a cup of tea, an offer I rarely turn down. He made a phone call and told me that it would be ready very shortly. He avoided the subject I wanted to get to, the two brick, and asked me how I had spent the previous day. Without mentioning who my fine guide had been, I gave him a run down and told him how impressed and awed I had been by all that I had seen. He told me that I had covered in one day what most visitors could just handle in two days. The tea came. We sipped in silence until I asked him about the Director of Antiquities and my bricks, which were still under his desk. Mr. Farid was full of apologies because, so he said, the Director was still out of town. I asked him for advice on getting the brick out of the country saying if the Director wasn't back by the next morning, I wouldn't have any more days left in Cairo and would have to forego my planned day, visiting Luxor and the Valley of the Kings, so that I could try and get an audience with President Nasser or the Minister of Culture. I told him that young "King Tut" would be upset if I didn't visit him. Farid laughed and said that the President was very busy with the visiting foreign ministers and there was no chance of an audience, that I should make shipping arrangements, and he would handle the matter the very morning the Director returned. I bent down and picked up the brick and smilingly, of course, pointed out that he hadn't handled the matter very well up to then.

We parted good friends and I found my way to the British Airways office where I introduced myself to the manager. Now, British Airways and I had a very good working relationship, and the Regional Manager in Washington, D.C. had sent a signal to Cairo advising them of my impending arrival with a request that all necessary assistance be given me. This was done whenever I went overseas. The manager, an Egyptian, was pleased to see me and, after ordering some tea, asked me if he could be of assistance. I assured him that he certainly could and recited the story of my problem with the two brick and the supposed absence of the Director of Antiquities.

He asked me to go with him to a box maker to whom I gave the dimensions of the container I wanted him to make. I made sure that he understood all the instructions which included a hasp lock with two keys and foam rubber installed on all sides, including the top and the bottom. For this he asked for ten pounds, a very reasonable amount. He said the box would be ready and turned over to the British Airways manager the following morning. The manager then led me not back to his office but to a small coffee shop where, over a cup of thick syrupy Turkish coffee, he told me about Customs formalities and, of course, baksheesh. The Customs would be issuing the export license which would cost three pounds but, if I wanted to make sure my box was passed through without any delay, another two pounds would be needed for baksheesh. I handed over fifteen pounds to the manager, ten for the box and five for Customs, and asked him what would happen if I decided not to hand over any baksheesh. He replied that, then, the Customs would find they couldn't get to my shipment for months. I asked him to make sure that one of the keys to the box was sent to me by air mail and that the other be wired to the hasp so the U.S. Customs could get at the contents for their examination. I handed him a small packet of "FRAGILE" labels which were to be stuck all over the box. I liked the British Airways chap and left him feeling that he would "worry" the Department of Archaeology until it disgorged my brick and then see to their safe packing and shipping. (Wrong again!)

Cairo has over a dozen museums but the most important is the Egyptian Museum which confines itself to exhibits from the Pharaonic period. I started at the Egyptian Museum which I entered with almost the same feeling of elation as I had felt when approaching the Great Pyramids. The entry fee was ridiculously small and the cost for a permit to take my cameras in was greater, although still a small amount. On entering the first hall, my first impression was of being overwhelmed by massive statuary, a tremendous amount of dust on everything, and a host of visitors. (My latest information is that the dust problem is now under control throughout the museum).

I wanted to see the Tutankhamen artifacts first, so I walked up to the first guard I saw and just said "Tutankhamen." He pointed up the stairs and off I went. Whilst looking for the boy king's exhibit, I passed case after case filled with small figures of gods, goddesses and scarabs, and ushwabtis. Concerning ushwabtis: In the days of the very early Pharaohs whenever one died it was customary to kill several of his servants, soldiers, and his wife. This was so the Pharaoh would have all the "comforts of home" during his after life. If the gods decreed that because of some misdeed during his life on earth the king should perform some menial tasks, then his servants entombed with him would be able to do the jobs for him. Later on it was deemed that the slaying of a pharaoh's entourage was unnecessary and that small figurines of his servants would serve exactly the same purpose. Hence the ushwabtis. The scarab was a representation of the scarab beetle, sometimes referred to as the "Sun Beetle." This creature is the dung beetle which can be seen rolling small balls of animal dung along the ground. Since these balls are perfectly round, and to the ancient Egyptians just like the sun, they became of great religious significance to them.

I found the rooms with Tutankhamen's treasure, artifacts of breathtaking beauty. The discovery of his tomb in the Valley of the Kings by Howard Carter and Lord Carnarvon is so well known that I don't need to repeat it, here. But there I was, standing amidst all the items they had found in the tomb over fifty years ago. My eyes were first attracted to the gilded wooden outer cover of the alabaster container of Tutankhamen's canopic jars with four gorgeous goddesses holding out their arms as though protecting the shrine. I managed to get one shot of this before the crowd filled my lens. There was a display of the pharaoh's daggers, with solid gold scabbards and one with a solid gold blade. His thrones were there. One with ivory inlaid back and seat and another with a solid gold back with a bas relief design showing the pharaoh's wife, Ankhesamun, putting soothing ointment on his arm. (Perhaps he'd been out in the sun too long that day). The couch with supports in the form of leopards stood there awaiting its royal owner to take a rest. Two very dusty cases were attracting. One showed one of the two tall protecting figures, armed with a club and a shield, that Carter had found just outside the entrance to the sarcophagus room. The other held a superb model of a solar ship for the pharaoh to travel in across the sky as he went through his daily after-life cycle. Then I looked for the solid gold mummy cover that had taken six men to lift. There before my eyes was not only beauty and craftsmanship but enough wealth to make its owner an instant millionaire.

There was much more for me to see but I wanted to see the second of Tutankhamen's mummy cases. It was there, in another dusty glass case. A finely crafted facemask of carnelian, obsidian, lapislazuli and gold that was a perfect portrait of the young pharaoh. That it was possible to tell that the resemblance was accurate was possible because when the mummy was unwrapped the face revealed matched perfectly with those on the coffins. After the mummy was removed from the last coffin it was covered with a head and shoulders mask that is now on display in the Cairo Museum. This, too, was made of gold, carnelian, obsidian and lapislazuli its lustre undimmed by the thousands of years of entombment. I stayed in one spot for fifteen minutes before I could get my photograph of this mask. It was worth it, though. Elsewhere, in Istanbul, I had to wait half an hour for a break in the crowd of visitors to take a photograph.

I left the Tutankhamen exhibit, my poor bitten arms seeming to be hurting more than ever making me wonder if perhaps, after all, the stupid story of the curse of Tutankhamen was real. The room with several royal mummies on display was open and after paying another small fee, about 25c, I went in. There they were, lined up in case after case. The remains of so many of Egypt's famous names. Ramses the Second was there lying proud and peaceful, while the bellicose Sekenere lies with his mouth opened in its death scream as his skull was cracked open by a blow from a battle axe. Another worth mentioning is the mummy of Tuthmosis the Fourth. He was a member of the 18th dynasty, the same as that of Tutankhamen, that helped bring Egypt to the greatest point in its history. This pharaoh, too, seems to have popped off peacefully. Having recorded all this on film I left the museum because I wanted to see some of Cairo's famous mosques and walk down a few streets.

It was still only noon so I dropped into a restaurant for a shishkebab lunch and then took a short walk in the center of the city. There is a small park there with plenty of benches and I thought it would be a good place to sit, and digest my lunch. Standing at the edge of the small park was an Arab dressed in an ankle length nightdress like robe. This typical arab garb is necessary in the Middle East. It protects the wearer from the burning rays of the sun during the day and provides insulation from the very chilling desert air at night. The man was a vendor offering peanuts and an oversize bread circlet that resembled the famous bagel. There was a building adjoining the park with its wall decorated with colorful paintings of ancient Egyptian symbols. After a while I moved on and entered a street that was more to my liking and expectations.

Although I was still in modern Cairo, there were street vendors selling everything from fresh vegetables from carts to a man with a large brass container, fastened to him by a wide leather strap slung around his shoulders, from which he dispensed lemonade into a glass from which all customers took their drink. Arab children in their little "night gown" clothes were darting hither and thither playing some kind of a game with much shouting and laughter. The buildings on either side of this street were well kept apartment houses which were occupied by some of the downtown merchants and restaurant owners.

I saw a taxi standing idly with its driver leaning against some railings. I approached him and said that I wanted to hire him for a couple of hours but needed a firm price before we took off. Although bargaining over the price of just about everything is said to be part of the enjoyment of traveling in places such as Egypt, I have neither the talent nor the inclination to follow this practice. Years of foreign travel had made me wise, when it came to purchasing anything from Italy eastward. I have a phrase that has saved me a lot of time and, surely a lot of money. Whenever I find something I like I say to the vendor

"I like this and MAY buy it from you but I never bargain. You have one chance to quote me the lowest price you want for it. If I think it is reasonable I will buy it from you. If I think it's too much I'll just leave you and perhaps buy it somewhere else. Remember, you have only one chance."

This approach usually takes the wind out of their sails and puts them on the spot. They would much rather give you a glass of tea and haggle until the customer is pleased to pay half of the original quoted price. Actually, a quarter is the fairest price. I have walked out of many shops with the owner calling out a lower price than the "lowest" he had just finished quoting. Other merchants who might be standing in their shop doorways hear this and courteously invite me into their place and quote me the rock bottom price. So it was with the taxi driver, I recited my formula and stood as though I was about to go looking elsewhere. It worked. The man shrugged his shoulders, mentioned a fair price and opened the door for me even before I had a chance to say that I agreed.

I told him that I wanted to go to the Islamic Museum, the 9th century mosque of Ahmed Ibn Tulun, the 14th century Sultan Hasan Mosque and the Mosque of El Azhar. One might think that I was on a pilgrimage and going to do a lot of praying. Actually, each mosque had some unusual feature or location. If there was time, I said I'd like to visit the famous "Musky" bazaar.

The Arab Museum turned out to be the repository of some of the most elegant Moslem artifacts I had ever seen. The ceramics on display rivaled part of what I had seen in Istanbul's Topkapi. The intricate wood carvings inlaid with ivory and mother-of-pearl were everywhere in the form of tables, chests and a host of folding screens. There were delicately chased silver and brass round tables on gorgeous inlaid stands. Then I saw a tremendous collection of mosque lamps, each more beautiful than the one next to it. There was a host of handsomely woven carpets and incredibly woven fabrics. Although every-thing was attractively displayed The lighting in the museum was not the brightest, probably by design, so I probably missed a lot of detailing. Out to the taxi and then on to the Ahmad Tulun Mosque which I wanted to see just because of its rare spiral minaret. I didn't go in but admired it from a distance and then close up.

The Sultan Hasan Mosque which, as I have already written, dates back to the fourteenth century has high fortress type walls and is built close to the Citadel which dates back to the time of Saladin. The walls Saladin had built in the twelfth century are still standing strong and proud along with some of those added by later rulers. I went inside this mosque and through a latticed window managed to get a couple of shots of the Mohammed Ali Mosque. This mosque dates back to just 1840 and is built on a high point of Cairo and its tall pointed minarets and huge dome dominate the city skyline.

My next stop was the "Musky", one of the world's most famous bazaars. Some of the shops in the area date back to the year 1400 and the whole area is heavily scented because of the streets of the spice and herb sellers and the street of the perfume sellers. I saw strange roots seeds and strangely pungent roots being sold wrapped in small twists of newspaper. I went down the street of the tentmakers to watch these famous craftsmen decorating the heavy materials used for ceremonial tents. The perfume sellers displayed their essences in the slimmest of bottles..all exotic scents that caused my eyes to water and brought on a paroxysm of sneezing since I am allergic to most perfumes. I hurried to get a glimpse of the copperworkers, leather-workers and the looms of the rugmakers. All these artisans have very small stalls which open onto the narrow street.

I had saved the best for the last. The El Azhar Mosque is the home of the Moslem University. Founded in 972 this is said to be the world's oldest university. After removing my shoes, I entered its vast sanctuary whose arches are supported by 380 columns. The adjoining buildings are occupied by busy students from all over the world because El Azhar is recognized as the most important center of Koranic studies in the world.

Since the next day was going to be my busiest and longest in Egypt, I had the driver return me to my hotel. They were still serving afternoon tea so I found a little table and ordered some tea and finger sandwiches. (Actually, I didn't ask for "finger" sandwiches because in foreign hotels that's the only kind they serve. Our U.S. heavy slabs are unique). Just as the waiter brought my order there was quite a hubbub in the lounge and everyone stood up and moved towards a small platform near the entrance. All I could see were two or three tables and three high ranking army officers who were standing at attention. At first I thought they had just noticed me but I was wrong because in came half a dozen more heavily bemedaled military and naval officers along with a large smiling man in civilian dress. Behold! President Nasser! The people pressed forward and stretched out their hands for him to shake. He obliged quite a few before he indicated that "enough was enough" and sat down for some refreshment. I looked around and saw that no-one was bothering to drink their tea, except me. They just sat and gawked at Nasser. Yes, there was the man the world held responsible for the Mid-East mess and sitting just a few yards from him was a nice Jewish man...the only one in the hotel, Me! If my presence had been known I would have been quickly ejected, or worse. After I had finished, as I walked out of the lounge the President of the United Arab Republic caught my eye and smiled at me.

I make a point of usually buying only three presents from each country I visit. One for my wife to display for a couple of weeks before she hides it in a drawer or hangs beside my basement work shop, another for my son and the other for my daughter. My son is easily taken care of with a wallet or a decorative dagger. My daughter has been rather hard to look after. Some years ago, one of my sisters generously gave her a solid gold charm bracelet and ever since I have had to scour around trying to find a gold charm representative of each country I have found myself in. In Turkey, after much searching, I found a miniature Turkish slipper. In Paris it was easy to find a miniature of the Eiffel Tower. However, in Cairo I was fortunate enough to find what I wanted right inside the hotel, at the lobby display. It was a solid gold charm-sized head of Nefertiti. There were a few mahogany colored wooden plates, ten inches in diameter with an ancient Egyptian scene inlaid in silver, brass, ivory and mother-or-pearl. One that I really liked showed a Pharaoh on his throne. The price was ten pounds, which instinct told me was rather high. I decided just to take the charm and wander around the tourist shops after I had a nap and dinner. When I got to my room I remembered that I would have to "take care" of my clerk before I went to sleep, later. So I decided to forgo my nap and just washed up, anointed my ever-swelling arms and went out to the shops. The regular shops are just like the booths in the bazaars, each selling the very same items next door to one another. They line both sides of the streets with their proprietors propping up the doorposts while they call out to those who are obviously looking for something to take to a foreign country. "Sir, in my shop you will find the best bargains" or, to make you feel more important using an archaic word "Effendi, please come and have some tea with me. You do not have to buy anything."

The merchandise consisted of large decorated copper tables on wooden legs or the same item with the copper having been coated with silver. Old looking prints and paintings, various kinds of weapons, replicas of ancient Egyptian statuettes, (although they tell you that they are ancient originals), mahogany tables in all shapes and sizes with the silver, brass, ivory and mother-of-pearl inlay. There are replicas of ancient wooden screens, replicas of the solar ships found in tombs, strings of "mummy" beads, (some of those to be found in antique shops are genuine), scarabs in a multitude of sizes and colors and, of course, a large number of the inlaid wooden plates similar to those I had seen in the hotel

I walked past a few of these shops trying to look at their displays without being pestered by the owners. Very difficult. Then a very strange thing happened. Well, not so strange in view of being in Egypt and having read many other travelers' accounts of their experiences there, including authors from the last century. As I approached one shop the owner stepped into the street and blocked my passage. Before I could tell him to get out of my way, he half whispered, "Mr. Basil please come inside I have something very special for you alone." At first I was really taken aback, but I followed him into his shop with a vague idea of what was to come...one of the oldest Egyptian tourist tricks in the book. It was so old that I thought that the whole world knew about it and that the Egyptian merchants, Greek, French and Arab wouldn't expect anyone to fall for it. He knew my name. Obviously the old grapevine and confidence tricks were still in style.

"Mr. Basil," he said "that new tomb you visited at Sakkara, yesterday. I know someone who has managed to get the foot part of the mummy case for you to take away with you and he only wants fifty pounds for it and he can help you get it out of the country."

This was the most expensive con of the three classics. The other two were having your guide at the Great Pyramids suddenly scrape something from between the blocks and tell you that he had just found some "Mummy Wheat" thousands of years old and that it would germinate, and pretending to find an ancient scarab in the sand.

I told the rascal that I didn't believe him and that I had heard of this trick ever since I was a child. I also told him that I didn't think the Chief Inspector for Hieroglyphics would do anything illegal. We parted company immediately and I walked into the shop next door. The plate I was looking for was there, among others, and I spouted my speech about only one price, etc. The seller asked me to stop talking business and to let him have his boy bring in some tea so we could become friends. I declined and asked him the price of the plate. Reluctantly, he wearily quoted me ten pounds, the same price the hotel wanted. I said goodbye and wouldn't stop even when he called out "For you, sir, eight pounds."

I crossed the street and decided to see what someone else would want. It's hard to understand but the moment I walked through the door the proprietor put a glass of tea in my hand and said, "You have come to the right shop, sir. All the other merchants cheat customers." I sipped my tea and looked around until I found the particular plate I was after. The quote was five pounds! The plate was identical to the others I had seen and I turned it over to look for some flaw. There was none.

"Tell me, " I said " why are you only charging me five pounds when you have seven pounds marked on the back?" Looking astonished the man remarked that he rarely met anyone from overseas who could read Arabic. (Arabic figures are easily memorized) He answered my question by telling me that if a guide had brought me in he would have had to pay a two pound commission, otherwise the guide would stop bringing in the tourists. As we spoke, a young man shouted something through the door and dashed off. The shop owner informed me that the word was out that a large cruise ship had arrived in Alexandria and that the passengers would be in Cairo the next day. He said there would be a lot of good business for him. I paid him for the plate and then photographed a couple of his more interesting tables to show my wife. Shipping would not be a problem, he explained. We shook hands and I wandered off to find a place to have dinner. I was quite hungry and found a nice looking restaurant with an international menu. However, I decided on soup, steak and chips again. With memories of the war, I said to the waiter "I want beefsteak not camelsteak." He was not amused. As I walked along the streets, after dinner, I happened to look out in the direction of the airport and saw a bright flash which was followed a couple of seconds later by the sound of an explosion.

My clerk was on duty by the time I got back to Shepheards Hotel and he asked me if I had heard the sound of the plane crash. What I had seen was an Al Misr airline plane trying to land ten miles short of the runway. This definitely was not good news since I was to fly up to Luxor early the next morning. I went up to my room and was surprised to find that the "police spy" and his chair were nowhere to be seen. I was due to return from Luxor early the next evening and would then have to wait until 2:30 in the morning to get the British Airways bus out to the airport to catch my flight to London. That left me a lot of hours of hanging around. So I called the hotel desk and spoke to the clerk, explained the situation, and asked if he would be able to find somewhere for me to nap the next night without me having to pay a full day's room fee. He told me he would take care of everything but that I should pack my bags, leave them in the room but arrange to have them checked at the airline office as soon as I got back. He reminded me that I should "talk" to him, and no-one else, on my return.

The flight up to Luxor, in a twenty passenger commuter type plane, was very smooth and pleasant. To clarify matters about flying "up" or "down" to Luxor since when one looks at a map Luxor is obviously south of Cairo, I should point out that the Nile flows DOWN to the Delta. Therefore, one travels "Up the Nile going south. It was interesting to see, on both sides of the river, verdant expanses which tapered off into the sandy, forbidding Egyptian Desert as far as my eyes could see. The 300 mile flight took just about two and a half hours, but from quite a distance away I could see the remains of ancient temples and other ruins stretched out between the little mudbrick villages which dotted the landscape.

At Luxor I took out my list of places to see, which I had compiled some years before. Since my main objective was the tomb of Tutankhamen, in the Valley of the Kings, on the other side of the Nile, I knew I was going to have to move very quickly. Taxis were available and I was besieged by five drivers the moment I got into the small terminal. I selected the least vociferous and asked him if he would be able, not only to take me around Luxor and Karnak but also have his car ferried over to the west bank and so stay with me all day. He said that he could get his car ferried over but that there was an agreement between the taxi drivers on each side to stay on their own side. I had to accept that and proceeded to tell the fellow just what I wanted to see.

First of all I visited the remains of the great temple built at Luxor by Amenhotep the Third who ruled Egypt from 1417 to 1379 B.C. The great hall of the temple had originally been over 600 feet long and as I looked at some of the massive columns I could see that Ramses the Second had been around because his cartouche was inscribed on many of them. Ramses had a number of his statues erected on the grounds. The temple was also interesting because in early Christian times it had been made into a church. Later a shrine to a Moslem holy man was built inside the great hall. Amenhotep the Third had several temples and palaces built elsewhere, at Thebes, (Part of which is now Luxor) and Karnak. He is probably best remembered as the father of Ikhnaten the pharaoh who threw out the priests and practices of the god Amen and introduced Solar Monotheism.

We drove to the famous Avenue of the Sphinxes which stretched from Luxor to Karnak. This avenue is just over a mile long with restored ram headed sphinxes lining the original pavement which had been uncovered. It leads to the great Temple of Karnak dedicated to Amon, originally the chief god of Thebes. He was often represented as a ram-headed human, hence the ram-headed sphinxes in the Avenue. (Sphinxes could be seen just about everywhere I turned, not just on this avenue) This temple has a great colon-naded hall, 388 feet by 170 feet, with 134 columns set out in sixteen rows. This is in the western half of the one thousand square feet which the sacred grounds occupy. I spent a short while looking at some of the elaborate wall carvings in the temple and then moved out to the eastern half of the sacred area which contained a bewildering complex of halls and shrines not all belonging to the same dynasty, one of them being dedicated to Tutankhamen. There was an obelisk bearing the figure of Queen Hatshepsut and, what I found most attractive, a limestone column known as the Lily Column of Tuthmosis the Third. It showed massive carved lilies and the king being embraced by a goddess, a truly remarkable piece of carving with cartouches and symbolic figures above and below.

I had the driver take me to visit one of the villages built on the Nile banks. It was like going back over three thousand years ago, even to a small weathered sphinx leaning at a precarious angle. Modern amenities were absolutely absent. The women were washing their clothes in the river while there were a couple of men carrying water in wooden buckets which were suspended from ancient wooden shoulder yokes. Some scrawny looking cattle were wandering around nibbling the scarce grass, yet the village was surrounded by handsome healthy palm trees from which the villagers not only got dates but fronds to cover the roofs of their small mudbrick houses. This was 100% primitivity. I was surprised to find that the only children in sight were in arms or just toddlers. Whenever I passed a man of the village I would greet him with either "Saide"...the Arabic for good morning...or "Salaam." However, as I walked back to the taxi I heard the sound of little voices emitting some kind of recitation. I quickly glanced through what normally would be a window of a home, sans glass, and saw what was obviously a schoolroom.

Back in Luxor I had little difficulty finding a nice place for lunch since it is a city of over 35,000 and "home" to hundreds of scholars of Ancient Egypt from many countries. There were many restaurants, and I had the driver stop outside one of the larger and paid him off. I didn't want to tarry over my lunch, but since I hadn't had any breakfast I thought it best to eat well. It was a Greek owned establishment so I ordered some grape leaves stuffed with meat and rice and more meat in the form of well cooked shishkabob. Relatively speaking, the bill was quite high. The price in Cairo would have been much less. Still it was good and I felt ready to cross the Nile and get to the Valley of the Kings.

When I emerged from the hotel the same taxi was still standing there and the driver offered to take me to the ferry "as a friend." (I had given him a nice tip on top of our agreed price for the morning's jaunt).I accepted the ride and took the ferry over to the west bank. There it was just like a small market right on the river bank. There were stalls offering everything from sweetmeats to "scarabs" and cork topees as well as a very practical item used in India and the Middle East, the chatty. The chatty is a porous earthenware container, available in many sizes, which one fills with water. Since it is porous the outside rapidly becomes wet and the heat of the sun causes evaporation which, of course, draws heat from the water inside. A small spout on the side enables the owner to get a nice cool drink on the hottest day.

Once again, I was besieged by several offers of transportation. However, this time I could select from an assortment of ancient taxicabs, mangy donkeys and even a camel. After my mad desert dash on the camel at Giza I dismissed the last immediately. The donkey ride was given a little thought until I realized that there were no saddles in sight and that all that would be covering the animal's back would be a cloth. So it was to be another taxi. Since there were only three other prospective riders, besides myself, the competition for a customer was fierce. It became even more so when the drivers discovered that the other three were a party. Again, I looked for the least "pushy" of the drivers and selected him. I was then subjected to a torrent of abuse, both in Arabic and English, from most of the others. They got quite a shock when I turned on them using some of my nautical Arabic which can be quite insulting. My driver was all smiles as he opened the door of his cab to let me in. I just told him I would be sitting next to him, in the front, and let myself in there.

Despite the fact that the road was paved, the ride was quite bumpy and even in the front I was sliding around. However, I hadn't come for comfort. I was there to fulfil another long awaited dream, a personal visit with Tutankhamen. We passed through fields of cotton, wheat and sugar cane all looking very healthy on the diet left behind by the regular autumnal flooding of the Nile. There were a number of mud brick villages, heaven knows how old, and here and there pieces of ancient statuary including more Sphinxes. We stopped at one field beside which were two seventy foot high statues of Amenhotep the Third. They were famous,despite the fact that they were in pretty bad shape from weathering, and I knew that Tutankhamen's funeral procession had passed by these colossi. I took my pictures and returned to the car. After passing through the fertile belt and entering the desert, we saw a lot more ancient statuary and then the temperature seemed to rise very quickly. I estimated that it was around a hundred degrees; still I was in the Valley of the Kings, and I had been in places where the temperature was 115 degrees so I wasn't uncomfortable.

We came to a spot where I could get a good view of the desolate peak that overlooked the valley and had the entrances to about twenty ancient tombs built into the hillside. It was amazing to realize that, even though almost on top of one another, none of the tombs ran into one another. There was a rest house operated by Thomas Cook and Sons which was very close to the tomb of Tutankhamen and the tomb of Ramses the Sixth which, in turn, was just above the entrance to that of Tutankhamen's.

My driver pulled up by the rest house and I proceeded on foot. Before going into the Tutankhamen tomb, I wanted to see the elaborately decorated entrance to the funerary chamber of Ramses the Sixth. I had seen color photographs of this entryway but could hardly believe that the colors weren't exaggerated. They weren't. A large "Ba," a human headed bird, was above the main doorway and every conceivable part of the door and passage ways were covered with religious figures, cartouches and hieroglyphics. Even the ceiling was lavishly decorated. From there it was only some yards to the entrance to the tomb of King Tutankhamen. There were guides available, too available, but I gave one several piastres NOT to guide me and keep his friends away from me while I went inside alone. (I was well acquainted with the book by Howard

Carter, the discoverer and excavator of the tomb, and owned quite a few fancy books on Tutankhamen). I tried to visualize Howard Carter walking down the thirty foot cleared passage through the antechamber and into the burial chamber. As I stood in the doorway I could see the large yellow quartzite sarcophagus with the four protecting goddesses carved at the corners and the paintings that covered all the walls. I walked over and looked down onto the colorful coffin which had been fashioned in the king's likeness. It was the first of the three coffins nested one inside the other. (I had seen the other two in Cairo). Seven feet long, it showed the boy king's hands folded across his chest holding the royal emblems, the crook and the flail, with the cobra and vulture resting on his brow. Inside, I knew, lay the mummy of the boy pharaoh...probably the only royal mummy finally resting in its original place of entombment. With my guide book to help me identify the meaning, I examined the wall paintings. The one behind the sarcophagus showed all the rituals of death and entombment. Another painting showed nobles pulling the sled carrying the mummy of Tutankhamen. Yet another wall painting showed Tutankhamen embracing Osiris, the god of the underworld, while his spiritual double known as the Ka stands behind him. All this in brilliant reds, greens, white and black. One intriguing painting showed the young king's successor, Ay, dressed in a leopard skin performing a priestly ceremony known as "The Opening of the Mouth."

I was taking a more detailed look at the carvings of the figures and the hieroglyphics on the great sarcophagus when in came the three people I had seen at the ferry. The first words uttered by them came from a lady who said, "I hope the 'Pharaoh's Curse' won't get us!" At this, my sore swollen arms began to bother me again. Lord Carnarvon, the wealthy amateur archaeologist who had funded Howard Carter's expedition, had died in Cairo as the result of an infected mosquito bite. This fact, coupled with the deaths of Carnarvon's half brother and A.C.Mace, Carter's partner, had given birth to the myth of the curse. To begin with, Lord Carnarvon was a sickly man who left England for Egypt for health reasons and in 1923, when he died, no medication existed to prevent secondary infections from developing. Then, Mace was also suffering from a long standing chronic illness. If there had been "a curse" surely it would have hit Carter first. Carter lived for seventeen years after he opened Tutankhamen's tomb. He died in 1939 aged sixty-six.

After leaving Tutankhamen, I walked to the rest house and had a snack after which I realized It was time for me to head back towards Cairo. So I had another bumpy ride back to the Nile, crossed over and caught my flight
in good time.

The first thing I did when I got back to the hotel, was to put on some warmer clothes (in readiness for England's spring weather) and set my little alarm clock for three a.m. Then I took my case over to British Airways where it was checked through to London on a Comet-IV plane run by East African Airlines. (British Airways was their agent). Then, it was back to the hotel and a friendly visit with my personal clerk. I handed him two pounds, which pleased him immensely, and was told I could stay in the same room until I left at 3:00-ish. Thanks to an official called Mr. Basil, (no relation of mine),I had no problems getting out of Egypt, complete with my modern sundried mud brick from Kharga Oasis, and fell asleep as soon as I had fastened my seat belt. I awoke just in time for breakfast, an hour away from London. There I showed my ballooned arms to the Doctors in my family and was given prompt relief. Within a couple of days I was back to normal and still alive. I had survived "The Curse."

What happened to my two ancient bricks? The story continues in Washington D.C. over two years later. In order to show our appreciation for all the cooperation we had received from many foreign countries which had made it possible for the General Shale Museum of Ancient Brick to grow from an idea into a well known reality, we held an Embassy Party in Washington D.C. Invitations were sent to the Ambassadors and Cultural Attaches of over two dozen countries to attend a showing of the museum at the headquarters of the Structural Clay Products Institute on 18th Street. A firm of caterers was employed, as well as the services of "Rock" group.

The precious specimens from the museum were packed and very carefully driven to D.C. where they were displayed on black cloth covered tables in the Board Room of the Institute. Each brick had a card giving the culture and country of origin, as well as its age. Also on display were several light boxes which showed enlarged transparencies of some of the photographs I had taken during my journeys.

Most of the diplomats and their Cultural Attaches accepted our invitation. The Egyptian Embassy informed us that they would have THREE Cultural Attaches at the party and I could hardly wait for the night when I would meet these fellows and convince them that unless they secured the release of the two bricks lying under Chafik Farid's desk, in Cairo, another plague, in the form of phone calls and cables to Nasser, would descend upon certain Egyptians.

It was quite "a bash" and it was quite a sight to see the Diplomats with a drink in one hand and something edible in the other walking around the tables looking, first, for the bricks that had come from their own country and then becoming fascinated by the entire display. The men from the Egyptian Embassy came in a group and I just stood back and watched them as they scrutinized each card looking for something from Egypt. There was nothing for them. I saw they were puzzled and went up and introduced myself. The leader of the Egyptians was Mr. Fathey Bahig who asked me where they could see the Egyptian display. I led them to one of the light boxes which showed a slide I had taken of a 4,700 year old mud brick wall at Sakkara. Asked about bricks, I told them that all I had from their country was the modern mud brick from Kharga Oasis covered with a mass of straw and without a history. I said I didn't think they would have wanted me to put that out as their contribution, and told them about the bricks that should have been there. Since I had a lot of people to meet, I made an appointment to meet Fathy Bahig for lunch the next day, Saturday. I must say that it was a pleasant meeting, up to a point. Fathy was very pleasant company but was terribly embarrassed by my problems with his country's Department of Archaeology. He said he would get onto the matter first thing Monday. I told him that there was no need for him to wait until Monday since Saturday and Sunday were not religious days in Egypt and that unless I heard that the bricks had been released by Monday, the president of General

Shale would send a cable to President Nasser to let him know that his wishes were not being followed. At the mention of Nasser's name poor Fathy became very agitated. He begged me not to write to his president. I asked him if, maybe, a cable would be better. He told me that anybody who was reported as inefficient, to Nasser, invariably found themselves in prison.

I stuck to my guns and told him that I had gone to a great deal of trouble trying to get the specimens, exactly what I had asked for, out of his country and that it was now three years since my visit and the "sands of time had run out." He vowed that I would hear something before the end of the day on Monday but asked me not to have anything sent to President Nasser before he, Fathy, had a chance to straighten things out. On the Monday morning, as I walked into our office building, the receptionist handed me a cable she said had just arrived. It was from Cairo and informed me that the brick had been shipped, that very morning. The cable gave me the flight number and the weighbill number.

The brick were delivered about a week later, after being held up in Customs. The box was sturdy, well padded and had two keys fastened to the hasp. As I placed the bricks in the museum, I felt that I had really accomplished something and the germ of an idea was growing that I could get even more out of Egypt. As mentioned previously, the two brick given to us, after all the trouble, represented Pharaonic Egypt and Roman Egypt. However, the Pharaonic brick was a rare fired brick and what we now needed was a simple, ancient sun-dried brick. My procedure to procure one was a little involved.

First I wrote a letter to the Director of Archaeology in Cairo enclosing an International Money Order for twenty-five dollars. This I had made out to him personally. The letter thanked him for past favors and requested one more. I told him I had seen a Third Dynasty wall at Sakkara and would be grateful if he would arrange for someone to drive out there and remove one from the wall and ship it to me in the box which I was sending him. He was given to understand that we would pay the cost of having this done, along with any other fees involved. As well as the money order, in the letter I enclosed a key to the box and a slide of the wall at Sakkara. He was requested to send the shipment "all charges collect." The box was shipped off to him, by air, a week before I mailed the letter. My cohorts at General Shale kept telling me that I had seen the last of the box.

How wrong they were! Six months later the box came home carrying a whole brick and half a brick. They were not from the wall I had photographed but from another. Obviously there was reluctance to disturb the wall I had indicated, but there was a document along with the shipping papers indicating that the brick were, indeed, from Sakkara, Third Dynasty and close to five thousand years old. The list of charges included, not only air freight but also a sum for travel from Cairo to Sakkara and one day's pay for someone to make the trip, plus an amount for the Customs charges

So my visit to Egypt produced a total of three specimens for the museum, a nice beginning for our Ancient Egyptian display.

CHAPTER 5

ENGLAND, FROM ROMANS TO SHAKESPEARE

$\mathbf{H}$alf a mile from my home in England there is a Roman wellhouse around which, as a youngster, I often played. From my earliest days I was aware of the many Roman relics in Leeds. Each time the main roads were repaired the workmen would discover that the base was originally built by the invaders who had arrived in 43 A.D. and stayed for 400 years. Each discovery was duly noted in the newspapers, as were those made at places like Bath, London and a hundred other old Roman settlements.

The Romans brought the art of brickmaking to Britain, a craft which slowly disappeared after their garrisons were recalled to Rome. Within fifty years brick was no longer made and remained a past building material until the twelfth century when monks made a few for fireplaces and for leveling the courses of stone which they used to build their magnificent monasteries. Then brick slowly came back into vogue for the wealthy to build their mansions and palaces. So I knew that England would be a country rich with brick for our museum, as well as being a country that did not have an "Antiquities Law."

All I had to do was select my sites and contact the curator of the museum which was close to each and arrange a meeting over in England. After some correspondence I had appointments at the Grosvenor Museum in Chester; the Roman Bath in Bath; a small Roman Museum in Doncaster; the Shakespearean Trust in Stratford-on-Avon; and in London with the Late Dame Kathleen Kenyon who was recognized as the world's foremost lady archaeologist.

No matter what else I do on my visits to England, I always make time to spend a few days motoring in Yorkshire, the largest county, where I used to camp, hike and bicycle. It is like a magnet which draws me to the county's famous dales, lush green wolds and heather and gorse covered windswept moors. In Yorkshire are to be found the stately, awe-inspiring remains of a host of ruined abbeys. They were not destroyed by nature but by Henry the Eighth who, after his break with Rome and his subsequent excommunication, commanded that the abbeys and monasteries should be made uninhabitable. Yet, even in their present roofless condition many are still stately and awe-inspiring with their soaring Gothic archways and heaven aspiring roof supports.

My favorite is Rievaulx Abbey, built in the lee of a northern hillside with its sixteen chapels; a 140 foot cloister around which one may walk in silence like the monks of old; the choir and transepts of the church; as well as the refectory. The tombstones of some of the abbots are still in place at Rievaulx. However, if you look into some of the nearby farmyards, don't be surprised when you see walls and pigsties built with stone from the Abbey as well as the tombstones of departed abbots.

I had read that there had been some recent archaeological excavation at Rievaulx, and on this particular occasion I hoped to be able to find some piece of discarded burned clay artifact that might fit nicely into our collection. Wan-

89

dering around the deserted ruins, I saw the meager remains of what had been vast decorated tiled flooring and, here and there, small brick fireplaces. I left all these untouched and merely picked up two fragments, mixed in with the gravel walkway, which I recognized as coming from some thin roof tiling. In vain, I searched for signs of the reported recent excavation and, having absorbed for the twelfth time the atmosphere of peace and tranquility of the Abbey, disturbed only by the cawing from a nearby rookery, started down the hill towards my car.

Before getting in, I looked back at Rievaulx in all its stately glory and noticed a group of workmen gathered together about a hundred yards away from the Abbey at the top of the hill. I could tell they were watching me, so I waved to them and received a couple of waves in return. I began to walk towards them and one workman detached himself from the rest and came to meet me. This fellow was carrying a spade. We met halfway up the hill and exchanged pleasantries. I asked what he and his friends were doing and was surprised to find that they were leveling off the ground where a team of archaeologists had worked the previous fall. I asked what they had found and was told, "Not what they had expected." It seemed that all that had been discovered was a pit of useless rubble. In a few minutes I was standing with the rest of the workmen looking at the disturbed ground. It was a long trench.

I told the men that I was hoping to find just one brick or even a tile that the archaeologists had discarded. Without a word, the chap who had greeted me stuck his spade in the loose earth and turned over a small pile of soil in which I could see the shape of a thick floor tile. I retrieved it and brushed the dirt off and was rewarded with a perfect tile bearing a cruciform design which was heavily glazed.

The first fellow and about three of his mates turned over a few more spadefuls of earth, but all we found was another tile that was chipped and pitted. I thanked them for their help, gave a five pound note to the man to whom I had first spoken, inviting them to "Have a pint on me, men," shook hands all round and trotted off down the hill joyfully carrying my lucky finds.

Standing by the car were my companions for the day, my sister and her husband with whom I was staying in Leeds. Despite my assurances that I wouldn't dream of disturbing anything that was a part of the abbey and maintained by the authorities to show as much of the original structure as possible ...bricks and floor tiles... they stayed away from me pretending they didn't know who I was. As we drove away, I showed them my "treasures" and suggested that we go into the nearby village of Helmsley and have lunch in the historic Black Swan Inn. We got there just in time, before they stopped serving lunch. After a good satisfying meal of roast beef and Yorkshire pudding washed down with half a pint of bitter ale, we drove to Sutton Bank from the top of which we were able to look out over the famous Yorkshire Dales a sight which made me slightly homesick for the land and county of my birth.

The next day, I went to Doncaster, a small town best known for its racetrack but which, as Danum, had been a military station along an old Roman highway. I was greeted by the curator, Mr. Lidster, who proudly showed me around his small facility. We then went into his office where I reminded him of my request for assistance in obtaining a Roman brick. He smiled as he opened his desk drawer and handed me a Roman brick which bore the clear marks made by a sandal whose wearer had walked over the artifact while it was still wet. It was quite a thrill to hold the brick and run my fingers over the sandal depression and I was just about to thank him for the 19 hundred year old gift when he took it back from me saying that it was his most exciting find and the prize of his personal collection. And that was that! He told me where the current Roman excavations were in progress and that he was going to attend a meeting of archaeologists, one week later, and would see what he could "dig up" for me.

So, it turned out that my "horse didn't come in" at Doncaster but I had a goodly number of other prospects to see and I made tracks for Chester, an old walled city in the west, which had been the headquarters of the 20th Roman Legion in 79 A.D. It had been an Ancient Briton settlement long before the invaders took over and, after the Romans left, was repeatedly raided and looted by the Saxons and the Danes. Early in the 10th century it was rebuilt by the weak king Aethelred who consolidated the old walls into two miles of ramparts and towers. Then, in 1070, it was besieged and taken by William the Conqueror. Today, Chester is recognized as England's best preserved walled city with a tremendous number of Tudor houses, medieval streets and elegant Georgian homes. Still standing is King Charles' Tower...he who was beheaded after losing his kingdom to Oliver Cromwell's Roundheads...from which the ill fated monarch watched the defeat of his army on Rowton Moor, just two miles away. The city is also famous for its 14th century galleried walkways. All this along with the extensive Roman remains and, if you're lucky, a band concert being held on the bandstand on the banks of the river Dee.

The Grosvenor is a small, but excellent, museum with a superb collection of Roman artifacts. In its cellars are a huge quantity of pieces that have not yet been thoroughly examined. I was fortunate in that the head of the orthopedic department of a hospital in nearby Buxton, a very close personal friend of some forty years standing, had already "gone to work" for me on the Director of the museum. Having a devilish sense of humor, my friend persuaded the director to put aside two very heavy pieces of Roman masonry for me, thinking he was presenting me with a weighty problem.

What the archaeologist turned over to me was a massive Roman burned-clay roof tile, weighing just over thirty pounds, and a large brick, of the same weight, which had come from the floor of a hypocaust room. (More on hypocausts later.) The good doctor, the director, told me that they both came from the barracks of the Praetorian Guards, on the Via Praetoriae, and were 19 hundred years old. Although my quest was really for bricks, I also gratefully accepted the tile since it was such a fine example of fired clay. Smilingly, the director asked me how I proposed to get them out of the museum and over to Tennessee. I told him that I had already, by mail, arranged with a firm of packers and shippers to pick up anything I got in England, at the various museums, and have them flown across the Atlantic. I told him that they would be calling at his museum to collect his generous gift within a week.

I spent the night at an old railway hotel, The Queens, and turned in after wandering through, and enjoying, the historic and peaceful spots in Chester and walking along the city walls. The following morning, I had my favorite English breakfast which included a nice large grilled Scotch kipper. A kipper is a herring which has been cured over an oak fire. They are obtainable in America but, since grilling them causes the emission of an odor which permeates the house persistently, my wife is reluctant to serve them very often. The kipper can be poached but the flavor is much weakened or, to put it better, watered down.

I caught the train to Bath, another city with strong Roman ties. The city nestles in a valley made by the bases of several steep hills. Although the area was known to the Celts, it remained for the Romans to settle there for over three hundred years. The Romans found the famous hot sulphurous springs and made very good use of them by building special lead lined baths. They named the place Aquae Sulis and it remained a spa until the baths were destroyed by the Saxons. However, in the early 18th century it entered a new era when the famous dandy Beau Nash turned it into England's most fashionable watering place. Today it is as popular as ever as a tourist attraction with the excavated Roman baths, the famous Pump Room which still has the atmosphere of Regency England, its Royal Crescent which is the finest and most beautiful of Georgian streets in the country.

The city has grown up the hills, the steepness of which I can physically attest to since my hotel was built at the top of one and I got some very strenuous exercise by walking to and from it, except when I had my luggage. My first night there, I walked into a candy shop about half way up the hill. As I picked out some picture postcards, I noticed that it had started to rain very heavily. I exclaimed, "Good heavens, it's pouring down!" The young lady behind the counter, who obviously was not paid by the Chamber of Commerce for any public relations activity, said, "Oh, this is nothing. You should see it when it really rains, the water comes down the hill like a torrent. This is a dreadful place."

A word about my hotel. It was old but very fashionable and where members of the Royal family would stay. The aged retainer who showed me to my room asked me, "What time would you like me to bring you your tea in the morning and which newspaper would you prefer?" My room was on the third floor..the English third floor, the American fourth floor. Not having seen any signs indicating the location of the staircase (I had been brought up in the elevator), I was wondering what one would do in case of fire. I went to the window and happened to catch sight of a device almost completely obscured by the drapes. It was called The Orkin Safety Fire Escape and consisted of several yards of nice white rope and instructions which told you, in case of fire, to throw the rope out of the window and climb down it.

The next morning I made my way down to the city center and to the Bath Museum where I met my contact, a Mr. Owens, who was the curator. I had spoken to Mr. Owens by trans-Atlantic telephone and knew that I was going to get a Roman brick. Mr. Owens personally conducted me around the baths and beneath where excavators were hard at work trying to release a piece of marble from the bottom of the trench in which they were working. My guide showed me their most recent find, the base of the statue of a Goddess of the Bath. He said that the archaeologists were positive that the Goddess, herself, would shortly be found. Looking along the trench I noticed something circular protruding slightly from the side and asked, "Is that a drain?" The answer was that it

12th century brick tower south of Kabul, Afghanistan. The entire facade is decorated with bricks carved in Kufic characters.

Kabul Street scene. Note woman in center wearing her chadri. Another is just in the picture at right.

Meat stalls near Kabul. Beef is sold at the left stall and lamb at the one on the right.

Pretty Afghan students from the American University in Kabul. This was the first time any of them had allowed themselves to be photographed.

Interior of 400 year-old caravanserai in the vast desert south of Isfahan, Iran. Note lavish use of fired bricks.

3,500 year-old Lion Gate at entrance to the ancient Hittite capital of Hattusas located 125 miles north of Ankara, Turkey.

One of two executioner's fountains in Topkapi, Istanbul, Turkey. Remains of marble post used for displaying the severed heads are still visible at both of them.

17th century Sikh barracks at entrance to the tomb of Jehangir. Lahore, Pakistan.

Interior of the Colosseum in Rome, Italy. Millions of bricks went into its sturdy construction, c. 70-79 A.D.

Colorful and ornate Jain temple in Bombay, India.

Giant sundial in Jai Singh's observatory, New Delhi, India.

The rajghat, place of Mahatma Ghandi's funeral pyre in New Delhi, India.

5000 year-old brick kiln discovered by Professor Sankalia near Poona (Pune), India.

Left to right: A bricklayer, a steelworker, and a water carrier, "Gunga Din," at construction site in Poona. Note the flimsy bamboo scaffolding.

Mohenjo-daro (Mound of the Dead), 4,500 year-old site in the Indus Valley, Pakistan. Here, seven cities were built of brick, one on top of the other. One wall is 60 feet thick!

Istanbul Bazaar. Captain Osman, one of Kemal Attaturk's Revolutionary Army which brought democracy to Turkey. (First photo he ever permitted.)

Awe inspiring Taj Mahal, Agra, India. Tomb of Shah Jehan and his bloodthirsty wife, Mumtaz.

Baby Taj, containing tombs of Mumtaz's parents and grandparents.

The sacred Bo tree at Anuradhapura, Sri Lanka. The single limb growing from the protected, truncated bole is visible on the right, supported by a metal rod with a "vee" top.

The author with the Bo Priest, Anuradhapura, Sri Lanka.

Ancient king's dagoba with a prince's tomb at its side. Anuradhapura, Sri Lanka.

was a skull dating back to the Celtic period. I saw the sacred spring which fed 80 degree Fahrenheit water to the baths. Later I was shown some of the objects thrown into the spring by Romans for various reasons. There were coins, possibly offerings as penance for some sin or other. The majority of the peccadillos must have been trivial because most of the coins were of small value. Some gold coins had been found, too. The Gods alone know what heinous crimes merited such expensive "donations."

Quite fascinating were small pieces of pewter which had been found in the sacred spring. These had curses scratched on and had been rolled up before being tossed into the water. They were all in similar vein and asked that whoever had committed a crime against the petitioner should die or, at least, become impotent.

The great bath is impressive with its steaming water and large diving stone, which was well worn at the water edge by the feet of ancient Romans. Looking up, I saw several classical-looking statues perched around the high walls surrounding the open air bath. Mr. Owens informed me that they were not very old, having been put up during the past hundred years. He said it wasn't certain that there were so many, originally.

Beneath the level of the bath was the hypocaust room. The Romans took their bathing very seriously to the point of ritual. Not only did they swim in the baths but they had to have hot rooms, almost like saunas, in which they could sweat while they sipped wine or water. To keep these rooms hot required a hypocaust room which contained a large fire tended by a couple of men who fanned the heat of the flames towards a series of hypocaust tiles. These were box-like clay tiles that were laid inside the walls of the hot rooms and formed a continuous network to carry the heat up and around the walls. The hypocaust room at Bath has dozens of columns, about six feet high and built of bricks, which supported the room above.

When I was sitting in Mr. Owens' office holding the Roman brick which he had presented to me, he asked me if we had one of the hollow wall tiles in our museum. On receiving my negative answer, he walked over to a large trunk and brought one out and said he wanted me to have it. Again, although it wasn't a brick, it was made of burned clay and I thought it would be nice as an accessory in our display and graciously accepted it. I was surprised at its weight, about four pounds, and intrigued by the several grooves that had been made in the sides to permit the wall plaster to adhere better to the tile. There were some pieces of plaster still clinging to it. (Just two years from the time of writing I was back at the museum and mentioned to one of the officials, with whom I was having a "Bath Bun" and some coffee in the Pump Room, that we had one of their hypocaust tiles. He was very much surprised and said we were very fortunate because they were very scarce and that he couldn't imagine the museum ever parting with one.)

Having spent a very interesting, and profitable, morning at the Bath Museum I marched up my hill, checked out of my hotel and caught a fast train to London where I had a dinner engagement with a most fascinating personage.

After reading "Digging Up Jericho", an account of Dame Kathleen M. Kenyon's 1952-1956 expedition, I had planned to try, somehow, to get to meet this famous person. She was recognized as the world's foremost biblical archaeologist and when one reads the list of young students who assisted in the "dig", the names of present day prominent archaeologists from many countries are there.

At Jericho Kathleen Kenyon discovered the oldest brick ever found, dating back some nine or ten thousand years. I had managed to persuade the late Awni Djani of the Jordanian Department of Antiquities to part with one of the large bricks found at what was called the "pre-pottery Neolithic B" level and I hoped that Dame Kenyon would help me obtain a brick from "pre-pottery Neolithic A" which was some three hundred years older. I also wanted to hear first hand about her work in Jerusalem.

I had contacted her by mail at Saint Hugh's College, a girls' college in Oxford where she was the principal. The old days of wealthy archaeologists financing their own expeditions, often to the detriment of the sites they dug up, are long gone. Today, just about every field archaeologist is a member of the faculty of some university which has archaeology as a course. Financing of expeditions comes from government and university grants and whatever sums large corporations care to donate. Miss Kenyon was very prompt in replying to my request for a meeting and agreed to meet me for dinner in London. The place I had suggested was Veeraswamy's, a well known Indian restaurant on Regent Street with authentic Indian food and decor. To get to it one has to walk about ten yards down a narrow side street and walk up to the first floor.

At the appointed hour, 7 p.m., I was seated in the restaurant "nursing" a drink with my eyes fixed on the entrance. At 7:15 there was no Miss Kenyon. At 7:45 still no sign of her, so I called through to Saint Hugh's College. A young lady answered the phone, and when I asked to speak to Miss Kenyon she giggled and said, "Miss Kenyon has gone up to London to have dinner with a gentleman from America." So I waited another thirty minutes and still not having met my guest called the college again. Once more, a young lady answered the phone and with a giggle told me the same thing I had heard on my previous call.

I realized that my "date" had, somehow, got lost so I asked the young lady to leave a message for her principal to the effect that I regretted whatever it was that had prevented her from keeping our dinner engagement and would call her the next morning and, if agreeable to her, I would come to Oxford and meet her for lunch. This done, I relaxed and "tucked into" an excellent dinner.

The next morning I called Dame Kenyon who explained that she had come to London but had forgotten the name of the restaurant in which we were to meet. She had walked up and down Regent Street expecting to see the name of the place prominently displayed so as to jog her memory. Unfortunately, she had failed to look upwards where she would have seen the name Veeraswamy on the windows of the place. She invited me to go to Oxford that morning and have lunch with her at "The Mitre," a 15th century inn. (It has since been demolished.)

At noon I was hanging around the small vestibule of the "Mitre". I had seen some pictures of Kathleen Kenyon and knew I would recognize her when I saw her. The vestibule of the old inn was dimly lit and most of the little daylight came in through the glass of the revolving door. I watched the few people that came through this door, but no Kathleen Kenyon. Then, at 12:30 the daylight seemed to be blotted out and through the entrance appeared my "date." Her pictures showed that she was of large proportions and I would have recognized her from that fact alone. She saw me standing there and came over and said, "Mr. Saffer, I presume. Sorry I'm late, but I always seem to be held up by innumerable meetings."

We went into the cosy dining room where we were seated by a window. I suggested that we order lunch before we started talking. The waiter handed us the menus and asked us if we wanted wine. I knew that this would suit my guest so I simply asked her if she would like some Liebfraumilch. "Excellent choice." she said. The waiter then asked if we wanted a half bottle or a full bottle. Before I could answer, the archaeologist replied, "A full bottle, of course." (I only managed to get one glass. Miss Kenyon polished off the rest. I had been primed by one of her friends in the States that Kathleen Kenyon enjoyed generous libations and many cigarettes.)

Our conversation went just the way I had hoped. Dame Kenyon expressed her great interest in the Museum of Ancient Brick and said that she was very pleased that someone in the world had realized the importance of preserving the history of bricks before many more ancient sites were destroyed by man and nature. I questioned her about the possibility of a brick from "pre-pottery Neolithic A" at Jericho and was elated when she told me that she would arrange for one to be sent to us within a matter of days.

She expounded, at length, about the Jericho dig and her work in Jerusalem. Her retirement was just a few years ahead and apparently she was looking forward to that event so she could work on the years of accumulated notes she had on Jerusalem. Over in Jerusalem, she had a number of Roman brick stamps and promised that she would rescue a couple for us and hand them over next time we met. This was most encouraging, since it seemed my barging in on her was no problem and that she wanted to be kept up to date on the progress of the museum. Roman brick stamps are hard to come by but the next time we met, again at the Mitre, she handed me a stamp which read "LEG.X FRET" which stood for THE TENTH LEGION OF FRETENSIS. This was one of the Roman legions that destroyed the Temple in Jerusalem in 70 A.D. (A legion took the name of the place where it was first formed).

On one of my later visits to Kathleen Kenyon, in Oxford, the bookshops had their windows plastered with banners promoting a new book by Kathleen Kenyon, "Jerusalem." My wife was with me on that trip and the rain pouring down made the pavement quite slippery; and as she came to see us off at the station the three of us hung on to one another to make sure we didn't fall. At any rate, my wife remarked that we would be certain to purchase a copy of this new book before we left Oxford. This brought the following response from Kathleen Kenyon. "For heaven's sake don't waste your money. It's a terrible book and the only reason I wrote it was because I have a contract with my publishers. I told them I wanted to wait a while longer but they insisted I publish." Needless to say, the book is in my personal library.

I kept in touch with Dame Kathleen Kenyon right until a few weeks before she passed away, just two years after she had retired. She gave me permission to reproduce some of her Jericho pictures in a slide lecture and expressed the hope that, some day, after the Arab refugees who were "squatting" on the site of the "dig" left she would try and get me a Middle Bronze age brick from Jericho.

After Oxford, I drove to Stoke Poges. Stoke Poges is a small, sleepy, village in Buckinghamshire that has been immortalized by Thomas Gray's "Elegy in a Country Churchyard" written over 200 years ago. The churchyard in its delightful rustic setting is delightfully peaceful. The church itself, the Church of St. Giles, dates back to Saxon times somewhere around 600 A.D.; and part of a wall and a window of that period may still be seen. The Normans built onto the Saxon structure in 1086 which has been in continuous use since it was founded. I was once informed by the sexton that prior to that it had been the site of a Roman temple. However, the present vicar, The Reverend Cyril E. Harris, who has written a detailed history of Stoke Poges Parish Church, makes no mention of this matter.

The sexton told me a fascinating story about the churchyard which I will get to shortly. The exterior of the main part of the church was rebuilt in 1588 using well fired bricks, and I asked the Sexton if I could go beneath the chapel floor and see if there might be an odd brick lying around. He said that he'd better do it since he had his working gear on. He did; and there was! (As a matter of fact, he came up with two but I got him to take one back). I carefully compared it with those in the wall, measured its dimensions, and was satisfied that it was "part of the family." It is now in the Museum of Ancient brick.

The churchyard is unusual because it has what the residents call "leaping Boards." In addition to the usual type of tombstone there are still a few made of wooden boards which look something like bed headboards. They got the name of "leaping boards" because, through the centuries, the boys playing in the churchyard have been jumping over them. (Actually, they were the original bedboards placed over the graves of the heads of Saxon families.)

Wandering around among the Saxon cross monuments and centuries'-old smaller tombstones, I noticed that a few had hour glasses engraved on them while others seemed to have bones, sickles and snakes. I had seen similar headstones in New England churchyards; however, lying on its back close to the wall, I stumbled across a headstone which had a skull and crossbones, the traditional pirate emblem. It was all by itself and really aroused my curiosity. After taking some photographs of it, I went in search of the sexton. I found him inside the picturesque little church and asked him about the skull and cross-bones.

According to him, late in the 1600's a new settler in Stoke Poges turned out to be a wealthy retired pirate who had decided to live out his remaining days doing good deeds and getting closer to God. The church and many of the villagers were in debt but the reformed pirate paid off all that was owed and, whenever services were held, could be seen standing outside the church listening to the singing and whatever words of faith from the vicar drifted out in the air. When he died and his will was read, it was found that he had left everything to the church and requested that he be permitted to be buried just outside the churchyard wall. The sexton concluded his story by stating that a meeting was held and the congregation voted to bury him INSIDE the church-yard.

Some time later during the writing of an article on the Stoke Poges churchyard, I contacted the vicar to confirm the sexton's story. Reverend Harris wrote and told me that he believes there is no substance to it. He averred that the 17th and 18th century tombstones had these strange symbols on them to indicate the transitory nature of life and the inevitability of death. About the burial, he wrote that only the unbaptized and those who had committed suicide were invariably excluded from churchyards. "If it excluded sinners," he wrote, "then no-one would have qualified to be buried in the churchyard."

However, the tombstone is there and causes some speculation that the sexton's account might be true.

Since I had not yet accomplished my task of obtaining a Tudor brick from the time of Elizabeth and Shakespeare, I headed towards Stratford-on-Avon, the Bard's birthplace, and hoped I could find a brick that was closely associated with him.

So much has been written about Stratford that I believe it would be superfluous to repeat much of it here. Each summer, for six years while in high school, I had spent two weeks at a camp in that lovely town. We had to attend plays at the Shakespearean Theater every day..sometimes twice a day..but we had plenty of time to canoe on the River Avon and flirt with the members of girls' schools who were camping there. Yes, those were truly idyllic, as well as educational, summers.

I had also spent a night in Shottery Lodge, a mansion used as a youth hostel which overlooked the original Ann Hathaway's cottage, before it was destroyed by fire and rebuilt.

On this brick hunting trip I spent the night at Alveston Manor part of which had been an old monastery, and after dinner strolled over the bridge and through the town passing famous 16th century inns and spending half an hour sitting on the banks of the river listening to the soft sounds of the flowing water and the occasional hoots of owls joined by the always distant sounding, throaty calls of cuckoos.

To say that the employees of the Shakespearean Trust were not at all overjoyed to see me the next morning would be an understatement. Having explained my mission, I was looked at as though I had come to tear down Shakespeare's birthplace. It was forcefully explained to me that every single brick in his birthplace and what they call The New Place, both museums, was securely in place with nary a one that could be presented to our museum. After I had placated everyone, I convinced them that destroying was not my modus operandi and that they need have no fear of my presence in Stratford. I asked if they could give me a person to contact who might be able to help me locate a brick from some ancient ruined Tudor residence.

I was told to call a Mr. Fox and permitted to use the Trust's telephone to call him. This gentleman was most understanding and, after reminding me that destroying Trust property was a criminal offense, told me to call him back in one hour. So I went down to New Place and, for the umpteenth time, went through

William Shakespeare's last home and looked at the memorabilia in the several glass cases. Someone from the Trust must have alerted the docents to the fact that a suspicious character was in town because wherever I went in the house, I was accompanied by two attendants. All I was carrying was one camera. No mason's tools at all. As a matter of fact the only time I took a mason's hammer with me was on my visit to Turkey. I only take an old sheath knife on my trips for loosening bricks I have been given permission to take and for protection. Still, the two ladies stuck to me like glue, and although other visitors were blatantly violating the signs which announced that "Photography is Forbidden" the moment I put a hand on my camera case, even to straighten the sling, I was told, "No photographs are permitted, sir."

When my hour was up, I asked if I could use their telephone and was refused permission. So I wandered over to one of the inns and called Mr. Fox from there. He had good news for me. He had contacted a building contractor who was in the process of demolishing an old residence and that if I didn't mind traveling five miles I could have two of the Tudor bricks. He gave me directions; and, thanking him for his assistance, I left town. I found the place quite easily and saw a pile of buff colored handmade bricks by the side of the wreckage of what had once been a proud and stately home. Approaching the fellow who seemed to be in charge, I handed him my card and told him what I had come for and that Mr. Fox had cleared it with the contractor. He looked at me with the usual "What's so special about old bricks? You must be weird." expression I had grown to recognize, and told me to help myself. I picked up the first two that came to hand and then asked him if he had any idea of the date the house was built. He asked me to follow him. Just behind the shell of the house was a stone lintel with the date 1550 chiseled into it. That meant the brick pre-dated Shakespeare by fourteen years. I photographed the lintel with my two bricks in front, shook hands with the foreman, gave him a pound note and told him to think of the crazy Anglo/American brick collector while he "supped his ale," and returned to Stratford where I called Mr. Fox and thanked him again and told him I would write an official "Thank You" from the States.

That small country had yielded me several fine artifacts, and I was well satisfied with that little expedition.

Four years ago I was paying a family visit to London when I decided to visit to St. Paul's Cathedral. I had been there before but had never found time to go down into the crypt. So accompanied by a niece and her stroller-riding daughter I visited Christopher Wren's finest creation. After "doing" the various chapels and, this time, the crypt we walked along to a part of London known as London Wall where there was a new museum devoted to the history of the city. It is called The Museum of London. Inside are artifacts from every level of occupation. Along with Roman sandals, armor and pottery, the museum had Celtic and Saxon artifacts, as well as a horned Viking helmet dredged up from the Thames river. Just outside the museum was a section of the wall erected by the Romans in the first century. It was nearly all rock and rubble. However, at the base I could see some nice large red burned clay tiles that had been used to form the base of the wall. Here and there were a few other of these tiles that had been used to level the structure when the stonework started to get out of alignment. I estimated that each tile was two feet long, one-and-a-half feet wide and three inches thick. I was fascinated by these artifacts and told my niece that I would be back the following year to pick one up. She laughed and told me that she didn't believe I could get my hands on one.

I looked at the sign which had been erected by the firm which was helping to restore the wall and noted its address. After a lot of letter writing and some transatlantic phone calls, just over a year later I was invited to present myself at the Museum of London to take possession of one of the tiles and, with permission, take enough pictures to go with an article on the museum.

On arriving at J.F.K. Airport at Newark, for the first time in years of bringing brick into the country, I hit a snag. One of the roving officers came up to me and asked for my customs declaration form. He looked at it and saw that I had listed the tile but under value had put N.C.V. (No Commercial Value).

He pulled the 35 pound tile out of the package, which was under my arm and breaking my back, and snorted "What do you mean 'No Commercial Value?' Everything has a value so what's it worth, a thousand dollars?" I said the only value I could put on it was one dollar and explained that it was worthless to anyone unless they had a museum like ours.

The rascal started to lose his temper and began raising his voice at which point I said, "You could stand on the Brooklyn Bridge all day and never sell the thing for even a dollar. If it will make you feel better I'll declare this tile as being worth $150. If that doesn't satisfy you, please take it away from me and give me a receipt. I'll get the matter straightened out through the State Department since this is a gift from the British Government." At that, he shoved the tile back into my arms, scribbled on my declaration form and told me to stop holding up the line and go.

Chapter 6

"WHO'S HOME IN ROME?"

It was time to go to Italy where there was a wealth of brick from all ages. My flight was pleasant and I spent most of my non-dozing time rememorizing a host of Italian nouns and verbs. At one time, when my eyes had grown tired, I closed my eyes and went back in my mind to where and why I first learned Italian.

July 1943 I was part of the invasion force that went to Sicily. My ship was in Syracuse harbor unloading all kinds of munitions into landing craft. The town had been well shelled and bombed and I thought that I might find a shop that might have some film among its ruins. So I went ashore although there were still German snipers at work there. I found a photographer's shop which was a mass of broken brick and scattered photographs. Stumbling around, I heard someone in the next room. It turned out to be a British Tommy who told me that if I was looking for film, as he was, I was out of luck.

Hearing the sound of rifle shots close by, I decided to get back to the comparative safety of my ship. However, as I picked my way out through the debris, the Tommy came over and handed me a large photograph saying, "At least you might like to have a souvenir." It was a picture of an exceptionally pretty girl who had been photographed with a halo. Back out in the street I walked past a couple of soldiers who had just dragged a no-longer-functioning sniper from a building across the street. As I looked down at the deceased German, I was handed another souvenir. This was a clip of his bullets. Down on the beach I wandered around looking for some craft to take me out to my ship. I saw an Italian boy, about twelve years old, who came running up shouting "Pane, pane." (This is pronounced Pannay.) The only word I knew pronounced that way was the Indian word for water. I shook my head and showed him the photograph at which he exclaimed "Lilliana Ricupero!" So he knew who she was, and I handed him a pencil indicating that I wanted him to write the girl's name and address on the back of the photograph. He smiled and repeated the words "Pane, Pane."

This time, by pretending to put something in his mouth and chewing, I got the idea. I wracked my brains searching for the answer until I realized it was so much like the French word "pain" for bread, and that was what he wanted. I said "Si, si." and pointed to my ship. I got back to my vessel, asked the cook for two loaves of bread and returned to the beach. The moment I stepped out of the front of the craft, the boy came running up to me. I put the bread into his outstretched arms and watched the tears roll down his cheeks. I patted him on the head and decided not to pester him with such a minor thing as a girl's name and address. I started to walk away to grab a craft going out into the harbor. The boy watched me and came running up shouting, "Signore!" I stopped and he indicated that he wanted to write something for me. I had left the photograph on board but handed him a piece of paper and a pencil. He wrote, "Lilliana Ricupero Via Roma."

That was that until three months later when I was back in Syracuse and had located Via Roma and the subject of the photograph. I gave her the picture and, in return, she gave me a much smaller copy. We couldn't communicate at all. Her father owned a small bar directly across the narrow street from their apartment; and that night as I walked with another officer to go in the bar, I found her father being arrested for breaking the curfew. The M.P.s were about to take him away but my friend and I convinced them that he was harmless and just looking after his business which was crowded with allied troops.

After an evening's futile struggle of trying to talk to this pretty young lady, I decided to learn Italian. The next morning I found a shop that had a book on Italian for sale and took it back to the ship. I spent the rest of the day and evening memorizing verbs, declensions in the present, past and future tenses and building a workable vocabulary. The next day, when I presented myself at Lilliana's home, her eyes opened wide when I addressed her in Italian. During the next several days we met and, closely chaperoned, had some very interesting conversations concerning her family and how they had fared, so far, during the war.

So, that's how I came to learn Italian and, after my brief brushing up, was looking forward to using it again.

I landed in Rome on an April Saturday afternoon and got a taxi to take me into the city. The ride was harrowing! The traffic around and in Rome was fantastic. Where there were two lanes of traffic the drivers turned it into three and four lanes, weaving in and out with their horns blasting all the time. As we got into the Eternal City we passed by a number of stately ruins, including the Colosseum and the Roman Forum.

My hotel was The Mondial, a small but comfortable place just off one of the main streets. After checking in, I went for a walk in the vicinity. I was only a couple of minutes away from the large fountain of the Naiads which is in the center of the Piazza della Republica and which, after later seeing the Trevi and other Roman fountains, I decided was by far the most beautiful. I took several photographs of the magnificent Rutelli creation putting my life in jeopardy when I crossed the traffic laden street to examine it up close. Stopping for a small glass of refreshment to keep the now-chilling air out of my bones, I then bought a large number of picture postcards from a dear little old lady who tried to short-change me by a nice amount. However, I just stood there with my hand out until, with a curse, she handed me the additional lire I had coming.

I went inside a centuries-old basilica, close to the Piazza and was awed by the simplicity of its architecture which didn't detract from the delicate mosaics, the giant size paintings and the marble and bronze statuary.

After returning to the hotel, writing and addressing the cards which I handed to the concierge for mailing, I went out to find a cozy restaurant in which to have dinner. The hotel had a nice dining room but I wanted something less formal. At the end of the street I found just what I was looking for and went in. There was only one occupied table with four diners obviously enjoying a host of antipasto. A waiter came up to me and addressed me in Italian. I replied in kind

101

as he helped me off with my coat and led me to a table. He handed me a menu with a long list of delightful sounding dishes, all written in Italian, as well as a wine list.

I asked him to bring me a glass of the "house's" best chianti and buried my nose in the menu. My chianti appeared in a couple of seconds. Not just a glass but a whole bottle from which the waiter poured a glassful for me. He stood there awaiting my order which I was ready to give him. Some antipasto, the famous Italian Zuppa (vegetable soup) and spaghetti with meat sauce is what I asked for. Without a word, the waiter took the menu from me and walked over to a side table and returned with another written in English! I felt somewhat deflated and asked the waiter, in English, if my Italian was so bad that he couldn't understand my order. He replied "Sir, your Italian is O.K. but I think my English is better than your Italian, since I worked in London for over ten years." I really didn't get the point since mine was a simple order. However, he pointed out that I would have difficulty ordering my dessert in Italian. In my best Italian manner, I shrugged my shoulders and let the matter rest.

Before and during my meal I kept an eye on the other occupied table. The waiter kept bringing them dish after dish without a break. Two tremendous bowls of spaghetti followed their antipasto and soup. (As I was leaving they were about to tackle four tremendous beef steaks and, from what I observed later in other restaurants, they probably were only in the middle of their meal). In Italy only two meals are eaten during the day. Lunch at about two or three p.m. and dinner from eight o-clock onwards. Breakfast is only for foreigners staying in the luxury hotels. The Romans, on their way to work, hop into small quick service bars where they first pay a cashier and then grab a croissant and a cup of coffee both of which are polished off while standing. The traffic in and out of these open trattoria is heavy.

The next day, I had an appointment with a professor Moretti at the Museo Villa Giulio, Rome's finest Etruscan museum. I got to the museum in the middle of the morning only to be told that my contact was out of town and wouldn't be back until late that night. One of the bricks I hoped to acquire was an Etruscan unit which I knew were extremely rare so I said I would be back the next morning. I had another contact, the Director of Antiquities, a lady archaeologist, but I knew that since it was Sunday her offices would be closed. Two strike-outs in one day, not so good. I hopped into a cab and went down to the Colosseum. The real name of this vast arena is the Flavian Amphitheater named after the emperor Titus Flavius Vespasianus, usually referred to as Vespasian, who started its erection in 72 A.D. After his death, his son Titus kept the construction going until it was completed in 80 A.D.

The name "Colosseum" came from a colossal statue of the emperor Nero that stood close to the amphitheater.

The foundations and ninety percent of the walls and vaulting were made of bricks. As I looked at the outside walls I could see the several recesses that had been built into the outside wall to act as anchors for the marble that had once covered the facade. Throughout the centuries, as all over the world, vandals had removed the marble to be used in their own palaces and villas.

Naturally, a brick from the Colosseum was on my "want list." Inside I went and was immediately overwhelmed by the millions of brick that had gone into the building of this place. Looking around, I could see where the authorities had replaced some marble seats to indicate just where the Roman emperors and the members of the Senate had sat to watch the horrible spectacles that were enacted on the now disappeared floor of the arena. There is scarcely a part of Roman history that is not connected with the Colosseum. In the 8th century the Venerable Bede said, "While stands the Colosseum, Rome shall stand; when falls the Colosseum, Rome shall fall: and when Rome falls, with it shall fall the world." After the sacking by the Normans in 1084, only a skeleton remained of antique Rome. The Colosseum was abandoned and was used as a quarry for building materials. It wasn't until the 18th century that Benedict XIV consecrated the Colosseum to the names of the innumerable martyrs who gave their lives for their faith. He had a black cross erected there which visitors cannot fail to see and remember why it is there.

I climbed to the highest point of the Colosseum and just sat staring down into the bowels of the place where the prisoners had been kept and re-creating all the terrible things that had happened in the arena above. After a while, somberly, I climbed down and started to examine the architecture of the place and wondering from which part I would be able to obtain permission to take a brick.

Around the entrance was a group of young men selling guide books and souvenirs. As I watched them operating I noticed that there was an elderly gentleman who seemed to be coordinating their activities. I walked up to him and asked him how much he wanted for a guide book, quickly saying that he could only make one offer and if I didn't like it I would get one in the city.

As usual, my little recitation threw him. He mumbled in English and Italian, scratched his head and was about to open his mouth when I stepped away from him. He was right there with me and gave me a price I couldn't refuse. While I was paying him, he asked me what part of England I was from and I told him I lived in Tennessee. At this he got quite excited and told me that he had a son at The University of Tennessee in Chattanooga. He then dragged out a sheaf of photographs of himself and General Eisenhower taken at the time the Allies liberated Rome. He showed me newspaper cuttings in which he was referred to as "Colosseum John." I found out that all the other vendors were either his sons or sons-in-law.

So we became good friends and I told him what I was looking for. He said that the only person who could help me was the Director of the Colosseum but, since it was Sunday, he wouldn't be out that day. Just as he finished saying this, he grabbed my arm and pointed to two men striding towards us. He indicated that one of them was, indeed, the Director. I hastened to meet him and greeted him, in Italian, handed him a brochure on our museum and asked him to help me with "Uno matone antiqua originale." (One genuine ancient brick.) He smiled and told me to wait. His companion got some keys from a guard, let himself through a metal gate which led to the nether part of the structure and disappeared. While we waited, the Director said that I was the first person ever to ask permission to get one of "his" brick. Others had been seen removing brick from the walls and had been arrested and fined. Since I had acted correctly and was an archaeologist (which I wasn't), his assistant had gone to get me a brick from the foundations of the Colosseum.

I invited the Director and his assistant to be my guests for lunch. He declined saying they always spent Sunday with their families. Just then up came the assistant with a triangular brick somewhat grimy but was obviously basically buff colored with dark brown specks all over the surfaces. I shook hands with the Director, thanking him profusely, and he started to walk away. The Assistant asked "Colosseum John" for a bag for the brick. This was produced and the artifact was handed over to me. More hand shaking and this fellow set off after his boss. "Colosseum John" told me to go after the assistant and give him a few thousand lire. This I did with the recipient accepting with a great deal of reluctance.

The stray cats of Rome are both innumerable and (in)famous. They are to be seen all over the city, especially around the entrances to restaurants where the ingoing and outgoing patrons have to "fight" with these felines to get through the doors. The Colosseum must have been their breeding ground, because there they were forever underfoot. This is the latest part of the saga of the place. During the past couple of centuries it had been used as an unofficial market place and, with its myriad secluded corners, had been the working place of Rome's prostitutes. I got away from most of the cats when I walked back up to one of the upper galleries to look out of the windows down on the people walking along the street and to get another angle of the seats.

As I moved away from one of the brick windows, I tripped over a rectangular brick. Picking it up I could plainly see that it had been made using a wooden form and that the maker had run his fingers along the wet clay. I looked at the window to see if it belonged there because, if so, I would have replaced it. However, there was no place for it, although it was just like others that had been used to build the opening. So, I just popped it into my airline bag, along with the brick from the foundations.

When I returned home to Tennessee, when I washed this brick I was astonished to find that the letters "VT" in perfect Roman letters had been carved into the side that had been laid face down in mortar. The artist had to have carved the letters whilst the clay was still wet. To this day, I have been unable to come up with a meaning for these letters other than they were the initials of the artisan's girl friend.

I was well pleased with my visit to the Colosseum. I had visited another of the world's most famous structures and was about to leave with two brick specimens. One from the foundation (c.72 A.D.) and the other from the top level (c.80 A.D.).

A couple of chocolate bars were bought from one of Colosseum John's family and I devoured them as I walked from the Colosseum over to the entrance to the Roman Forum and a wonderful encounter.

The Roman Forum is the name given to a tremendous number of ancient ruins whose marble columns and stones were witnesses to the rise and fall of many empires and show that Rome was present during some of the world's greatest epochs of art, history, religion and humanity. Here are the remains of a large number of pagan temples, as well as sturdy triumphal arches honoring Constantine, Settimus Severus and Titus.

When first entering the Forum, one gets the impression of being in a marble quarry with pieces of fallen columns and slabs with fragmented inscriptions strewn all around. Several of the temples, at one time or another, had been converted into Christian churches such as the Church of Saints Cosma and Damiano whose vestibule rises over what had been the Temple of Romulus with the original bronze door and lock still accessible. The three soaring columns balancing part of the cornice, the remains of the Temple of Castor and Pollux appear in most posters inviting foreigners to visit Italy. The remains of the House of the Vestal Virgins still has several of the original statues standing around. I noticed, with great interest, that the walls were built with bricks and I decided that I would ask the authorities to give me one.

With my guide book in one hand and my Italian dictionary in the other, I started my passage through the Roman Forum. I passed up nothing, going from side to side as I progressed. Everything had a sign at the site. However, about one and a half hours after my entry, I came across a piece of marble embedded in a hole over which had been placed a small galvanized roof. This was unmarked, which was rather frustrating. I looked around to see if there was anyone around who might be able to help me and saw two black-cassocked priests just a short distance away.

I went up to them and addressed them in Italian and asked if they would mind having a look at the unmarked monument. They were only too pleased to oblige and told me that it was called Umbilicus Urbis, the navel of the world. These two priests, it so happened, were Spanish and were taking some special courses in E.U.R. Seminary. One of them had recently arrived from Peru, where he had his own church. The other had his church in a small town in Spain. The Father from Peru asked me how much of the Forum I had seen and decided that I must have missed quite a lot (I hadn't) and insisted on taking me all the way back to the beginning and giving me a wonderful history lesson. His friend came with us but left when some Spanish speaking ladies came over with some questions of their own. He took them on a personal tour.

By this time we were conversing in English in which the priest was fluent. However, at one place he was fishing for some words and asked me if I spoke French. I did. From then on that was the language we used although I had to keep asking him to slow down since he was far more fluent than I. It was a nice warm day and I was getting a wonderful lecture.

Eventually, we came to the Arch of Titus with its famous bas-relief of Roman soldiers with their plunder from the Temple in Jerusalem, with the carts being pulled by Hebrew slaves. I got my photographs and pointed to a word in Hebrew which had been recently chalked inside the arch. The priest said he didn't know what it was. I told him that it was the Hebrew word for Sabbath. He was surprised that I could read it and asked me if I had seen "The Mose." I realized he meant the famous Michelangelo statue of Moses. On learning that it was on my list he took my arm and insisted that I see it with him. It was in the church of Saint Peter in Chains. On the way he took me into another church, which I have never been able to find again and whose name I didn't get. He wanted me to see the fourth century mosaic over the altar. It was truly breathtaking. It showed Jesus, in the center, with six lambs on either side. These were, obviously the apostles. Then at one end was the figure of a man wearing a regular halo whilst at the other end was another figure wearing a square halo. I stood back and admired this work of art and asked about the square halo. The priest told me that it showed that the mosaic had been commissioned by a Pope who was still alive at the time it was completed.

We went into three other churches so I could see the glorious works of art inside of each, mosaics, paintings and statues, and then arrived at San Pietro in Vinculo where I saw the famous "Moses." It was truly impressive and somewhat overpowering. To me, it appeared as if the great leader was not exactly seated but about to get to his feet. I noticed the horns on his head which represented, according to my College of Art instructor, the power of the Almighty connecting with his servant. When I was there, that time, the statue was roped off with velvet covered ropes. So I could get an uncluttered shot, my friend told the other visitors to step back whilst he moved the ropes and stands back. I examined the detailing of the statue and then took time to enjoy looking at the two statues on each side of Moses. One was of Rachel and the other was of Leah. The priest took my arm and led me over to the altar where I saw the ancient chains that had held Peter. While I was still visualizing the past, my reverie was interrupted by my guide's request to follow him.

I was taken to a dark room where the priest felt for the switch and turned the lights on. The four walls were covered with dozens of paintings on which he proudly gave me a quick run down as to the subjects and the artists.

When we got outside, I looked at my watch and found that it was six o-clock. The priest said he had to get back to E.U.R. in a hurry. We exchanged addresses. My companion had been holding a plastic brief case all afternoon and, as he moved, I could hear the clink of money. I knew he would be offended if I offered to pay him for all he had done for me, so I told him that I was very grateful for his assistance and, as a token of my appreciation, wanted to make a donation to his church. He objected very strenuously but I insisted and he only gave in when I said, "Father, how can you refuse me the pleasure of helping your church in its good work?" We shook hands and parted. (Heard from him twice, after he had returned to Peru.)

I returned to my hotel, cleaned up, and then went down to dinner. After that, I wandered around the streets, again, and got myself thoroughly sprinkled by staying close to one of Rome's famous fountains for too long.

I had an interesting conversation with the elevator operator at the time I returned. There were three other passengers in the cage with me and one of them, in English, asked the elevator boy a question having to do with the hours of operation in the dining room. The operator, about twenty years old, just looked at the questioner blankly and made no response. I told the other passengers what I had found out about the restaurant. Turning to the operator, I asked him in his own language if he knew any English at all. His answer was negative. I suggested to him that if he were to learn even a little of the hotel visitors' language he would get bigger tips and faster promotion. His reply was that people coming to Italy should learn HIS language not the other way round!

On another occasion, I asked him if he had seen the statue of Moses or ever been inside the Colosseum or in any of the famous buildings that were within a couple of hundred yards of the hotel. To my surprise it turned out that he had never heard of the statue of Moses and that the name "Michelangelo" meant nothing to him. One of the other elevator operators told me that his associate had mentioned our conversations and that all "my" operator knew was where the pretty girls lived and felt if I could speak his language why couldn't other tourists learn it.

The following morning, Monday, I returned to the Museo Villa Giulio only to discover that Professor Moretti was still "not at home." A secretary made phone call and then told me to go down to the Colosseum where, in a shed used for piecing together fragments of inscriptions, I would find a Professor Panciera who would be pleased to meet with me if I could get to him before he had to leave for a meeting. Naturally, by the time I had found his "office" he had gone! However, he had left a message with an assistant telling me to return to the Villa Giulio where Professor Moretti's assistant, a Dr. Mario Torelli, would be waiting for me.

At last I found someone at home! Dr. Torelli was "a gem." He was a younger man who spoke perfect English and who invited me to visit with him in his office. Coffee was brought in and for two hours the good Doctor, who was a specialist in Etruscan archaeology, held forth on brickmaking in ancient Rome. During our session, in came the elusive Professor Moretti who apologized for not being at the museum when I had shown up the previous day and, since my original letter indicated that my main interest was bricks, Dr. Torelli had volunteered to look after me. After a few minutes, the professor left us, and Dr. Torelli continued with his fascinating "lecture." Just 13 miles from Rome, he said, was the site of an Etruscan town known as Veii. Bricks had been found there but, since they were just mud bricks, after being left exposed to the elements from the time of the initial excavations, they had dissolved. However, he told me if I wanted to see Etruscan statuary, then it would be worth my while to travel out there. If not, he would arrange for one of his field assistants to bring in some pieces of burned clay roof tiles from the site. This intrigued me. If they could fire roof tiles, why were there no fired brick? The answer was that the Etruscans hadn't discovered how to make lime mortar, so they had to use mud units held together by mud mortar. Something else that came out during our meeting was the fact that the archaeologists had discovered a number of small gold and silver squares, neatly folded and nailed to the walls of a temple. When opened up, these items were found to be prayers and curses, just like those discovered in Bath, in England.

I told Dr. Torelli that I still wanted to get a specimen or two from the Roman Forum and would pass up Veii. On hearing this, my host picked up the phone and called Dr. Pancieri who had now returned to his shed in the Forum. He arranged for me to return to the place where someone would wait for me and assist me in every possible way. Before we parted, I accepted an invitation to have dinner, that night, with Dr. Torelli and his wife. They were to pick me up at my hotel at eight o-clock.

Back to the shed in the Roman Forum where I just had time to shake hands with Professor Pancieri and thank him for his forbearance before he disappeared leaving me in the hands of another assistant who spoke only Italian. The assistant insisted on showing me the large number of broken Latin inscriptions they had laid out on tables and on the ground. He was proud of the progress they were making, and I congratulated him on this job which would take decades to complete. Then I got him out of the shed and into the Forum. I led him to the House of the Vestal Virgins and pointed to a fine triangular brick which was lying on the ground and asked if I could put it in my flight bag. He smiled, shook his head and disappeared behind a wall returning with another triangular specimen. He explained that the one I wanted was from a later structure whereas the one he handed me dated back to around 50 A.D.

My young guide was most agreeable when I asked him to show me a portion of the Forum that was closed to the public. After receiving my promise not to use my camera flash, he took me into what seemed to be a large cave although this had brick walls and vaulting, as well as having a floor that was tiled with thousands of thin clay tiles, similar to miniature brick, which had been laid edgewise. The place wasn't too deep and was obviously only the beginning of an archaeological exploration. After scouting around and handing me another triangular brick, the man told me that it was believed that we were standing in the exit from a tunnel it was suspected started in Nero's "Gold House" which he had built on the Palatine Hill but which had not yet been discovered. The cruel emperor had never had the chance to live in the place since he had, with help, taken his own life (in 68 A.D.) before it was completed. Thanking him profusely, I took leave of the young archaeologist and walked out of the Roman Forum.

I noticed a tall brick tower not too far away, along the Via Cavour. My guide book told me that it had two names. The first was "Torre Delle Milizie" and the other was "Torre Nerone"..("Nero's Tower.") A legend has it that Nero climbed this very tower, playing his zither during the burning of Rome in 64A.D.and sang his song about the fire of Troy. Half the city was destroyed during this conflagration the starting of which was blamed on Nero. However, certain recorded facts are inescapable. True, he was probably responsible for having the fire arranged and blaming it on the Christians, but at the time he was many miles away giving one of his many concerts. False, he couldn't have climbed the "Torre Delle Milizie" because it wasn't built until almost eleven hundred and fifty years after his death.

I paid a small fee and was admitted to the place. On several levels there were deep alcoves, each bearing a number, which were originally barracks and later used as shops by merchants. There was a rickety wooden stairway leading all the way up to the top. It swayed as I walked and I was not a little nervous about whether or not it would crash before I got to the top and back. It was well worth the effort, though. From the summit I could see the entire city and, despite a smoky haze which hung over it, managed to take some panoramic pictures. It was a fascinating aerie and I spent at least an hour up there. Reluctantly, I decided I had better get down since the sun seemed to be going down. So, once again, I faced the prospect of walking on the rickety stairway. Heights do not bother me but it was still a long fall. At the bottom, I made my way to the gate only to find that it was locked and chained with the guard nowhere in sight. The iron fence was unclimable, my bag of brick wouldn't even go through the railings, I was locked inside a solidly built fort.

I walked around looking for another way out. Nothing doing! I came across a tremendous clay jar about four feet high which was quite photogenic and then, from "out of the thin air", there appeared a small boy who held out his hand and asked for 500 lire to show me the way out. That was twice as much as it had cost me to get in! I handed over the money and followed my guide around a balcony and down a short flight of stairs which led into a courtyard surrounded by the backs of several apartment buildings. There was a locked gate leading to the street and the boy told me to stand by it and wait. He ran over to the doorway of one of the apartments and standing on his tiptoes pressed a button. A buzzer sounded in my ear and the gate was unlocked. Out I went and seeing the almost unbelievable traffic jams decided that the quickest way to my hotel was on foot.

It is worthy of note that I found Rome to be the home of the craziest drivers I had ever seen. Traffic lights meant nothing to them. Crossing the street was an act of bravery. The cars were bumper to bumper and woe betide the pedestrian who was slow in slipping between two cars. On one occasion, it took me half a dozen attempts to cross the road to get to the Colosseum. As a matter of fact, after the third try I bought and ate an ice cream cone before setting off again. I saw several fender benders and heard the screaming of the involved drivers as each attempted to lay the blame on the other and appealed to passers-by to support their claims. That is my only criticism of the Romans (with the exception of the dear little old lady who tried to short-change me). Otherwise, everybody was so helpful and especially patient with my broken Italian.

After I had cleaned up, changed my clothes and done some dictating I went down just in time to catch Dr. Torelli coming into the hotel lobby. He took me out to his car, introduced me to his very beautiful wife and told me that they were taking me to a restaurant which was usually only frequented by Romans. This was what I really wanted, to sample the true Italian flavor. The restaurant was called Da Mea Patacca and was in a part of the city I would never have found by myself. The establishment had two floors. One was on street level and the other was one flight down. The noise inside was incredible. I couldn't decide whether it came from the diners or from the band and singers roaming around the restaurant. The three of us had to shout across our table to converse with one another!

Before long, I started to become hoarse and had to stop talking for awhile. I looked around the filled restaurant and took in all I could see: the tremendous amount of gesticulating that is a part of Italian conversation, the tremendous amount of food in front of each diner, and the heavily laden waiters who had to ballet dance around the room to avoid having their arms hit by those of the conversing customers.

I must admit that I found most Italians easy to understand whenever I had occasion to ask for directions in Rome on this, and later, visits. A single turn of the right wrist followed by two of the left meant "Take the first street on the right and then make a left turn at each of the next two streets." People have told me that the Italians pretend not to understand tourists who try to speak their language. That has not been my experience. I know that they are proud of their musical tongue and resent it being "torn apart"; but when they meet someone who has obviously worked hard at it, they are Kindness itself. The secret is to stress the penultimate syllable of most of the words. That is enough to endear one to them.

The menu was a large work of art with a listing of dozens of line illustrated dishes and I had a hard time deciding on what to order. The food was served and suddenly the noise subsided, considerably. I realized that the roving musicians had disappeared. I told the Torellis that it made conversation much easier. Dr. Torelli told me that the break was only for a couple of minutes during which time a band which had been playing on the floor below changed places with our departed entertainers. How true that was! Just as he had finished telling me about the second band, it started up. It had more brass instruments than the first and didn't have a singer so they could play louder. All I could do was eat my dinner and smile at the Torellis. Mario (Dr. Torelli) shouted that there would be plenty of time to talk after we had left the place, so I relaxed and enjoyed my food realizing that the atmosphere, now referred to as "ambience" is what I had really wanted with my meal. After a terrifically large dinner, well wined and topped off with ice cream and pastries, we left that wonderful ristorante with me clutching a rolled up copy of the menu. On my next visit to that city I took my wife and Mrs. Torelli, and the place was later visited by my sixteen year-old daughter and a school friend. They were followed, two years later, by my son and his friend. All voted it the highlight of the eating places they visited during their trips to France, Italy and England.

The hour was getting late and I had an appointment with the Director of Archaeology, in Naples, who was responsible for Pompeii, so I suggested that I be taken back to my hotel and that, possibly, Mario and I could meet for dinner the following evening after I had returned from Pompeii. This was agreeable and I soon staggered into my hotel feeling that I wouldn't want to eat another thing for several days. When I got inside my room I discovered a very heavy brown paper wrapped package lying on the floor. When opened, it disclosed several fragments of clay roof tiles obviously brought in from the field by Dr. Torelli's assistant. I was too tired to do much more than look them over and slide them under my wardrobe. I had my bath, dictated the day's events and flopped into bed.

Came the dawn of what turned out to be a day during which I was cheated, lied to, abused, insulted, trodden on and well, we'll get to the full story shortly. It started off with my train to Naples being 40 minutes late in leaving Rome station. I grabbed a quick cup of caffe latte and a croissant at one of the stand-up bars on my five minute walk to the station and was sitting in my dingy carriage long before departure time. I was joined by a well dressed young man who remarked that the early morning trains were always very late. (Visions of the English milk trains which stop at every station for milk-can pickups.) I asked him if we could get some coffee in the station. He stuck his head out of the carriage and spotted a man wheeling a refreshment trolley along the platform.

So I had another cup of coffee and croissant, treating my companion to the same.

We conversed in English since this fellow, an electrical engineer, had worked in the U.S. for a couple of years. He said that he had a good job but had left it to return to Italy where he felt he really belonged. However, despite all his qualifications, the job he had obtained in Rome was far from satisfactory and he was trying to get back to The States.

Eventually, the train started on its way ..the time was 6:40

Although we made several stops along the way, no-one else got into our carriage. As we progressed towards Naples the young man kept pointing out the many fortified little towns perched on the tops of steep hills. Once, long ago, they had been independent Dukedoms full of intrigues and treachery each nearly always at war with one or several others. I could imagine what they must have looked like behind their ancient walls and promised myself that one day I would make a trip to see some of them. The valley through which we traveled was healthy looking and fertile. One of the good things that Mussolini did for his country was to drain what had been uncultivatable swampland into this rich valley.

When we reached Naples, my companion asked if he could help me. Knowing that he had an appointment, I told him I would be able to get around without any difficulty and that I would be able to keep my own appointment in good time. As I walked towards the street, I was besieged by a swarm of skinny little boys who fought one another as they tried to wrest my flight bag and camera bag from my hand. "ANDARSENE!" (Go away!) I shouted. They all stood back and I was congratulating myself on getting rid of what was universally known as one of Italy's greatest pests, the street boys. Not that I didn't feel sorry for them, but what could one do for a dozen of them?

I stopped and looked around me only to find that the picture postcards of beautiful, clean Naples were just lies. True, the buildings were neat looking but that's where it ended. They all seemed to be in need of paint. The streets were littered with everything from newspaper pages to apple cores. The empty cigarette packages were numerous enough to form a thick carpet. I wondered if the authorities had a massive clean-up before the start of the tourist season. There were a number of small tables out on the sidewalk surrounded by participants in some kind of gambling game.

I looked for the street names but couldn't find the one I was looking for. Stopping a passer-by, I asked for directions to the Muzeo Nazionale which he started to give me when one of the street urchins, who had been following me and heard where I wanted to got, piped up with "You give me 500 lire, Joe, and I'll take you to the Museo Nazionale." I checked my watch to see how much longer I had before I was expected by the Director. It was getting close, so I told the youngster to lead the way. He grabbed my hand and proceeded to take me with him. I had expected the place to be close by but I was taken across the piazza, down a side street and three or four other streets. We approached a large building where my guide asked for his money. I gave him the money and went inside the building to a policeman who was standing by the head of a line of people who were awaiting permission to go in.

I noticed that there were four or five other officers of the law close by and wondered why the Museum needed regular police guards. The fellow I spoke to didn't know the whereabouts of the Professor I asked for and pointed to the group of fellow officers. One of them asked me where I thought I was. When I mentioned the Museum he told me I was in the wrong building and should go back outside and make a right turn. This was accomplished and I found myself in a crowded courtyard. That didn't look right, so I went up to another uniformed man who seemed to have an air of authority. Asking him where the professor could be found, I was told to go back into the building I had just left and go straight up to the second floor. I did as I was instructed and, when I got to the second floor, was amazed at the large number of policemen and rough looking civilians. There was a frame elevator which came up through the middle of the floor and out of this stepped some men wearing handcuffs and leg irons. I was inside the Criminal Court! I darted down the stairs and found my way to a busy thoroughfare and hopped into a taxi which deposited me outside the museum after a very short ride.

Here the fun began again. At the entrance to the museum, after I had announced that I had an appointment with the Director, I was referred to another entrance next to the main doorway. Inside I found a gate blocking my passage. Behind the gate sat a couple of characters who looked as if they spent their days napping. One of them stood up and loudly asked me who I was and what I wanted. I showed him my letter granting me a meeting with the Director. He read it, showed it to his companion, and handed it back to me and sharply told me that I was not permitted to go inside the building. I asked him to produce someone who spoke English. No luck. Then, the second man asked me why I wanted to see the Director. I explained the situation and was told that the Director was out of town and that I should go next door and speak to his assistant whom I would find by going back out and in through the main entrance.

Back inside the Museum, I was permitted to sit on a chair while they located a secretary. For forty minutes I sat there, the object of everybody's curiosity. Finally, a man appeared and introduced himself as the secretary to the Director. Shown the letter stating that I had an appointment, the secretary apologized and said the Director had to go out of town and that, normally, the matter of permission to remove a brick from Pompeii would be handled by one of his subordinates. Unfortunately, he hadn't come to work that day and there wasn't anyone who could help me.

I reminded the secretary that I had traveled several thousand miles in order to keep this appointment and that, surely, there must be a deputy Director. There was, but he, too, wasn't available. The secretary told me to "Go back to Tennessee and write for another appointment." I thanked him for his "help" and with an "arrivederci" departed the premises.

Directly across the road from the Museum was a small shop that sold groceries and sundries and I marched inside and putting down some money asked for telephone tokens. I had the Director's telephone number on his letterhead and I dialed knowing that this man was "home" in the Museum and that I had been given the run around. A secretary answered, and speaking as rapidly as I could muster, in Italian, and putting the word "dottore" before my name I asked to speak to the Director urgently. Yes, he was there! I reminded him of our appointment and told him of the misinformation given me as to his whereabouts. He apologized, mildly, and said he had just that moment got back into town but would be unable to see me until my next visit to Naples. I assured him that when I returned to Naples I would not have time to see him, and then hung up the phone. I got a cup of coffee at the shop and went out to look for a taxi which would take me to Pompeii which was 12 miles away on the super-highway. The first cab I waved to became my transport since he offered to take me out there, wait for me to do whatever I had to do there, and return me to Naples station for 75% of what his meter read.

I asked him several questions about some ancient tombs we passed, as well as what happened during the war. He said that many Italians resented the bombing of Pompeii by Allied planes, although not too much damage was done. However, he thought it had been justified because the Germans had artillery batteries there believing that the Allies wouldn't attack the ancient site.

The story of the destruction of Pompeii by the eruption of Vesuvius in the summer of 79 A.D. has been oft told and well documented so I will not repeat it here. A prosperous seaport and resort with a sordid reputation, it reminds me of the end of Sodom and Gomorrah. As you enter through one of the city gates, there is a small museum which rapidly puts you in touch with life almost two thousand years ago. On display are ancient dishes full of meal, grain and eggs..yes, eggs..that were buried, and preserved, by the combination of pieces of lapilli (small pieces of volcanic rock), ashes, and heavy rain which had covered the city and had formed a protecting shell over everything that was exposed.

The museum had plaster casts of complete human bodies, as well as one of a dog which had obviously died in agony. Each cast contained the complete skeleton. The figures showed almost every detail of the deceased's clothing, facial expression, and position at the time of death. Many of the deaths in Pompeii, when Vesuvius erupted, had been caused by asphyxiation from the fatal fumes that drifted down upon the place. Most people got away but others, who either through stubbornness or overloading themselves whilst trying to rescue their valuables, were trapped and fell prey to the fatal cloud.

They are still finding places where bodies were buried. The way the archaeologists handle the situation is to drill holes at each end of the body and pump in plaster. The bodies, of course, decomposed long ago but they left their impressions on the plastic material which buried them. The skeletons, though, are still in place.

There were many other fascinating items in the museum including all kinds of pottery, household items, personal grooming needs and one case devoted to erotic figurines.

I had a good map of the city and visited most of the places of interest including the hypacaust room next to the baths. I was interested to see, showing through a breach in the plaster, some hypacaust tiles running through the walls. I stopped in at the House of the Vetti Brothers, the best preserved of all the buildings yet excavated. There was the House of the Faun with a small bronze naked figure on a platform in a pool. However, I knew that what I was looking at was not the original. That was in the museum in Naples along with several beautifully painted walls removed from Pompeii and replaced by copies. In quite a few countries, original artifacts have been removed to museums where they are safe from vandalism and polluted air with replicas being placed at the open sites.

Having trodden down a number of "closed" streets, I decided it was time to see about a brick for the museum. I walked over to a couple of the many guards and asked where the site director might be found. One of them pointed towards a small refreshment shop out of which had just emerged a genial looking man dressed in a business suit. I ran over to him and introduced myself while I handed him my letter of appointment with the fellow in Naples. "All I want," said I, " is one, or possibly two, bricks which I could easily remove from the top of almost any wall in the "closed" section. He shook hands with me and told me to take whatever I needed. It was as easy as that!

I walked down one of the streets and came across a world famous mosaic which showed a ferocious dog along with the words "Cave Canem" (Beware of the dog). Standing sentry over the mosaic was one of the uniformed guards, while lying right on top of the mosaic was an ancient looking, worn out dog that didn't even look up when I spoke to his master. The guard let me take a picture of the mosaic with and without his pet. I gave him a few coins and proceeded along the street noticing that an ancient, broken, lead water pipe still ran along the bottom of some walls while others had the remains of burned clay drain pipes.

There was a good looking building, walls only, that looked as though it would yield a nice brick to my hunting knife very easily. The problem was how to get to the top of the wall. There was no way to do it unless I had help, so I went back to the mosaic guard and explained my predicament. He was most obliging and followed me back to my wall where he bent down so I could stand on his shoulders. With my feet on his shoulders and my hands balanced against the wall, the guard straightened up and there I was slipping my blade under a brick which popped up very nicely. Back on the ground, I gave the guard another tip and trotted along. I picked up a small piece of drain pipe, another brick which had fallen from a wall into the lane and a small pie-shaped piece which had obviously been part of a circular column.

The weather was perfect, the sun smiling down on my fruitful efforts, and I had a host of fascinating photographs. Above all, I had received the "blessing" of the Director of the famous archaeological site.

Slowly, I took a circuitous route back to the main gate into the city taking time to admire the terrific excavation work done by the archaeologists which included reconstructing the gladiatorial arena, and the exposing of the two thousand year old vineyards. As I walked past the faded paintings on some of the exposed outer walls and through the palm trees that straddled the entrance, I knew that I would be returning to Pompeii. I found my driver, climbed into the taxi and was driven back to Naples where I caught the train back to Rome.

This time I had another young man as a traveling companion. He,too, had lived in the U.S., working for NATO. He had stayed there for eight years, married an American girl and had to return to Italy when his tour of duty was over. Again, here was a man who wanted to get back to the United States where, as he put it, "Life is so much better there."

Mario Torelli picked me up at my hotel that evening and the two of us went to a slightly quieter place for dinner. After our meal we drove to a place that enabled us to look down on a great deal of Rome. We got out, walked awhile, and then sat on a grassy bank with an ancient brick wall to our backs. From our vantage point, with the aid of a full April moon, we were able to make out the remains of the buildings that had once been the pride of Ancient Rome. Mario did most of the talking while we discussed the glories and the shame that had been Rome, and the lives of the twelve great caesars. The title of Caesar, as a ruler, was not used until Julius Caesar's successor Octavius (later known as Augustus) adopted it. After that, it was used by all the other Roman rulers until Hadrian. He used the title "Augustus" permitting the heir apparent to be called Caesar. This, of course, led to the universal use of the word and its foreign translations Kaiser, Czar to be synonymous with the word ruler. However, the "Caesar" in Julius' name was merely a part of his family name.

Rome, Mario informed me, had been destroyed by local fires for hundreds of years because of the fact that the masses of poor, freedmen and slaves alike, lived in wooden shacks crowded on top of one another lining the narrow streets. Eventually, a law was passed that all buildings in the great city had to be built with bricks or stone. (After the Great Fire of London, in 1666, a similar law was passed.)

The subject of Veii came up. Mario had a pass to permit me to visit the excavations and remove some pieces of tile; but since I already had some that his assistant had delivered to me, I told him that my time in Rome was almost up. Then he told a strange tale of how Veii, which was Roman, had been built on and around the ruins of Etruscan Veio. The archaeologists had discovered some statuary, above ground, on the site of an Etruscan temple. They identified them as being pieces of the god Apollo and so they named the site the Temple of Apollo. However, when they got down to the main building, all indications pointed to the fact that it was dedicated to Diana, and refusing to admit an error refused to rename the temple ruins. So, if you go to Veii to visit the Temple of Apollo, remember that it didn't belong to him but to Diana.

We drove down into the city and stopped at a restaurant on the Via Veneto, popular with Roman intelligencia, and sat at an outside table sipping coffee and watching the activities along this famous street. These included two protest marches by University students; a scuffle between two young men over a young lady; and a continuous stream of swaying hips dressed in the tightest fitting skirts I had ever seen. That was my sampling of La Dolce Vita.

Checking with the Concierge the next morning, I got the numbers of the two buses I would have to take to get to the Catacombs of St. Calixtus several miles outside Rome on the famous Appian Way. First, though, I turned my brick and a couple of fragments I knocked off the Etruscan tiles over to the airline for shipment back to the museum. Then, I was on my way.

My second bus stopped right outside the gate of the catacombs so, before going inside, I went for a stroll along the ancient road, The Appian Way, which stretched all the way from Rome to Brindisi, on the southeast coast, a distance of 350 miles. It was built in 312 B.C. and enabled the Roman legions to move across the country at a remarkable pace to repel any invaders. It was indeed a thrill to walk along the edge of the road on the massive blocks. I had passed the ruins of several tombs and sepulchers which spanned some twenty generations of Patrician families.

There were several guides in the yard leading down to the catacombs and they were calling out in various languages so visitors would attach themselves to a tour suited to their needs. The catacombs of St. Calixtus was the first cemetery of the Christian community of Rome and named after the first administrator. They are over eighteen hundred years old.

I followed my group underground into the labyrinth in which one could quite easily get lost. The guide kept telling us not to lag because he would have to come back to collect any stragglers and lead them out. There were galleries, with body cavities hewn into the rock, leading off in every direction. The bodies would have been laid four to five above one another. We were led deep into the bowels of the earth and the heat became quite oppressive and after thirty minutes it seemed that we had all had enough of walking in a line, two abreast, just looking at what had become boring sameness. Eventually, we started to climb and were led out into the courtyard where I had an opportunity to talk with my tour leader. He said that the Salesians are the custodians of that sacred place but have a few very special outsiders who act as guides. He pointed out a tall guide who was surrounded by a large group, the members of which were trying to get close enough to him to give him their tokens of appreciation for "a job well done." There was something strange about the man. First, he was so much taller than any other Italian I had seen and, second, his gaunt features were whiter than most Italians. My guide told me that the fellow belonged to a small group of Jews directly descended from the Hebrew slaves brought to Rome by Titus in 70 A.D. These people, he said, kept to themselves and wouldn't permit their children to marry outside their own group...even though the "outsiders" were Jewish. On top of this, I was told that the guide spoke ten languages, fluently, and was looked up to by the Salesians because he was an outstanding scholar. I moved over towards this unusual man to take his photograph, but by the time I got there he was already heading another group moving towards the entrance to the catacombs.

I stepped outside and walked along the Appian way taking in the scenery which was dotted with the famous Roman Pines. The pines of Rome are somewhat stunted with very little growth on most of the trunks and a tendency to lean. I put all this down to the effect of the salty air and prevailing wind. I heard a bus coming behind me and managed to get it to stop for me. This took some doing and I had to run alongside the vehicle for some twentyfive yards before being allowed aboard and suffering a lecture having to do with regular bus stop signs. A few lire on top of my regular fare quietened down my noisy driver.

I got off my bus close to the too elaborate marble monument dedicated to King Victor Emmanuel the Second. Several sculptors worked on this project which took twenty-six years to complete. A Venetian sculptor, Chiaradia, worked for twenty years solely on the equestrian statue of the king!

116

A couple of minutes away I came to the famous "Trajan's Column." To celebrate his victory over the Dacians Trajan decided to build a forum that would surpass all others in size and splendor. As well as two libraries, a temple, a basilica, arches and statuary he had a column that has stood for almost two thousand years. Consisting of 19 blocks of marble, it has a spiral staircase that goes right to the top. However, the most important feature is the helicoidal band of figures which depict a documentary view of the arms and costumes of both the Romans and the Dacians. It shows the bridges Trajan built, his camps, and the enemy fortresses he destroyed. After the Emperor's death his ashes and his statue were placed on top of the column. In 1587, his ashes were buried under the column and his statue replaced with that of St. Peter.

I meandered along the Via Nazionale, towards my hotel, stopping every now and then to wander into the courtyards of some small apartment buildings. In each I found something lovely and photogenic...a small fountain built into a wall...small well-tended flower gardens just turned green...and a strange peace in the air although the heavy honking traffic was but a few yards away.

One block away, I saw the Quirinale, the home of the President which I had heard was open to visitors. I looked through the gate and saw an impressive parade of Italy's National Guard, the Carabinieri. Each man is over six feet, slender, and when seen on the streets are always in pairs. Anyway, there they were lined up in many ranks waiting for me to dash in and get a handsome photograph. I got halfway to the building entrance when an officer, waving a pistol, came tearing down the steps yelling at me and waving his arms. I looked at the hundred men around me but none seemed to blink an eye although I could tell they were amused. When the officer got to me he shouted "No pictures. No pictures." I got the message and backed out believing I had "visited" the wrong building. I felt I had enough excitement for one day and quickly walked to the peace and quiet of my room.

I had dinner at the hotel and spent a couple of hours dictating what I could recall of Mario Torelli's remarks about the Etruscans...the fact that their language had only just begun to be translated, thanks to the writings on the wrappings of a fair haired Egyptian mummy shipped home by a Yugoslavian. This happened over a hundred years ago but translation was a very recent occurrence. Then there was the matter of the fact that the pottery produced by the earlier Etruscans was so much smoother and generally better made than that of their descendants.

So it turned out that once I had found those who were "at home" in Rome they treated me very well indeed. My one failure had been my inability to get below ground level at the Colosseum and as my plane took off, the next morning, I was already planning a return visit which would get me down below the level of the long gone wooden arena and into the cells there.

Two years later I was back in the Eternal City. This time, though, I had arranged for the services of a young lady who specialized in helping making advance arrangements for archaeologists. I was accompanied by my wife who had never visited Rome. Here I should mention that my wife is ten years younger than I, a matter which twice became a source of amusement to us.

I had contacted the guide, Madelena, through the Director of one of America's leading museums and had asked her to "work her charms" on the Director of Antiquities in Rome and secure permission for me to get down to the foundations of the Colosseum. When Madelena picked us up at our hotel, the same one I had stayed at previously, this time minus the unambitious elevator operator...she told me that she hadn't been able to find anyone in authority who would grant this permission. The story was that the water-table had risen, placing the entire Colosseum in an unsafe condition. For almost two years, the edifice had been closed to the public and although once again open, the ground was treacherous to tread on and crevassed. Even the Director only went down when he had a group of surveying engineers with him trying to work out a plan to save the place from collapsing. There is an old saying that as long as the Colosseum stands, Rome will be great.

We had lunch in a restaurant controlled by a famous American fast food company and over our hamburgers and french fries I told Madelena that I wanted her to take us to the Colosseum first and then to visit the vast subterranean rooms, all that remained of Nero's "Domus Aurea" ("Gold House").

I didn't need any more brick from the Colosseum but I was determined to do everything in my power to get through the iron gate guarding the steep stairway down to ground level. I was pleased to see that "Colosseum John" and his family were still peddling their wares. If visitors were to believe all the peddlers told them, they would think that all of them were talented ivory carvers. The most popular items with visitors are cameo brooches; and each peddlar lays claim to the fact that he, personally, carves his own wares. To prove their veracity each shows potential customers a piece of horn with an almost completed cameo ready to be cut off. The truth is that they are mass produced.

Having sighted "John", I told my wife, Judy, to let Madelena give her a short tour of the Imperial Roman marvel whilst I had a chat with an old friend. Both of the girls knew what I was up to and pleaded with me not to try to "go below." I danced away from them and cornered "Colosseum John" and asked him how his son was doing at the University of Tennessee in Chattanooga. The old fellow recognized me, threw his arms around me, said he was glad to see me, his son was now in medical school in Memphis and asked if I had come back to get another ancient brick. When I told him that my goal was merely photographs of the cells, he became quite concerned and warned me that it was exceedingly risky. I took out my roll of Italian currency and asked him to talk to the guard who had the keys.

He walked over to a small office where a guard was standing and told him what I wanted. The guard shook his head emphatically and told "John" that if the Director were to come by and see me going down or coming, up his job would be lost.

At this point, I spoke up in Italian and asked how long it had been since the Director had his walk through. It had been less than an hour. "John" laid twenty dollars' worth of lire on the narrow counter of the stable-type door. That's all it took. The guard took a large key ring from a nail in the wall and led us to the locked gate. "John" told me that the Director only came around twice a day and the guard's job was safe.

The key turned in the lock, I went down a couple of steps and heard the lock click again. I was on my own. There was only enough daylight coming through the iron gate to let me see down to the first bend. When I turned this corner all was pitch black and I couldn't even see the steps. Below me was just a black void and I tried to descend by resting my shoulder against a wall I couldn't see. I hadn't brought a flashlight or even a few matches so I managed to get back up to the gate and attract "John's" attention. "John" came over to find out what my problem was and I asked him if one of his group might have a flashlight I could purchase. He disappeared for a couple of minutes returning with a flashlight and the guard. The guard opened the gate, came inside, locked the door and took me by the arm. He led me down through the Stygian darkness until we came out into bright sunlight.

I took several photographs of the Colosseum from below and then started looking towards the rooms that had probably been the cells. The guard told me to say, if we were caught by his Director, that I had lost a lens cap from above and had asked the guard to help me find it. The fellow pointed to a small opening in a ruined wall and said it had once been a one-man cell in which the prisoner could neither lie nor sit, only stand. We moved around until I came into an open section with a number of large rooms along a large wall. These had been the main cells; and as we approached them, the guard pointed out that there was a chasm between us and the cells. I knew he wouldn't let me jump over...if he knew...because the width of the chasm varied from three to five feet and getting into the rooms would entail an additional vertical movement of a couple of extra feet. I took some photographs and, without warning, jumped into one of the rooms. The guard screamed at me "pericoloso" and begged me to get back to him. I did as he asked, but not before I had taken more shots from inside. When I jumped back out, my angry companion grabbed me by the arm and picked up a piece of broken brick which he dropped into the chasm. It took four seconds before I heard it splash into the waters that were creeping into the foundations and destroying them.

I promised the guard I'd behave myself but he kept a tight grip on my arm. At one point I wanted to walk through the tunnel the Ancient Romans had used to drag away the slaughtered. The ground looked firm and had a good growth of grass and weeds but the guard bent down and picked up a piece of stone and threw it about five feet ahead of where we were standing. As we watched, the stone slowly sank out of sight!

I had seen enough and been away from my wife too long and knew she and Madelena would be worried about me. I told the guard to get me back up to where the sane people were walking around. To salve his hurt feelings I gave him a little more money and he delivered me back to "Colosseum John" who refused to accept any money for the use of his flashlight. (This famous character died a few years later, a fact that was reported world wide.) I had enjoyed the excitement of "rushing in where angels fear to tread" and appreciated the look of relief on the faces of my female companions.

From the Colosseum, at the risk of our lives, we scuttled across the road to the mound known as the "Colle Oppio" which is the only way to get to the subterranean rooms of what is left of Nero's "Gold House." The main part of the palace was destroyed by fire in 104 A.D. and over the ruins were built the Baths of Trajan of which almost nothing remains. Long after Nero's "Gold House" had disappeared, the marvels of the palace were talked about. Grecian temples and cities were robbed of their finest sculptures and paintings, and gold and precious stones were said to have adorned its walls. Down in the cavernous rooms that are left, thanks to the dim light of a single lamp some faint remains of frescoes could be made out high up on the walls of one room. In what was probably meant to be the Emperor's dining hall, the gilding and painting on the ceiling was also just made out.

I asked Madelena to drive us to the Church of Saint Peter in Chains so my wife could see "Moses." Although the giant figure still dominated the interior of the church, I was disturbed to find that since my previous visit a large souvenir shop had been installed behind this masterpiece. Having taken an art course in college, my wife was aware of the history of Michelangelo's masterpiece. The two flanking figures of Rachel and Leah were also carved by him. We went over to look at the actual chains which are under the main altar.

We had arranged to take Dr. Torelli's wife, Rita, to dinner that evening so we returned to the hotel where she picked us up in the early evening and off we went to Da Mea Pataca for another truly Roman evening of dining to the music of two bands. We ended up drinking coffee at the same place on the Via Veneto I had been with Rita and Mario on my previous visit to Rome.

Madelena, in her little car, arrived at 8:30 the following morning to take us out to Ostia Antiqua at the mouth of the river Tiber. On the way, we passed innumerable interesting ruins and broken pillars and obelisks, as well as the pyramid tomb of Caius Cestius close to the English Cemetery. Each year this cemetery attracts thousands of visitors who go to pay homage to two of England's greatest poets whose bodies are buried there..John Keats and Percy Bysshe Shelley. Concerning the Pyramid; in medieval times it was known as the Tomb of Romulus...one of the twins who founded Rome...even though there are two inscriptions indicating that the "inhabitant" is Caius Cestius Praetor, a member of the tribune.

We passed by the church of Saint John built right on the spot where the apostle was buried. The original building was built by Constantine with a larger basilica being added towards the end of the 4th century. It was destroyed by fire in 1823 and was rebuilt on the same foundations and on the same design as the original. Time didn't permit us to visit the church, and we arrived at Ostia Antiqua in good time.

Ostia was founded in the 4th century, B.C. and became the port for Rome. It was a bustling prosperous place until it started going "downhill" in the 3rd century A.D. There is so much to see in this excavated city: sepulchers of many periods, baths, the ruins of one of the Western World's oldest synagogues, a theater, a mill, warehouses, residences and a beautiful theater originally built by Augustus. Here a host of taller than average Roman pines added some color to the excavated landscape, but I was there to examine the brickwork which I started into immediately after Madelena's guided tour of the ancient port.

I poked around some low ruined walls photographing as I went.I was able to look right down into the cavity of one of them which graphically demonstrated how the triangular brick were best used. I wandered over to a grotto with a small stream running through it and picked up one of the bricks which was lying in the water. Madelena thought I was going to take it. She was right. I was. However, before doing it I had to find someone who could give me permission to take it away. Several yards away from where we were standing, I noticed a couple of archaeologists who were working on their hands and knees. I went over to the men and found they were unearthing a mosaic using tiny trowels and soft brushes.

I introduced myself and explained my mission. One of the men told me to take any brick that was merely lying around and, obviously, not part of a restoration job. Explaining about my Roman guide who was doing an excellent job of guarding everything movable, I asked if one of them would come with me and hand me a brick. One of the fellows got up, walked a few feet and bent down, picked up a triangular brick and handed it to me. Thanking them, I returned to rejoin my party.

My brick hunting in Italy was, thus, concluded. The rest of the second visit was purely vacation. From Ostia Antiqua we drove to Vatican City where we had a delightful tour of the museum, the Sistine Chapel and Saint Peter's. Lunch "had gone by the board "and we had a remarkable session sitting in the Sistine Chapel. Here, Madelena was in her element. She pointed out every single detail of the Michelangelo ceiling and then took on the frescoes one by one. She became indignant when discussing the three painted by Botticelli, criticizing not the artist but the terrible damage done to them by the restorers. So much of the restorers' colors were far too vivid and made the frescoes look artificial and not at all Botticellian. We sat in the chapel for almost two hours before moving into St. Peter's.

This is not a book on art, but all the beauty with which we were surrounded in the Sistine Chapel and St. Peter's cannot be dismissed in a couple of sentences. It was inspiring to see, in person, the famous "La Pieta" even behind its protective shatterproof screen put there after a maniac had tried to damage the statue in 1972; the gilt-bronze throne above the main altar which was designed to incorporate a wood and ivory chair which is said to have been used by Saint Peter; the magnificent tomb of pope Urban the Eighth; the bronze doors of the main entrance; and the high altar before which ninety-five lamps burn day and night. It had always been believed that the high altar had been built over the tomb of Saint Peter, but it wasn't until June 26th, 1968 that the pope announced to the world that skeletal remains discovered over forty years before were indisputedly those of Saint Peter. So much to see that in an hour we only "scratched the surface" before going down into the crypt with its simple tombs, in front of which visitors were kneeling and praying, and marble chapels. From the crypt we walked straight on out into the sunlight and Saint Peter's Square.

We parted company with Madelena at our hotel. She, to go out to the airport to meet some English archaeologists; we, to have a leisurely dinner and an early night in preparation to a trip to Pompeii the next day.

The visit to the ancient city was uneventful. I wasn't looking for any brick, so I took my wife on a tour of the site turning down several streets that were overgrown and not part of the regular tourists' itinerary. We came to one wall with a closed wooden gate which bore the notice "CHIUSO" (closed.) This was a nice invitation to go in! We found ourselves in the courtyard of a ruined residence that was in the process of being excavated. On two tables we saw two freshly dug up plaster casts of victims of the 79 eruption. The plaster was still in the process of being dried out. I took some photographs and we left.

The train journey back from Naples to Rome provided us with the first of two good laughs, that day. Sitting opposite us in the carriage was a couple obviously very much in love. They appeared to be about thirty years old and were both uncomfortably dressed in new clothes. The young woman kept constant hold of her companion's hand while she tried to figure out who we were without making it obvious that she was looking at us every couple of minutes. Eventually, in her own tongue, she asked me "Are you and your daughter from England or America." I smiled at her while her young man realized she had made a mistake. I told her that the lady was my wife and, to help her overcome her embarrassment, asked her if she and her companion were going all the way to Rome. Her boy friend joined in the conversation and said that they were from a small town near Naples and were going to Rome to be married. In answer to my comment that I thought they would want to be married in their own church, the man said their priest who had known them all their lives had been transferred to Rome a short while before and that he was going to perform the ceremony.

That happened in middle of the afternoon. A few hours later, my wife and I were browsing around an Italian type pharmacy looking for some picture postcards. Also, browsing were a man, his wife and a their son. The son walked over to my wife and told her that he was a member of the U.S. Armed Forces and stationed in Turkey. He was on leave and his parents had flown to Rome to spend some time with him. My wife said she hoped they were having a nice time, whereupon the young man said to my wife, "How about a date tonight?" (Since the shop was small, every word could be easily heard.) My wife said, "It's nice of you to ask me out but you'd better ask my husband!"

These two episodes made up for my wife's complaint that despite the romantic reputation of the Italians, she hadn't been pinched, even once, on the Via Venito.

CHAPTER 7

THE MOUND OF THE DEAD

Anyone who has an interest in archaeology or just ancient cities has read of Mohenjo-daro, which translates into "The Mound of the Dead," in the Pakistan portion of the Indus Valley. This is the site of the extensive remains of a 4,500 year-old city of the Harappan civilization where seven cities were built one on top of the other as the water table rose. The construction was entirely of bricks, millions of them, and the site drew me like a magnet for several years until I could resist no longer. I had to go! An archaeologist who had worked at the site for many years told me that there probably wouldn't be any trouble getting there, but as for getting permission to retrieve even one brick for the museum that would be virtually impossible. The Pakistan Department of Antiquities was adamant in its refusal to permit a single brick to leave the site, he said as he gave me the name of the Director of Archaeology for Pakistan who was one of the most respected and famous persons in Pakistan. His name was Dr. F.A. Khan whose office was in a compound in Karachi.

First of all I obtained a visa from the Embassy of Pakistan, in D.C. and then I wrote to Dr. Khan explaining who and what I was and requested an interview with him when I arrived in Karachi. In reply I received a most cordial invitation to meet with him at the compound at ten a.m. on a certain date. It should be mentioned that, at that time, the state of affairs between India and Pakistan over Kashmir was so bad that martial law was in effect in Pakistan.

As I have mentioned, the British Airways office in D.C. always signaled ahead when I was to arrive at a certain point, requesting all necessary assistance for me. I was never let down. Arriving at Karachi airport at three a.m. as I got off the plane a young man wearing a British Airways badge came up to me and handed me a long letter from the local manager. I stopped to read it in the light of the airport's floodlights and found it to be an apology for the manager being unable to greet me, since he had to attend a relative's funeral. By the time I had read the epistle, all the other passengers from my flight were already through Customs and Immigration; and, as I walked towards the terminal, an officer came up and asked me what I was doing out on the tarmac. The boy from the airline started to explain only to be chased off by the officer who grabbed my arm and escorted me to the terminal. I handed my passport with its stamped visa to another officer. He looked at it and handed it over his shoulder to the stern faced fellow who had almost dragged me in. They could find nothing wrong with it, and it was duly stamped that I had entered Pakistan. The next desk was the Customs who merely asked for my Currency Declaration. (The strictest regulations were in force, and visitors were only allowed to take 80 rupees..about seventeen dollars...into the country. I had just one 50 rupee note purchased at a money changer's in Rome.) The same "arresting" officer was following me down the line and he was the one who took my Currency Declaration. He looked at it and said, "Where are your 50 rupees?" I took out

123

the bill and handed it him. He looked at it and, with a nasty grin asked, "Where did you get this and how much did you pay for it?" I told him that I had paid the Italian money changer ten dollars for the Pakistani rupees. Then both he and the customs officer on duty started to give me "the third degree." Over and over they asked me where I got the money and how much had I paid for it? At one point I managed to get a word in and told them that their own regulations permitted me to bring in 80 rupees and here I was with only 50. The response was that it was alright to have 80 rupees but only in ones, fives and tens. Incoming fifties, hundreds and thousands were black market money. I was asked if I knew the official exchange rate. I did. It was 4.75 rupees for a dollar.

(I had got a quarter of a rupee per dollar extra!) The questioning was kept up. The same questions and the same answers over and over. I was out on my feet, all I wanted to do was grab a cup of tea and go to bed.

After over half an hour of this nonsense I said, "There are two things you can do. One is to keep the money and let me go to my hotel and the other is to take me to prison and call Dr. F.A.Khan at his home and tell him that his guest is a prisoner." The magic words! The first officer said "You are here to see Dr. Khan?" I nodded my head, and the two officers had a quick conference after which I was handed the 50 rupee note and told to leave and spend it quickly and to realize that they were only doing their job.

I left the terminal as quickly as I could, got in a taxi and was driven to my hotel where I checked in, had some tea sent up to my room, put a Halazone tablet into a glass of water (for brushing my teeth) and "dropped" into bed. The time was 4:30 a.m. and according to his letter Mr. Fernandez, the Manager from British Airways, was coming to have breakfast with me at 9 o-clock.

At five minutes to nine I was called on the house phone by Mr. Fernandez and went down to meet him. He was a very friendly gentleman who said that he and his staff were at my service. Over breakfast he told me that he had made an appointment for me with the director of the Karachi museum at ten o-clock. I told him that I was going to see Dr. Khan instead. He told me that he was certain Dr. Khan wouldn't see me. He had his car and driver outside, and we went to the airline office where I dropped Mr. Fernandez telling him I would see him in a few days. I left my suitcase with him and just took my flight bag and cameras. Then it was "on to the compound."

On the way there, my driver turned around and told me that they wouldn't let us into the compound and that we should go back to the office. I requested he continue to the compound. Arriving at the gate, my driver had a few words in Urdu with the guard. I stuck my head out of the car window and told the guard to ring Dr. Khan and tell him his guest from America was at the gate. This done he saluted me and opened the gate and told the astonished driver how to get to the Director's office where I got out, thanked the driver, grabbed my belong-ings and walked up to the curtain over the entrance. As I got there a minion appeared and drew the curtain aside and indicated the way to Dr. Khan's Office. I stood in his doorway and surveyed the gentleman who could do so much for me. He was a very pleasant looking fellow who got up and greeted me by name while he gave me a nice warm handshake. He invited me to sit down and asked if I would join him in a cup of tea. We sipped tea and chatted for some time, and

124

he expressed his admiration for my company for its efforts in preserving the history of the brickmaker's art. He told me that I would be permitted to remove a brick from Mohenjo-daro and that he had a brick from Harappa, the capital city of that era, brought in for me. We talked about how I was going to get up there. When I heard how much it would cost to rent a plane, I quickly decided to go by train, a journey of some nine-and-a-half hours. Dr. Khan apologized for being so tied up as being unable to do as he had hoped, accompany me personally. He called the railway station and told them to reserve a seat for me in a first class carriage. Then he made a telephone call to the director of the excavations at Mohenjo-daro and told him that he knew there was a German archaeologist staying at the rest house but he would have to be turfed out to make room for me and that a guard should meet me at the station when I arrived.

The good doctor, the man who built up a fine organization from scratch, (in the beginning all his staff were volunteers and everyone had to provide their own table, chairs, paper and ink.) led me outside to his car and had us driven to his favorite restaurant. Now, it was eleven o-clock and my train was to leave at noon, so it was quite a bit before his regular lunchtime. When we got to the restaurant he had a fit. There were only four men inside, sitting around the center table--HIS table. He berated the poor manager and the other men scuttled over to another table in a corner. Dr. Khan turned to me and said, "How do you like that for action?" We had a fine Pakistani lunch, for which he insisted upon paying, and then he had us driven to the station. He stayed very close to me to make sure that everything went smoothly. The train was standing in the station and we found my carriage and both of us got in. Dr. Khan asked me if he should purchase something for me to read on the trip,but I told him I had quite enough to read. Instead of hurrying off he stayed with me until just a few minutes before it was departure time. He saw the guard (conductor) and told him to lock the carriage door as soon as the train was ready to leave and that he was responsible for my safety. He told me to be sure to go and see him on my return from "Mohenjo-daro." Just after this generous and friendly gentleman left, a businessman from Quetta got into the carriage. He was in western clothes as was the next man in. However, as soon as the train pulled out of the station the second man pulled down a bunk, climbed onto it and changed into regular Pakistani dress.

The compartment had one bench type seat long enough for three people to sit on comfortably. Just beyond the seat was the entrance to a small toilet while opposite two pull-down bunks were fixed on the wall. There was a vent for the Pakistani type "air conditioning" system. This consisted of a large ice receptacle built on top of the single compartment with a ship type wind scoop facing forward. As the train traveled along the air went down the scoop and was cooled by the ice before entering the compartment. Unfortunately, "the iceman had not cometh" before departure time so we had to put up with uncooled air conditioning. I didn't mind it at all. Still, as you will see, others weren't as understanding.

The first stop came about one hour after we had left Karachi. During this time I had been chatting with the man from Quetta, and I recalled the horrible Quetta earthquake of 1935 which destroyed three quarters of the city with great loss of life. The man was surprised, and pleased, that I knew about his city. At any rate, when we stopped at the first station the guard unlocked the carriage door to permit the entry of another passenger. This man was about six feet seven, weighed somewhere in the region of 300 lbs and was carrying a tremendous bedroll that seemed to be about as big as its owner. He, too, was dressed in western clothes and he dumped his roll in a corner of the carriage and addressed himself to all of us in English with a "Good afternoon."

There are actually four languages used in Pakistan. The official language is English. Then there are the two dialects Urdu and Sindhi. On top of all these a small amount of Hindi is still spoken by some of the older people who had to move from India to Pakistan at Partition in 1947. Noteworthy is the fact that the English spoken by the literate, and many of the illiterate, is for the most part beautifully grammatically correct. The newcomer asked me where I was going and how long I was going to stay in his "fine country." In turn, I asked him what his calling was, adding a statement that I imagined that he was a government official. He was a tax collector. Hearing this, I told him that he had the right physique for the job and I doubted if he had too much trouble collecting. He laughed and agreed with me.

The man in the bunk had long since gone to sleep, and after another couple of hours the train stopped at another station where, once again, the door was unlocked. This time there was no new passenger, just a small boy who had brought me something to eat. I was handed a china plate which had a mound of rice upon which rested a leg of what must have been the scrawniest chicken ever created. The whole was covered with a nice curry sauce. This was handed to me along with a single chapati--the thin tearable round bread which one uses to grab a handful of food and eat along with the curry. I had changed some travelers checks at the hotel before I checked out earlier, so I was able to give him some money. While I was eating my meal the man in the bunk awoke and complained about the "unendurable "heat and lack of air conditioning. The other two agreed with him that the situation was dire and that the guard needed to be reported. This made me feel rather disappointed in my fellow travelers because if I, used to much less heat, could stand it surely they who lived with it year round could take it.

Enter "The Black Book." This was a British innovation to ensure perfect performance by all the Indian people they controlled. Anyone with a complaint could ask for the "Black Book", (which was carried by all important functionaries) and enter his complaint. The book was scrutinized regularly and woe betide anyone deemed to have done less than their best. My fellow travelers called to the guard and told him to bring his "Black Book." The poor fellow started to explain why there wasn't any ice in the unit. The deliveryman hadn't shown up before it was time for the train to leave Karachi and the timetable had to be adhered to. Nothing doing! These chaps were out for blood. The book was brought and each wrote his version of the situation. Then it was handed to me, along with the pencil. I demurred but they were insistent so I looked at what they had written. The three entries went like this: "The guard is a terrible man who wants his passengers to suffocate by refusing to let ice be placed in the air conditioner."

"I have almost fainted several times because the guard didn't get ice into the air conditioning. He should be sacked."

"I don't know how I have managed to live in the hellish heat of our carriage. This could have been avoided by having a different guard."

I started to write in the book and looked up to see a pleased expression on each of the other men's faces. I wrote "I am a visitor from the United States of America, and I do not agree with the other gentlemen. The guard is excellent and he waited until the last minute before signaling for the driver to pull out of the station hoping that the ice would arrive. The fault is with the ice company. Also, if I do not find the atmosphere too hot, surely these three native Pakistanis can more easily withstand it. They have all exaggerated." Having done that I closed the book and handed both book and pencil over to the guard who looked as though he could see his employment being terminated.

The tax collector got out at the next stop; and as he unlocked the door, the guard gave me a nice smile. Underway, the man from Quetta looked up at the man in the bunk to make sure he was asleep again and then sidled up to me and whispered, "Is it true in America if you do not like your President, you can say so without being punished?" My reply was, "That is true. In public I can say he is terrible and ought to be kicked out and even call him nasty names. Nothing will happen to me. The only thing I cannot do is verbally threaten his life. Even then the authorities would think I was crazy and just give me a slap on the wrist." The Quetta merchant's eyes opened wide and his jaw dropped.

This allowed me to tell him than I thought the guard was an Anglo-Indian, saying I even detected some Irish in his speech. My companion disagreed so, at the next stop where the man in the bunk got out of the carriage, I walked along the platform and told the guard what I had told the man from Quetta. "You are so correct, sir." he said. " My mother was Indian and my father was an Irishman in the British army. Thank you very much, sir, for what you wrote in the Black Book." In between my little chats with the Quetta merchant I had been able to look at the countryside through which we passed. It was, for the most part, truly barren. A few trees could be seen here and there dotting the arid landscape, with an occasional village or small town being observed situated a couple of miles or so from the railroad tracks. There was little land under cultivation. Only small patches on which were growing crops too far away to identify. On one occasion I got a glimpse of a man tilling the ground with the aid of a couple of yoked oxen.

I was amazed at the tremendous amount of activity at each of the stations at which we stopped. The noise of hundreds of people thronging the platforms was amazing, and above all the babble could be heard the blaring of a radio playing Sindhi music. (We were in the state of Sind.) Only a few of the people at the stations were passengers for our train. Mostly, they were hawkers of sweetmeats, bangles and other baubles, as well as vendors of hot tea and lemonade. The sound was raucous enough for me to capture on my recorder and later incorporate in a lecture. I partook of some tea at each of our few stops, making sure that the vendors were using boiled milk. The seat in the train was soft and comfortable and I was able to catch an odd nap in between talking and reading the literature I had on "Mohenjo-daro."

The daylight faded and night fell and a light had come on in the carriage as we sped northwards. The man in the bunk left us without a word, although he did shake hands with me, at what turned out to be the penultimate stop before my destination. My remaining companion informed me that we were behind schedule by almost two hours. At 11:30 p.m. the train stopped at the small station at Mohenjo-daro where I shook hands with my friend from Quetta and left the train to be immediately greeted by a tall khaki-dressed young man who was armed with a pistol. He took my bag and camera case and led me to a tonga, a one-horse drawn conveyance. I had ridden in this type of wagon years earlier on the other side of the continent and didn't look forward to riding in it. At first I was placed on a seat at the rear of the tonga facing away from the way we were traveling. The road was unpaved and I was most uncomfortable. After a few minutes, I turned around and called to my escort who was sitting alongside the driver and asked him to change places with me. This done I found that in order to stop myself from sliding off the seat onto the road I had to put my arm around the driver's shoulder. (My reward for this was the garnering of a colony of fleas with which I had to live for several days.)

The moon was mostly obscured by clouds and everything was dark. I couldn't make out anything except the dim shapes of what were the walls of part of Mohenjo-daro. It was about a ten mile ride to the rest house and I was happy to get off the tonga. My escort led me to a small building, up a flight of stairs and into a darkened room. He struck a match and lit a kerosene lamp which enabled me to survey my surroundings.

My quarters were cramped, with the only equipment being a camp cot under which was a "pot-de chambre," a table on which stood a small water carafe covered with a glass tumbler, one chair and a busy buzzing mosquito. I was asked if I wished for anything and quickly requested a cup of very hot tea made with boiled milk. My famous guard (that's what he turned out to be) returned before too long with the tea and a couple of stale English biscuits to find me in my pajamas trying to ease the itch of a multitude of flea bites with some antiseptic ointment. Before he left he asked me at what time I wished to be awakened and what I would like to have for breakfast. I told him that I was very short of sleep having arrived in Pakistan very early that same day and that he should let just let me sleep undisturbed. As for breakfast, I asked him to have the cook prepare a couple of curried hard boiled eggs and some chapati for me. Sitting at the table I sipped my tea while I dictated the day's events into my recorder. A mosquito, or some other flying creature, had decided to join me in my cup of tea and drowned. I was too tired to fish it out so both the tea and its visitor disappeared down my gullet. After dropping a Halazone tablet into the glass, which I filled with water from the carafe, and covered with a book I crawled onto the camp cot and melted into the arms of Morpheus.

When I awoke, daylight was streaming into my room, and I found a ewer of hot water, a basin and soap and towel had been put on the table. My toilet completed, I picked up my camera bag and went downstairs. I found my guard standing right by the stairs. He hoped I'd had a good night's sleep...it was 9 o-clock... and led me into the dining room which had two tables. No sooner had I sat down than he started to serve my breakfast which was most tasty and satisfying. He told me that Mr. Rasul, the director of the small museum and the "dig", was ready for me to receive him at my convenience. I washed my curry down with the usual hot tea and, as I got up from the table, was surprised when my "man" came up with a bowl of water and a towel. I rinsed my hands and reached for the towel only to find my hands being dried for me! All this reminded me of the days of the "White Raj." (I never addressed him by his name, Mohammed, because he was always at hand.)

When I stepped outside a blast of 100 degrees-plus hit me in the face but I had been in much hotter places such as Abadan, in the Persian Gulf with 120 degrees and Peshawar, Pakistan, with its 115 degree heat. I saw the small modern museum building a few steps away and strolled over to meet Mr. Rasul. He was a very pleasant young man in his early twenties and very eager to please. However, he refused to go with me into the ruins until late afternoon because of the heat which he said would increase during the day. He opened the display case containing some of the artifacts discovered in the city. Some pottery, several children's toys in the shape of animals and others on tiny wheels. One of the many mysteries of Mohenjo-daro was the meaning of several carved stone seals discovered during excavations. Each bore the form of an animal with four yet-to-be undeciphered pictographs above it. The animals on the seals were a crocodile, an antelope, an elephant, a tiger and a rhinoceros, which indicated the kinds of wild animals known to the Indus Valley people. In the museum were a few of the eleven steatite sculptures discovered. These showed men with beards, who it has been hazarded were gods or priests. No one knows, really. I was permitted to handle these most rare and valuable items as Mr. Rasul made sure I knew the known history of the city.

Built on a vast alluvial plain on the banks of the Indus river, the site had been buried completely by silt from the many floods and the drifting sands. Until it was excavated all that could be seen on the site was an ancient Buddhist stupa (shrine) built of mud bricks. This turned out to have been located at what had been the highest point, the citadel, of the last of the seven cities built some two thousand or so years earlier. The original shape of Mohenjo-daro was a square, but the continuing rebuilding had slightly altered the form. Just a few yards from where I was standing I could see the high brick wall, some three miles in circumference, that had finally enclosed the city. The fate of the inhabitants of this, and other, Harappan cities is still unknown. Very few graves have been discovered. Some thirty skeletons were found in and near a well house, each showing signs of its owner being killed by the sword. But thirty skeletons do not comprise the entire population of such a tremendous city and the theory is that due to the constantly rising water table, which made it impossible to farm and also damaged their homes, there had been a mass migration to-? No one knows even that.

I told Mr. Rasul that, heat or not, I was going to enter the city and walk around by myself and would come out for lunch after a couple of hours. Then, perhaps, he would be brave enough to go back with me as my guide. No sooner said than done. I found myself in "Brick Heaven" oblivious to the heat and only looking for a spot where there would be a loose brick...not part of a struc-ture...that I could pick up and take back to my museum in Tennessee. There were so many such spots that I quickly stopped searching and devoted myself to wandering down broad streets and narrow lanes, all surrounded by 2,500 year old brick homes. I climbed a long flight of steps which took me up to the Stupa mound and looked down on the ghostly deserted city. For the few non-archaeological visitors that showed up from time to time, there were large signs written in English and Urdu which read as follows: Public Baths; Main Street; Crooked Lane and Chief's House. From my vantage point I could see a large ritual bath and a thirty foot high brick well wall. Descending, I made my way over to a large wall which was 60 feet in width and all solid brickwork. (Dr. George Dales of the University of California at Berkley who excavated at Mohenjo-daro for over a dozen years had once sent me a picture of this wall.)

The time passed so quickly that when I looked at my watch I discovered I had been in the ruins for two hours. So I headed back to the museum where Mr. Rasul was patiently waiting for me. We had lunch at the rest house. A welcome highly spiced chicken curry that really made me perspire, chapatis and a couple of cups of tea were served by Mohammed who, once again, brought me a bowl of water and dried my hands for me after I had rinsed them. Trying to delay our visit to the city as long as he could (until the sun started to drop down), the director dawdled over lunch.

I asked Mr. Rasul where the German archaeologist I had displaced from the bedroom was. His reply was just a shrug of his shoulders and outspread arms as if to say, "Who knows?" I learned from him that living in a couple of bungalows half a mile away were an electrical engineer and a construction engineer, and he promised to introduce me to them that evening. They were both involved in developing the area into a regular tourist attraction. A brick-surfaced landing field had already been laid out and was to be lengthened and illuminated.

Eventually, we moved away from the table and my trusty guard dashed to open the door for us. We entered the city, which was spread over twenty-four acres, where Mr. Rasul started us on a fine tour. Nothing was missed. We came to the line of cubicles by the sign "Bath Houses" and he pulled a flashlight from his rear trouser pocket and took me inside one of them. Proudly, he pointed out that the bricks used on the floor were all glazed. According to him, these brick had been specially glazed for bath house use. However, I had noticed that many of the brick in various walls were also glazed. I decided that the glazing was accidental, although the ancient folk had realized they were ideal for the floors of the bath houses. The clay used to make the brick had a very high salt content and in the course of drying, before firing, the salt "migrated" to the surface and became a glazing compound. From the little cubicles we went to the ritual bath where bitumen had been used as the mortar instead of the gypsum and mud mortar used everywhere else. The bath measured 40 feet by 23 feet with a depth of 8 feet and seemed to have been built on a platform. As I walked down the steps, I remembered that there was a similar bath at Harappa, the capital city of the ancient civilization, and realized that there must be a connection between the ancient bathing ritual and the present day Hindu ritual bathing in the Ganges river. Doubtless, it had all started in the Indus Valley at least 4,500 years ago.

My camera had been at work all day recording the wonders of this mountain of brickwork, and my photography was definitely slowing us down. Still, I wanted to see as much as I could. Many of the bricks in most of the walls were covered with a white powder--efflorescence--which was again caused by the brick absorbing moisture from the rising water table and bringing the salt to the surface. This was a serious matter because the brick were beginning to deteriorate. (Some years later, when it was learned that I was going to be on the Indian Continent I was invited to a UNESCO conference at Mohenjo-daro which was to determine how the brickwork could be rescued. Unfortunately, I had an important appointment in India and was unable to go north.

Down the middle of each street, both wide and narrow, a clay pipe was let into the ground and there was a connection to each of the houses. Yes, it was a sewage system. Those builders of the city were excellent planners and paid great attention to sanitation. Mr. Rasul told me that in some of the houses they had found primitive toilet seats. That was four-thousand-four-hundred years before the Englishman, Mr. Crapper, developed his system.

We walked in and out of several of the buildings, and I marvelled at the tremendously fine job done by the excavating archaeologists. Again, time flew and before we knew it the daylight began to disappear and we had to backtrack and get back to the rest house. I had asked for more curried eggs for dinner and started in on them as soon as I had washed up in the downstairs bathroom. The cook had also prepared some kind of custard but before I devoured it I had "my man" find out what was in it and if it had been boiled before being allowed to set. It was o.k. for me to eat it and it topped off the meal nicely.

After dinner Mr. Rasul came in and took me for a walk down to the bungalows of the technical people. We were accompanied by the guard who was, again, wearing his pistol. I decided not to ask any questions about having to have an armed guard. We were miles away from any town and I couldn't imagine anyone trying to attack us. I was introduced to the electrical engineer, a pleasant visaged person, who welcomed me into his abode. He produced some cold beer which went down very nicely. We chatted about his work at the site for awhile before we were joined by his neighbor, the construction man. The four of us sat and talked, and partook of our beer, for a couple of hours. We discussed everything but international politics. I made sure that subject never came up since, as I mentioned earlier, the country was under martial law. The electrical engineer promised to take me to see a local village the following afternoon. He said I would have a chance to compare the past with the present.

I was quite tired after my two visits to the ancient city and the enervating heat so I went for an early night. Back at the rest house I washed up at the ground floor washroom and exited to find a cup of tea and some more English biscuits awaiting me in the dining room. The lantern had already been lit in my bedroom, and all I had to do was prepare my Halazone treated glass of water before turning in.

The next day I was able to drag Mr. Rasul out right after breakfast and enter Mohejo-daro. I won't go into any more details of the city other than to state that I picked up the brick for the Tennessee museum; got right up to the 30 foot well construction and learned that it descended another thirty feet, all the way to the water level; that I saw two circular brick constructed threshing floors; and found that the street named "Crooked Lane" was a long street with a dog-leg turn which was believed to break the force of rushing water during torrential downpours. Finally, the archaeologists had, at that time, dug down 60 feet and hadn't reached the base of the walls. (At that level, water prevented more digging.)

During my tour of the city I discovered that I had lost the metal lens cap from one of my cameras. This, of course, was troubling since there was so much dust around. However, just after lunch while I was getting ready to make my way to the electrical engineer's bungalow accompanied by my guard I saw a tall khaki dressed man emerge from the ruins. He came up to me and with in strongly German accented English asked me if the lens cap he had in his hand was mine. Amazing! 24 acres and he had found this insignificant looking object! I thanked him and apologized for having taken over his room at the rest house. Asked where he had spent the previous two nights, he said he had a sleeping bag and had slept in one of the ancient dwellings in the city. I had planned to stay in the room until midnight since my train wasn't due to leave until 3 a.m., but I felt that I should return the room to the German. So I told him I would not be using the room after dark since I could stay a few hours in the station waiting room. My guard muttered something about "Too dangerous!" but I ignored his remark, shook hands with the archaeologist and walked off towards the bunga- low.

Soon, after being joined by Mr. Rasul and the construction engineer, there were five of us riding in a tonga with the electric expert driving. I soon began to hope that he was a better in his field than as a tonga driver. He kept having trouble controlling the horse and when we rounded a bend in the gravel road only to find we had run head on into a long line of wagons loaded with wood (fuel for some underground brick kilns), the horse moved towards a deep gully. In a twinkling of an eye we had all jumped off and started dragging the horse away from the steep drop. If we had failed, both the animal and the tonga would have been gone forever. Our "driver" took his whip and chased after the man driving the lead wagon that had "dared" to block our way. I took three photographs at the time. One was of the amateur driver lashing out with his whip at the driver of the offending wagon just before the accident. Another was of him chasing the poor man, while the third was of the horse and tonga in the ditch we were able to get them into.

We climbed back aboard our conveyance and, before long, came in sight of a small lake, called "Hottenwan Lake" just a short distance from a very small village. We stopped while I photographed a man and a small boy in a boat, rather large for such a small body of water, casting a very heavy net hoping to catch some fish. During the 15 minutes we were there they hadn't netted anything at all. As we turned back to the tonga I found that all the children from the village had come up, dressed in a variety of colors of clothing, and were standing on a bank smiling at me. I walked around to meet them while Mr. Rasul told me to "watch where you step." Looking down I realized what he was talking about. Even though just a short distance away was an ancient city with an excellent sewage system, here they had nothing other than the outskirts of the

132

village. The youngsters obligingly stayed together as I took some photographs of them, and then they surrounded me and escorted me into the village itself. The first thing I noticed was a small mosque with blue tile adornment. The youngsters wanted me to go inside, but without any Imam in sight I wisely declined to enter and just took a picture.

The homes were so primitive, just shacks, that it was obvious that whatever little money they had went to support the mosque and the Imam. Standing against a wall were two four-foot tall pottery urns. I got two of the small children, a girl and a boy, to stand in front of them while I took a picture. A few feet away I found an old woman making pottery. She was sitting on the edge of a small pit which enabled her to use a foot to provide the power for her potters' wheel. She smiled at me and handed me a small jug she had just finished. Obviously she wanted me to keep it but it was still wet and impossible for me to take away. I handed it back to her and gave her a five rupee note. The electrical engineer had just come up and he told me I had given her more than she could earn in two days. Five rupees--one dollar!

An event in my past came back to me, something I could never forget. During the war, my ship was being coaled at Karachi and I watched as both men and women walked up a wooden plank with a basket of coal on their head which they emptied into the coal bunker. Then they walked down another plank where the empty basket was replaced by another full one. It was heartbreaking to see the mass of ragged, emaciated human beings working so terribly hard. At midday they got a lunch rest and I squatted beside one man who was eating some rice which had been put on a broad palm leaf. I asked him about his life. He earned 5 annas (a nickel) a day! Questioned as to how he was able to live and provide for his family on such a small amount, he told me that his wife earned 3 annas a day and that the total of 8 annas just paid for enough rice to feed them and almost nothing for clothing. Hearing this I felt ashamed to be a part of the system that exploited India's population so selfishly. Even today the memory of that discovery disturbs me.

There wasn't anything else to see in the village, so we climbed into the tonga to return "home." The electrical engineer invited me to a party, in my honor, that night at his bungalow. He promised me a special treat.

While I was changing my clothes, the guard knocked on my door and told me that there was someone outside with a present for me. Standing at the small gate let into the low wooden fence surrounding the rest house was a lad holding out a large bream like fish resting on a piece of newspaper. Without a word, he offered it to me. Turning to my smiling attendant, I asked him what it was all about. He said that the boy and his father had seen me watching them fishing on the lake and wanted me to have their catch as a gift. I was in a quandary. Firstly, I wouldn't dare eat anything that came from the polluted lake and secondly, I couldn't possibly take the food that the fishermen had worked so hard to catch. So I smiled, took the fish and then handed it back to the boy who was bewildered by my action. I asked the guard to explain to the boy that I really appreciated the generous present but that my dinner was already being cooked and I couldn't take the fish onto the train with me. As my words were being translated into Sindhi, I took another five rupee bill and stuffed it into the boy's shirt pocket. I managed to shake his hand and gently hugged his shoulders. His face showed understanding and gratitude and he trotted off in the direction of Hottewan. I was genuinely touched by such generosity. That fish was big enough to feed a whole family. I went back and washed my fishy hands, since the newspaper had been quite soggy and the clammy fish had come through as I held it, and sat down in the dining room where I was, again, served my egg curry.

A short time later Mr. Rasul came by and, accompanied by the guard who was again wearing his pistol, we made our way to the bungalow. That was an evening to remember. There were several people at the "do" inside while a crowd of about thirty men who worked on the airfield squatted outside. The beer flowed and there was a good supply of English biscuits and toffee. The conversation dwelt on all the countries I had visited and my philosophy of mutual respect. Then in came a poorly dressed man carrying two flutes and a two-stringed instrument. I started my recorder as the man performed for us. First of all he played the two flutes at the same time. One was stuck in the corner of his mouth and gave out a single bass note. The other was like a regular wooden flute on which he played his melodies. The plaintive Sindhi music filled the room and was heard by those outside, since the window and doors were open to give the mosquitoes a way in. Following the flute music, the performer picked up his stringed instrument and accompanied himself as he sang a number of songs. This went on for half an hour until the man bowed towards me and moved outside.

I followed him so I could thank him. The outside assembly stood up as I got out. I went up to the entertainer and shook his hand and thanked him for his music. Then I started my tape playing. The look of astonishment on the faces was as if they were hearing music from heaven. Suddenly, I noticed that the musician had tears rolling down his cheeks and I wondered what was wrong. I stopped the tape and moved towards him. There was a young man standing beside him, and sensing he could speak English, I asked what I had done to make the old man cry. The young man said, "Sir, my father has been playing for more years than I have been on earth and this is the first time he has ever heard himself. Thank you. Thank you." What with the fish episode and the expression of gratefulness from the musician's son, the day had been rather an emotional one, for me. I was due to leave for the station in a short while and felt I was leaving behind some good, sincere friends.

At 10:30 I asked the guard to bring me my bill. It came to about $10:00! I offered him a tip which he refused, saying it had been his privilege to be with me and look after me. The cook came out and he accepted a little money from me. Then it was off to the station in the tonga. The guard was still wearing his pistol but I noticed that, now, he had opened the flap of his holster. At the station I started to say "goodbye" to the guard, but he told me that he had instructions to stay with me until my train arrived, at 3.00 a.m.

He led me to the waiting room which we found to be occupied by six Pakistani teenagers who had obviously been drinking. As we came inside, they moved to the other end of the room and stared, or rather glared at me. There was a chaise lounge just ahead of me and I put my flight bag and my camera case on a table next to it and started to sit down. Before I got on it one of the boys ran over and slipped under me and stretched himself out on the chaise. I was somewhat startled and stood aside. My guard started shouting at the young men and managed to get the chaise free for me. The six of them then came over together and started to get into a shouting match with my protector. Suddenly, he had his hand on his pistol, but before he could draw it I had got up and put my hand on his hand so he couldn't draw it out of the holster. I told him that there was no need for any violence and that he should leave me and go back to the rest house. He remonstrated and said his orders to stay with me had come from Mr. Rasul. Nevertheless, I told him he now had new orders, from ME, and I was in no danger from the young Pakistanis who realized I was a visitor in their country and would do me no harm. Reluctantly, he departed and I got back on the chaise but, just in case, I slowly opened my flight bag and felt for the scout knife I always carried on my trips to help when a brick had to be removed from a wall. I slid it out of the sheath and kept my hand inside the bag.

The noisy and slightly intoxicated youths came and stood around me making catcalls. One of them was the word "yankee-doodle." I smiled at them and said, "salaam." This quieted them down a little but one of them with deep brown eyes and a scowl on his face said to me, "Who are you? Why do you speak like an Englishman but wear American clothes?" To this I replied, with a smile, "I was born in England but now live in America."

One of the others said, "In Pakistan we dislike the British and hate the Americans."

I asked why the bad feeling towards America and was told that America had given more arms to India than to Pakistan. To this I replied that it was only natural since India was so much bigger than Pakistan. They stared at me intently and then looked at one another as if to say "What do we do now?" I let go of my knife and took out my recorder saying, "Would you like to hear some Sindhi music?" One of them asked me if I liked Sindhi music. I nodded my head and started the recorder. The music I had recorded earlier that evening filled the waiting room with pleasant sounds and all six of my tormenters started smiling at me. After a few minutes I stopped the tape and told the boys that it was a recording of one of their local musicians made at Mohenjo-daro.

Then one of the boys asked, "Would you like a cup of tea?" I replied in the affirmative but asked how tea could be obtained at such a late hour. There was no answer but one of the boys left the waiting room. The tension had certainly been eased. The fierce looking boy came right up to me and took a cardboard cigarette package from his pocket. He took out the cigarettes and put them back in a pocket and proceeded to tear the container in pieces. He ended up with two rectangular pieces and proceeded to make some scoring with his thumb nail. I asked one of the others what he was doing and was told he was making a gift for me. (All of these fellows spoke excellent English.) Five minutes passed in silence and then the thumbnail artist handed me the cards. One had an excellent outline of a long haired western girl while the other had the outline of a Sindhi farmer complete with the type of cap peculiar to Sind. I thanked him

135

and told him that they were excellent and that I would proudly show them around when I got back home.

The door opened and in came a small boy, about ten years old, carrying a large tray on which were seven cups of tea. I reached into my pocket but one of the other fellows told me that I couldn't pay for the tea since I was their guest. While we drank the tea I told them why I had come to Pakistan and that, thanks to Dr. F.A.Khan, I had received permission to collect a brick from the ancient site. This also was in my flight bag and I took it out and showed it to them. One of the boys told me that if I was a friend of Dr. Khan's, then I must be a very important person. I told them that I would be seeing Dr. Khan as soon as I got back to Karachi and asked where they were going. It seemed that they were catching a train to a small town further down the line where there were "many pretty girls and a lot to drink." The artist, obviously the leader, invited me to join them in a night of pleasure. In answer I stated that if I didn't have my appointment with Dr. Khan I wouldn't hesitate, to join them but I had to keep my promise to the doctor.

I took a photograph of the group and set my camera so I, too, could get in a group shot. Shortly thereafter their train could be heard coming into the station and I had just enough time to get the address of one of the young men so I could send six copies of the pictures back, get a hearty handshake from each and then they were gone.

It was shortly after midnight and I got back on the chaise lounge and closed my eyes. No sooner had I relaxed when two things happened. As the train pulled out of the station, someone closed the waiting room door and locked it from the outside. I got up and walked to the door just as the lights went out, not only in the room but along the station platform. I tried to open the door, without success. Then there was a clatter right outside the door. There was just enough illumination from the moon for me to make out the figure of a man with a rifle stretched out on the ground.

I managed to make my way back to my chaise wishing that there had been a rest room adjoining. So I tried to make the best of the situation by closing my eyes again, hoping I would be able to sleep until my 3 o-clock train to Karachi. It was difficult and I was only able to doze, fitfully.

It was the ringing of bells along the platform followed by the return of the light that got me up. I dashed to the door and found it unlocked. Out I went, looking for the station master's office. Finding it, I walked in and asked the fellow what he thought he was playing at by locking me in and putting a guard outside the door. It was the station master who had the last word. He told me that I was very wrong to send the guard back to the rest house, that he wasn't armed for nothing. He pointed to the strong iron bars screwed inside his windows and then to dozens of bullet holes all around the place close to the ceiling. I learned that there were bandits in the area and that they came down to the station almost every month to rob any passengers they could find. The previous month, apparently, they had found an Englishwoman in the waiting room and had made off with her possessions after first slitting her throat. I was definitely chastened and apologized for my stupidity and asked where the rest room was. There was more ringing of bells and I heard my train coming in. Once aboard, alone, the guard locked the carriage door and off we went.

Sleep finally came and I awoke to find the daylight streaming in. I washed and shaved in the small bathroom just before we pulled into a station. I couldn't get the window open and had to wait for the guard to come along and, in response to my rapping on the heavy glass, unlock the carriage. He was expecting me to want to get out because along came a boy who brought me a plate of rice covered with a nice curry sauce. I asked for some chapati so I could get the food in my mouth and he dashed off, returning within a couple of minutes with two chapati and a cup of tea. The train was in no hurry to leave so, after having my breakfast, I got out and stretched my legs. Even though it was only seven a.m. the station was crowded and noisy including the blaring radio. After a half hour stop we got underway. There were just two stops before we got to Karachi actually right on time.

I got into a taxi and went to the British Airways office. Mr. Fernandez was out but had left a message for me that Dr. Khan had been called out of town to one of his "digs" and regretted his inability to meet me. However, he had sent over the brick from Harappa. I seemed to have developed the start of a cold, so I decided to walk into the city center so I could buy some extra handkerchiefs. I made certain that I did not take my camera with me. I knew that the sight of all the vendors and people such as letter writers; astrologers; barbers; ear cleaners; etc. squatting on mats as they conducted their business would be hard to resist photographing. However, as previously stated, the country was under martial law and I didn't want to be arrested because I might have pointed my camera in the direction of some government building or other. Yes, it was as picturesque as I remembered from previous visits. I strolled along until I came to a row of stalls where I was able to purchase the handkerchiefs. Feeling rather peckish I looked for a restaurant, found one which really seemed like a club; and although the only non-Pakistani there, and looked at curiously, I had a good lunch.

Returning to the airline office, I found Mr. Fernandez had returned. We talked about my trip to Mohenjo-daro, but I omitted all mention of my not realizing that my guard was really that and that I had been somewhat foolish. I told Mr. Fernandez that rather than wait for the British Airways' plane the next day, I would like to try and get out that same night. He told me that K.L.M....the Dutch airline... had a flight at midnight and he was sure I could get on it. He had one of his men go with me to secure my ticket and stay with me while I did a little sightseeing and shopping.

The place fascinated me and I dawdled along taking in all the sights and absorbing the atmosphere. The airline man insisted upon walking half a step behind me until I stopped and told him that he was embarrassing me and I would send him back if he persisted in the "old way." We went into a store where I was able to purchase some recordings of Sindhi popular music as well as some traditional music. It was hot and dusty so I stopped at a stall that sold cold drinks. I ordered two lime drinks and insisted on my companion standing beside me instead of out in the road. The "locals" standing around just stared at us for a moment and then resumed their conversations.

Finally, we arrived at the K.L.M. counter at the airport. I handed the young clerk my British Airline's ticket, my passport and my yellow book in which was recorded my vaccination and inoculation against typhoid. I told him I wanted to get on their midnight flight to Cairo.

He looked at what I had handed him and told me that I needed an exit permit before I could leave the country. Also, a signal had come through that Egypt had just decided that passengers from Pakistan required a certificate showing they'd had cholera shots. That was a mess! Cholera inoculations required two injections four days apart. I asked if there wasn't an error since my doctor in the U.S. had checked to make sure I had all the shots I needed. There was no error. Apparently the Egyptian authorities had found a case of cholera among some recent passengers from Pakistan. What to do? The clerk told me not to worry but just to leave my yellow inoculation book with him, plus twenty dollars, and he would get a doctor at the Karachi hospital to help me. I gave him the money and he returned my passport and ticket telling me to check in at eleven p.m.

From K.L.M. my companion took me to the offices where I could get an exit permit. I had been in the country more than 72 hours and that was why it was required. At the entrance to the office complex we were stopped by a police officer who demanded to see my passport and had me tell him everything I had done whilst in his country. Where had I been? To whom had I spoken? He had both the Pakistani and me sign a register and then, after holding us up for fifteen minutes, he permitted us to enter the courtyard. We found the correct office on the second floor. It resembled a post office with a long counter and three tables each occupied by a clerk. One of them got up and came over and asked me what I wanted. When I mentioned exit permit he shook his head and said I was too late because they couldn't be issued after four p.m. I looked at his wall clock. It showed five minutes past four! I told the man that I had been held up by the police officer for more than a quarter of an hour otherwise I would have been there before four. He said he was sorry but there wasn't anything he could do and that I could get the document after nine the next morning. At this my escort started shouting at the official, in Sindhi, and all it did was to irritate the man. I decided that a little diplomacy was called for and grabbed one of the waving arms of the British Airways man and said, "Please be quiet. This official is only doing his duty. If the law says he cannot issue exit permits after four p.m. then there is nothing that can be done. I'll just have to cancel my seat on the plane and miss my appointment (which I didn't have) in Cairo."

This did the trick. The official, nicely, asked me why I had come to Pakistan. I told him I was there at the invitation of Dr. Khan and had gone to Mohenjo-daro to take slide pictures so I could lecture on this amazing place back in The States. I said I hoped my lectures would stimulate more tourism for Pakistan.

The official opened a drawer and took out a form which had already been signed and showed it to me. According to him I was absolutely correct and he didn't have the authority to give me a regular exit permit after four p.m., however his superior always left some signed forms that could be given to foreign diplomats who were on official business. He said that I qualified and taking back the form and my passport proceeded to fill in the blank spaces. When the

138

document was back in my hands, I asked the British Airways man to leave me alone in the office and, after he had started down the stairs, I turned to the now-friendly official and proffered a ten rupee bill stating that it was a gift he had earned by being so astute. He smiled, took the money and shook my hand wishing me a pleasant flight to Egypt.

We went back to the airline office where I checked the packing of my two ancient brick and had them shipped by air to The States. Then Mr. Fernandez and I put my suitcase, flight bag and camera bag in his car and went to have dinner at the hotel in which I had spent the first night in Karachi. After my dinner companion had left me I asked the hotel manager to let me take a bath in one of his empty rooms and suggested that he might do me a great favor by permitting me to rest on the bed until ten-thirty p.m. He was most agreeable and I revelled in the nice hot steamy water which went a long way to alleviating the constant itching I had been experiencing since my night ride with one arm around the tonga driver. My arms, back and stomach were a mass of infected bites and I began to realize that what I thought was the onset of a cold was some kind of infection caused by the flea and mosquito bites. At any rate, at ten-thirty-five I was in a taxi and on my way back to the airport.

I was the only one in line at the K.L.M. counter and handed my exit permit and my ticket over. The attendant worked on my ticket transfer handing it back to me with my yellow inoculation book under the folder. Peeping inside I saw the official stamp of the Karachi hospital with a doctor's entries showing that I had, indeed, received two cholera injections four days apart. Thanking the helpful young man for his accomplishment, I offered him a couple of ten rupee notes, the last of my Pakistani money. He refused to accept saying he was just doing his job of being helpful to a K.L.M. passenger. I shook hands with him and went into the departure lounge to await my midnight plane.

Now this wasn't the end of the story. Whenever I go on an extended trip, I always make a note of the names and addresses of those whose photographs I take and the names of the people who go out of their way to help me. I also make a note of the names of people who are unpleasant and obstructive. On my return home I send out photographs and letters of commendation to the employers of the helpful ones and letters of criticism to the employers of the "nasty" people. I wrote to the Chairman of the Board of K.L.M., in Holland, and without going into the details highly commended the young man at the K.L.M. counter in Karachi. Some two months later I got a letter from the young man telling me his manager had called him into his office, shown him my letter, and given him an immediate promotion.

The plane arrived on time and off I flew to Cairo where, once again I found myself walking into Shepheards Hotel at three-thirty a.m. This time there was no problem, even though my one night reservation was for the following day.

I just wanted to spend one whole day revisiting the Cairo Museum losing myself in the days of ancient Egypt. That night I caught another plane and slept all the way to London. By the time I eventually got back to the U.S., my brick from Mohenjo-daro and Harrappa were safe and sound in my office.

CHAPTER 8

PERSIAN MOSQUES AND CARAVANSERAIS

In 1971 the Shah Of Shahs, Muhammad Riza Pahlavi, ruler of the country of Iran...formerly Persia...threw what was probably the most lavish party the world has ever seen. It was given to celebrate the 2,500th anniversary of the founding of the Persian Empire by Cyrus the Great. The capital city, Tehran, and the remote ruined remains of Persepolis were jam-packed with very special guests. A fantastic white tent city was erected out at Persepolis with every modern convenience, with thousands of servants and foods, entertainment and luxuries of every possible description on hand for the convenience of the guests. These included most of the crowned heads in the world; ambassadors; film stars; famous actors and actresses; and members of the "Jet Set". In fact, anybody who was close to being "somebody" was invited to the birthday party.

After it was all over, all that was left as a reminder of this great event were a cleaned up Persepolis site and a massive archway called Shahyad Arymeher which was erected in Tehran. This is a fabulous piece of masonry which is impressive whether seen during the day or at night time when it is floodlit.

One of the past Deans of the University of Tennessee had presented me with a beautiful book on Persian architecture. It was fascinating and had several color photographs of mosques with exquisite tiled domes and interiors. Shortly after I had received this gift, I had lunch with a prominent Washington, D. C. architect whose hobby was the study of Persian architecture. He told me that in order for me to see the world's most beautiful brick and tile work, I had to go to Iran and visit the city of Isfahan. Our museum had one forty pound sun dried mud brick from that country dating back some three thousand years. That had been obtained through the Department of Antiquities in Tehran after two years of correspondence. When the brick arrived it was accompanied by a document written in Farsi, which uses the Arabic alphabet, and had six signatures appended. The document was quite lengthy and turned out to be the minutes of a meeting of the Archaeological Commission. The Commission had no head and all its members were considered equal, a fact important to this story.

I arrived in Tehran early in 1978 less than eight months before the late party-giving Shah was overthrown, but I saw nothing to indicate the turmoil going on among the country's leaders. To the contrary, all the people I spoke to, including some Iranian university students, were lavish in their praise of their ruler and his accomplishments.

An archaeologist from the University Museum in Philadelphia had given me the name of one of the members of the commission, and I had written to him and had an appointment the morning after my arrival. The flight over had been long and tedious with only one stop at which I could get off and stretch my legs, London. To make matters worse, the lady sitting beside me was an Iranian who had emigrated to the U.S. and was returning to Iran to try to collect some money from some government agency or other. According to her she and her husband, a diamond merchant, had owned a large farm which had been expropriated under an edict by the Shah and they were being poorly compensated. In fact, she said they were paid a pittance once a year and she or her husband had to travel to Iran to get the money. She "bent my ear" for thousands of miles. I did venture to suggest that if her husband was occupied with the usually rewarding business of diamond dealing, then it seemed logical to me that the farmland should be sold to several poor farmers who had no land of their own. That remark didn't sit well with her but it didn't stop her from cursing the Shah and everything Iranian.

Going through Customs was like being in a "flea market." Everyone had to put their luggage on a table and open it. Those who were Iranian born had all their belongings scattered all over the tables and on the floor by the officials. All packages had to be opened and their contents subjected to close scrutiny. Foreigners, like myself, were simply told to take our belongings and leave. As I departed, I saw my traveling companion engaged in a shouting match with one of the Customs men who had actually upended all her bags. I found a taxi and went off to the Tehran Intercontinental, checked in to a nicely furnished room, had dinner and slept until morning.

The next morning, a Monday, I strolled out of the hotel to see what the city looked like. The first thing I noticed was its beautiful setting with the snow covered Elzburg mountains stretching away to the north. The doorman of the hotel came up to me as I gazed upon the scenery and pointed out what he said was a very special mountain, Mount Demavend. The hotel was situated on a nice wide boulevard with a constant stream of cabs flashing by. As I walked along, I found it difficult to realize that I was treading the streets of Persia. Nearly everyone was wearing western clothing, and the streets had the same European look that I had, surprisingly, found in Turkey. A few women were to be seen, but no veils. The Shah's father had outlawed the veil some fifty years earlier. (When the Revolution came, nine months later, I wondered where all the veils the women shown on TV marching through the streets of Tehran had come from.)

For thousands of years this city had been a major trading center along the Spice Route from India to Egypt, and I was eager to start looking for some of the old caravanserais that had been standing in Tehran for many centuries. First, though, I had my appointment at the National Museum; so after three or four attempts, I managed to get a taxi to pull over and agree to take me there. Needless to say, that taxi plus the others I had hailed, had other passengers along.

As is common, Mondays are the days many museums are closed. This one was no exception, but I managed to get one of the guards at the entrance to look at my letter of invitation. He didn't speak English but he recognized the archaeologist's name at the bottom of the page and let me in. Using his arms and hands and fingers as indicators, he managed to direct me to the second floor and the correct office. I knocked on the door and a voice said, "Come in." The man inside obviously knew who it was that had arrived.

Entering, I found myself in a spacious, well furnished office with a tall smiling man standing behind a large desk with his hand extended in greeting.

I shook his hand and, using my name, he asked me to sit down in one of the comfortable leather easy chairs. First he asked how his friend in Philadelphia was, telling me that he had known him for many years. Then he asked how he could help me. I told him that I was particularly interested in obtaining one or two specimens of glazed ancient Persian bricks and was prepared to travel anywhere within the country if this was possible. He replied that there were many sites that had glazed bricks but, at that time, it would take the permission of the entire Archaeological Commission for me to remove any. Then he told me to be patient and leave the matter to him. It seemed that the Shah had decided it was time to appoint a Director of Archaeology, with all the attendant authority, in place of the six man Commission and that the Shah had told him, quietly, that he was going to get the appointment very shortly. When that happened, I was told, he would personally see that several glazed brick were brought in from various sites and sent to our museum. He asked me not to mention to anyone I might meet in Iran about his impending elevation. I stayed with the archaeologist for another half an hour during which he kept asking me about my travels collecting brick for the Museum of Ancient Brick and my relationship with various Directors of Archaeology, all of whom he knew.

After parting company with the fellow in the museum, I walked back down the strangely empty halls and out onto the street. As I had approached the museum, in the taxi, I'd noticed a car hire business close by, so I went in and enquired about renting a car with a both a driver and a guide. One of my stipulations was that the guide, at least, be a university student studying English or an English teacher. The rate was very reasonable, and I asked that the car pick me up at my hotel at two p.m. that afternoon. Since they had a branch in Isfahan, I asked them to make similar arrangements for me there. Then I found a nice looking restaurant where I had a Persian lunch. After that, I managed to get a cab back to the hotel where I washed up, checked my cameras and then went down into the lobby where I told one of the receptionists that I was expecting someone to ask for me and that I would either be sitting in the lobby or in a lobby shop which sold antiques. Promptly at two I heard my name as a page walked around. At that time I was in the shop but left immediately to meet my guide.

He introduced himself as a university student in his last year of majoring in English and Persian history. He said he was at my service for as many days as I needed him. Outside stood the car in which we were to travel. It wasn't much to look at, and when I saw its almost treadless tires I was rather skeptical about its reliability. I told the guide that I wanted to visit several caravanserais in the area and would probably need him until noon the following day. To his surprise, I got in the car and sat next to the driver while he had no option other than to sit in the back seat. I explained to him that this was my usual practice because I always seemed to slide around when in the back seat. He introduced me to the driver, another young college student who was also fluent in English. The two of them had a conversation in Farsi after which I learned that all the old caravanserais in Tehran had been demolished or converted to warehouses that were difficult to get to. The closest of these ancient buildings was at the small town of Karej located a few miles outside Tehran. "Good." I said, "Let's go."

142

We were soon on the way and I had a good chance to see a good cross section of the peoples in the area. In and close to the city nearly everyone looked European as they walked along the sidewalks past attractive looking shops. The guide, proudly, kept pointing out various industrial plants including a large Ray-O-Vac building, a couple of automobile assembly plants and a tire factory. He told me of a Russian-provided steel mill his country had just obtained. I noticed one plot of land on which stood a big rusting metal building skeleton. When asked about that I was told it had been another steel mill provided by the British but had never been completed. Whenever he pointed out the signs of progress he always gave credit to the modern western-thinking Shah. (Again, in light of the marches by university students against the Shah, just months later, this was really interesting.)

Not far away from Tehran, I began to notice more and more women wearing shawls over their heads. Then I started to see an occasional veiled woman. Obviously, as in Turkey where the wearing of the veil had been banned, the law wasn't strongly enforced beyond the metropolis.

Soon the driver stopped at my first caravanserai, literally an inn for caravans. Actually, this one was only half of the original building. The rest had been razed when the road was widened and paved. There was no way for me to get inside since the authorities had built a brick wall across the front of the half that was left. It was an unusual looking building and, from the road, I could see that the roof had been designed with several humps as though it had been designed to accommodate a camel under each. This wasn't the reason, though, because the roof was much higher than any camel. It was just the whim of the architect responsible for the design, some three or four hundred years ago. Along one of the earlier existing walls I could see that the sun dried mud bricks used had been laid in several attractive bonds (patterns).

Photographs taken, we drove on into Karaj where I saw several women wearing the veil. It was here I got a good look at a complete caravanserai, at least from the outside. It was built of well formed and well fired bricks; outside I walked right up to one of the many small alcoves built for the use of the camel drivers. While the animals and goods were under good cover, the drivers had to cook, eat and sleep in one of the arched alcoves. I saw an elderly man sweeping the ground in front of these alcoves, and I asked my guide to ask him if I could go inside the main part of the complex. Angrily, he denied permission. Then I tried offering him some money and that only made him madder. He had a conversation with the man who told him that there was nothing I would be able to see inside since the place was a filled warehouse. The man's wife argued with him but he wouldn't relent and went on sweeping. The wife, who was unveiled, had a little girl with her. The child had on a grimy cloak which even covered her head; and when the mother saw me photographing the alcoves when her husband's back was turned, she indicated to me that I could take a picture of the little girl. The mother removed the dirty dress from her daughter revealing a pretty curly haired youngster dressed in a spotless orange dress. I took my shot just as "papa" came up and shouted at me. The guide and I smiled at the woman and her child and got back in the car where we had a conference.

All the two students could come up with was that I be driven back to Tehran and shown the sights.

On the way back into the city, I had the car stopped at a very old brick bridge and asked the guide to find out from some of the old men gathered on the street how old the bridge was. As I watched, the fellow went from man to man until he came back and told me that no one knew the age of the structure. One of the men had told him that the bridge "had always been there."

We drove through the streets of the capital, stopping so I could get some photographs of the Shah's arch. I was really impressed by the design, its size and the quality of the workmanship that had gone into erecting the monument. We visited a couple of mosques where I took photographs of the amazing stalactite tilework. At one mosque there was a crowd of people standing around outside, and the guide told me that exactly one year previously an abortive attempt had been made upon the Shah's life and that this day they were having a special service of thanksgiving.

(A word about stalactite tilework. This is accomplished by attaching beautiful handpainted tiles to thin pieces of wood which are suspended from the ceilings of mosques, and other religious buildings' entrances.) Asking about visiting a bazaar, I learned that the bazaars were a development from the past when there would be two or three caravanserais built close together. While the caravans rested, the members would visit others to see what goods they had that could be bought or exchanged for some of what they were carrying. I roamed through one of the bazaars and then had the car drive me back to my hotel, telling the students to pick me up again the next morning. In the meantime, I told them to do some research and locate a caravanserai in another direction and that after seeing it, I had to be back at the airport for my flight to Isfahan.

Just before my car arrived, the next day, I checked out of the hotel making sure that I had a reservation for one night after my return from Isfahan. Into the car, and off we went. The guide had located a goodly sized caravanserai some miles outside Tehran in the opposite direction from that taken the previous day but, as we were driving on a narrow pot-holed road which passed through a small section on the outskirts, my fears about the threadbare tires materialized. There was a loud bang and the rear of the car swung around as the driver brought it to a halt. We all got out and examined the remnants of the right rear tire. I told the driver to hurry up and put on his spare. He said he didn't have one! The narrow street seemed to have quite a number of small repair and machine shops along both sides, and my two companions went from place to place trying to get someone to part with a tire and inner tube. It took them over an hour before they managed to persuade someone to let them have one. (It seemed that tires were very scarce in Iran, despite the fact that there were three tire plants in the country. The tires they produced were for military and export purposes, mainly, with barely a handful available for domestic use.)

By the time the haggling was finished and a new tire put on the car, it was time for me to repair to the airport for my flight to Isfahan. So the caravanserai was deprived of my presence. Of course, I was also deprived of my first look inside a complete ancient deserted desert inn.

During the 300 mile flight to Isfahan, I had to fill out a police form indicating my reason for going to the religious center, where I would be staying, and for how long. The form indicated that if I changed my address, I had to notify the police immediately. I put down the name of the hotel at which I had my reservation, the Shah Abbas. It was my understanding that this hotel, a converted 300 year-old palace, was really comfortable and staying there gave one the atmosphere and service of past palatial living. However, on my arrival at the crowded lobby desk I was informed that the hotel was full and that I should go elsewhere. This despite the fact that I was holding my reservation confirmation.

In company with about a dozen others in the same predicament, the manager was tracked down and cornered. He was most apologetic and said the hotel had been over-booked but there was nothing he could do about it. Having said this he bolted into an office and locked the door. While the other bedless people...a mixture of French and Italian visitors...hammered on his door, I decided to look elsewhere very quickly. I walked down the main street and quickly came to another hotel called the Ali-Qapu, pronounced "gapoo." It wasn't at all prepossessing but it was a place to sleep. The lobby looked rather dingy, and beyond I could see a glass screened restaurant with neatly dressed waiters. Behind the reception desk stood two very pretty girls, both about 18.

I asked for a room with a bath and was given a registration form. When the girl who took the form from me saw I was from America she said, "We like Americans staying in our hotel. I am Jewish and my friend here is Armenian." To this I replied with the Hebrew greeting used by Jews in Iran, not "Shalom" but two words that translate into "Blessed is the NAME." The girl's eyes opened wide and she replied, also in Hebrew, "Blessed is he that has come," meaning me. Then she announced that I was the first American Jew she had ever met and didn't think there were many in America. I was handed the key to my room to which I was shown by a smiling young porter.

The room was far from palatial, in fact it was dark with a double bed that sank in the middle. The paper on the walls was ready to pop off and the bathroom was in need of some new fixtures. As I surveyed my domain, the phone rang. It was the girl at the desk and she asked if I could go down at once. I thought there was a problem and went there immediately. What she wanted was to ask me if I would visit her home with her after she left work. This was a nice tempting offer which would give me an opportunity to see how the Iranians lived and I accepted the invitation on the condition that another member of her family would come to the hotel and agree to my visit. She said her brother would be coming shortly and he would extend the same invitation. I thanked her and returned to my room.

Then I remembered the instructions on the police form and decided that I should go around to the police station, immediately, and tell them of my change of address. Back at the desk I asked for directions to the station and the girls both asked me if something was wrong with the hotel. I explained the situation and both of them told me not to bother about it because the police rarely checked on tourists. Still, to me,"the law is the law" and off I went to make my report. The directions given by the girl at the hotel were rather sketchy; but I decided that the place couldn't be too far and, if I did get lost, I would be able to find someone who spoke English or French. (Many Iranians are fluent in French.)

Although the city center is small, it took me half an hour to get to the police station where nobody spoke anything other than their native Farsi. It was impossible to communicate anything at all. I was led into a room, which held a single chair, and locked in!

After about fifteen minutes the door was unlocked and in came two uniformed officers accompanied by someone in plain clothes. The last was, apparently, an officer who tried to get some sense out of me but there was no mutual language. The fellow became exasperated and spoke to the two uniformed men who came over, each taking an arm, and led me into an office which contained a desk, two chairs and a telephone. I was invited to sit down while the officer made a phone call. He spoke for a few minutes with his voice getting louder and louder and his free hand waving in all directions. Finally, he hung up and sat staring at me obviously wondering what to do next. Suddenly he called out and in came another uniformed policeman to whom he gave some instructions. This fellow then smiled at me and beckoned for me to follow him. We went outside where he removed a bicycle from a rack, took hold of my arm with one hand while he wheeled the bike with the other. We went down the alley, at the end of which the police station was situated, and out onto the main street.

I had no idea of what was in store for me other than the faint hope that he was taking me to someone who could speak English. This was correct. We came to a bank in which was a young lady who spoke fluent English. She listened to the officer first and then asked me what trouble I was in. I explained that I just wanted to report my change of address, but she wanted to know why I had gone to the second hotel. When told of the failure of the manager to provide me with the accommodations I had reserved, and paid for in advance, the young lady said that the policeman would take me to the Shah Abbas hotel and get the matter straightened out. I told her to tell the officer that I was quite satisfied with my room at the Aliqapu and to forget the whole thing. Nothing doing! As she translated my words the policeman became angrier and angrier and the bank girl told me that the Shah Abbas was going to give me a room or the manager was going to prison. So I was led back to the hotel. On the way, I managed to look around me and saw, dominating the scene, the gorgeous dome of the mosque of Shah Abbas the Great, (ruler from 1587 to 1628) which had been the main drawing attraction for my visit to Isfahan.

The manager was in the lobby when we got to the hotel; and when he saw me with the policeman, his jaw dropped. I walked over to him and said,

"So, you refused to honor a prepaid reservation and now you will find out what the penalty is for mistreating overseas visitors." I had no intention of having him dragged off to jail but I wanted him to squirm for a few minutes.

The policeman started to berate him and four arms started to wave violently in the air as the conversation continued. The manager appealed to me and said he didn't have any room at all and didn't know what to do. I told him to let me have his personal room and that would satisfy me. He rolled his eyes and told me he had a special suite for the use of his family and they would all have to leave if I insisted on that course.

Deciding he had been sufficiently scared, I told him that if he would refund the money I had paid in the U.S. for my room, I would agree to go elsewhere. He protested that he didn't have the authority to give me a refund and it would have to be handled by mail. I turned to the policeman and shook my head, pointed to the manager and crossed my wrists to indicate handcuffs. That worked. The manager shouted out "O.K.! O.K.! Sir, I will give you your money" and I uncrossed my wrists and put my arm between the two men. The manager disappeared through a door and came out behind the registration desk. I got my money back, in Iranian rials, at the correct exchange rate and left the hotel after shaking hands with both the manager and, of course, the policeman.

It is interesting to note that a couple of days later when I was photographing some old palaces and gardens, I met a group of French tourists who had been in the Shah Abbas lobby at the time I had checked in. When I asked the leader if he would object if I asked one of his pretty young charges to stand so I could get her in the foreground of one picture, he agreed and said he remembered me from the hotel and the fact that I had been unable to get a room. He told me that I was very lucky because even though the lobby was nice, everything else was terrible. The toilets were mostly stopped up; the water pressure was so poor that the showers didn't work; the food was bad, with some of his girls complaining of finding insects in their food; and the service was very poor.

I walked back to the Ali-Qapu where I found the Jewish receptionist, and her brother, awaiting my return. The brother, a university student, greeted me and said I would be very welcome at his parents' home but he thought I would enjoy meeting his uncle more. So I left the hotel with just the girl, who insisted upon holding my hand as we walked down the street. At first, I was embarrassed but soon resigned myself and warmed up to the situation. She led me through a maze of streets to a door in the middle of a row of two story shops. Upstairs we went and through another door which opened into what seemed like a doctor's waiting room. That's what it was! Her uncle was a pediatrician and around the room sat half a dozen women with one or two children with each of them. After a few minutes just standing there, the inner door opened and out came a woman with a child followed by the doctor in his white coat. His niece ran up to him, kissed him and led me into the office. Despite the fact that he had patients waiting, in flawless English he asked me to have a seat. The girl said she would see me later that night and left us.

The doctor asked me what part of the States I was from and told me that he had practiced for over three years in Maryland. He commented on my accent and said I was obviously from the north of England, possibly Yorkshire. Asked how he could tell so accurately, he said he had also been in practice in York, England, for a few years. York is only 23 miles from my birthplace and our conversation turned into an "old hometown reunion." He told me that he wanted me to visit his home that evening and then go with him to a Jewish wedding. It was arranged that he would pick me up at six-thirty. I left him and, surprisingly, managed to find my way back to my hotel. Once there, the first thing I did was to telephone the car rental office to tell them that I was to be picked up at the

Ali-Qapu and hoped that they had a good guide for me and, equally as important, a car with good tires plus a spare. Then I went into the dining room and had a very tasty Middle Eastern dinner complete with my favorite, stuffed grape leaves. The waiter was pleasant and efficient and, after the meal asked me if I would take his photograph. (He had seen me photograph the girls on the reception desk, earlier.) I told him I would do it when I came down for breakfast the next morning.

So, I was going to a wedding! What a stroke of luck. The Jews in Persia (Iran) had been there for two thousand years ever since Cyrus the Great had released them from their exile in Babylon. At that time he let those who wanted to go back to the land of Israel return there, while those who wanted to go and live in his land of Persia were welcome there. For the two millennia they had been there, the Jews in Persia had led an almost trouble-free existence.

Promptly at six-thirty I was picked up by the Pediatrician and driven to his home. It was nice and comfortable and there were Persian carpets and rugs all over the place. In his living room, where I was introduced to his wife and children, there were six carpets underfoot. Carpets were draped over a settee, rolled up and set on end in corners. I asked the doctor the reason for so many beautiful carpets and rugs. He told me that apart from oil, Persian carpets were Iran's only things of value; and a lot more stable than bank accounts. I felt that he was trying to tell me something and I got my first hint that all was not well with Iran. I recalled that, during the war, I had sailed into the Persian Gulf and had been in the port of Abadan, then operated by the now non-existent Anglo-Iranian Oil Company. I had found out from the British residents, who would serve seven year terms before going home on leave, that gasoline was free, water was a nickel a gallon and that the Britishers would put all their money into Persian rugs which brought a goodly profit back home.

My host's wife served a delicious dessert which the doctor and I put away with a couple of drinks. Then, after a couple of cups of Turkish coffee we left for the wedding. I told the doctor that I felt like a gate-crasher but he shut me up by saying that the bride was the granddaughter of an old friend of his who knew I was coming and that I was to be the "guest of honor." A short drive and then we parked the car. We walked down a couple of side streets and came to the entrance to a large walled garden. Two policemen were acting as guards and they greeted my host with handshakes. Through the gate I found the entire garden covered over by a large tent, some twenty feet high. Around the garden were a large number of benches and chairs which were occupied by women and girls. The doctor and I walked on towards the back of the house which had, somehow, been opened to expose all the inside rooms. Just before we came to the steps leading inside the house, my girl from the hotel desk popped up from a bench, gave me a peck on the cheek and said I would enjoy the wedding.

Inside, the place was crammed with small tables with four people to a table. They were seated in a strange way. Two men along one side and one at each end. The fourth side was unoccupied. (Remember, the women were all outside. In Orthodox Judaism the men and women are separated during religious services and ceremonies.) A few moments after the doctor and I were seated at a table, with our backs to the wall, the bride's parents and grandparents came up to us and, as they spoke in Farsi, the doctor had to translate for me. They were welcoming me and said they were very honored that I would take time to attend their celebration. I asked the doc to tell them that I was the one who was honored and very grateful to be invited.

The night was cool and even inside the house it was a little chilly. Even when a group of half a dozen belly dancers started wriggling their way throughout the crowded rooms, pausing to give a couple of extra shakes at my table, it didn't take the chill off. Patiently, I awaited the beginning of the marriage ceremony. I looked in vain for signs of the traditional wedding canopy. Then, after about an hour, I heard the sound of chanting and could make out the words of the ceremony in Sephardic Hebrew. Then I saw the canopy. It was formed by four men upon whose shoulders sat a small boy each holding a corner of a prayer shawl. I was able to follow the short service which, in this case, had two breaks. I heard the Rabbi chanting the blessing over wine and before too long a large metal bowl of wine was passed around the tables. Each person took a sip and when it arrived at our table I looked at my companion who could understand my apprehension because he said, "It's alcohol so the bowl is sterilized." I took my quick sip and passed the wine along. Half an hour later, the ceremony was continued and, again, the bowl of blessed wine was passed around. This time I took a good drink hoping it would warm me up.

Food was brought to the tables. It consisted of roasted chickens accompanied by scallions, parsley, large slices of strong raw onions and bread. There were no knives and forks. It was a matter of "fingers were made before forks." I had just torn into a chicken breast when up came the brand new bride and groom who not only thanked me for being with them on their special occasion but also asked me to honor them by signing the wedding contract, which was being carried by the Rabbi. I wiped my greasy fingers clean and took the pen and signed my name in Hebrew. This caused quite a bit of amazement. An American who could write Hebrew! Whatever other miracles still existed? The food kept coming, but nothing hot to drink, and the belly dancers were at it again and again. I had never before seen so many writhing navels at one time. The doctor and I had kept up a running question and answer session for hours, and I had learned a lot, but when midnight came I told him that I was about to fall asleep and asked him to take me back to my hotel.

It had been quite a day, starting in Tehran with the blowout, the flight to Isfahan, the mess at the first hotel, the experience with the police and, finally, the four hour wedding celebration which was attended by 300 people. I deserved a good night's rest, and I got it.

The next morning, true to my promise, after breakfast I took a photograph of my waiter and then one of a second who came up and asked for one to be taken of him. My cameras were loaded and I got back into the lobby just as a young man came in and asked for me. It was my guide. This fellow, like my previous guide, was majoring in English. The driver of a healthier looking car than that in Tehran also spoke English.

The guide told me that he had been told by the office in Tehran that I was interested in going into the desert to visit an old caravanserai. The fellow said he knew just where to take me but suggested that, first, I spend some time in

149

Isfahan which he said was popularly known as "Half the World." This was fine with me and we started off by visiting a couple of mosques. They were both located in what the Iranians call "The Maidan," a huge rectangular park some 550 yards long with flower gardens and pools.

The most imposing of the mosques was the Shah Mosque which stood at the end of "the maidan" and was entered through a huge gateway covered with blue tiles decorated with geometrical patterns. Inside, the mosque was beautifully tiled and had some attractive calligraphy overhead. The Sheik Lutf Allah Mosque, situated halfway down the "maidan," was built by Abbas the Great in honor of his revered father-in-law and was used as his private oratory. The interior had the ceiling and walls covered with blue tiles except where verses from the Koran had been painted in the beautiful script of a famous calligrapher. Here, I managed to get a photograph of the ceilings and the calligraphy. How I managed to end up with a nice detailed slide when my flash did not appear to reach too far, I don't know. Luck, I guess.

There is a special reason for the preponderance of blue tiles. The minerals from which the blue pigment was extracted were the most expensive of all and the builders of the mosques wanted nothing but the best for their places of worship. Another interesting fact is behind the reason for Persia having so many mosques, many of them deserted and unused. Each shah, on succeeding to the throne, wanted to build a mosque of his own that would outdo those of his predecessors.

After returning to my hotel for lunch, I was driven out to where stood some 16th and 17th century palaces. There was the palace of Ali-Qapu, after whom my hotel was named, which used to be the seat of government. It stands on a large piece of land, has a reception hall capable of holding over 200 courtiers and which gives one a great view of all of Isfahan's mosques, domes and minarets. The interior is covered with murals executed in polychrome relief and I spent quite some time moving around examining the simple designs. The grandest sight was the Chihil Sutan, generally called the "Palace of Forty Columns." The name is really misleading because when I looked across its reflecting pool, I could count no more than 20 columns, each made from a complete sycamore trunk. I tried hard to find extra columns or places where they might, once, have stood. Then my smiling guide told me to look at the reflection of the palace. There they were! The extra 20 columns, a reflection of those above the pool. The palace interior walls were covered with large paintings of a shah doing a little entertaining with plenty of loaves of bread, jugs of wine and the "usual." It was at this place that I met the French group, and my conversation with the leader made me change my plans for my evening meal. I had decided to have my dinner at the Shah Abbas Hotel; but after hearing the Frenchman's recitation of the problems at that place, I decided to eat "at home" at the Ali-Qapu.

In the cool of the evening I wandered the quiet streets of Isfahan stopping to purchase a hand painted tile at a special tile shop. The prices of their tiles ranged from about a dollar to thirty dollars! I found a bazaar which was a little noisy due to the banging of the various metal workers. Not surprisingly, the place was just like a Turkish bazaar.

My car with the driver and guide was waiting outside for me when I stepped out of the hotel the following morning. As usual, I hopped into the right front seat and we drove down to the Zaindeh River which we crossed by driving on a solidly built three-tiered stone bridge some 300 years old. As we crossed I saw another very handsome bridge, used on our return, which had 33 arches. Within a matter of minutes we were in the desert. Talk about barrenness! Over to the west, miles away, I could see desolate mountains while the ground on either side of our road was nothing but sand and stone. Very occasionally, I saw a small weedy looking plant. Then, some five miles out I espied a stone enclosure above whose walls I could see lush green tree tops. This, I was told, was one of several in the area which were communal garden plots laboriously watered by the group bringing buckets of the precious liquid from their wells. I asked about fruit thieves. Yes, they would climb inside; but whenever one was caught, he somehow was never seen again. Sand and more sand that's all there was.

After about an hour the car left the road and veered westward across the sand where all I could see was what appeared to be a collection of very large anthills a few mile away. As we got closer, I found we were approaching a mudwalled village with several ancient watch towers built into the walls. My guide told me that the village, called Mariya, was over five hundred years old and worth looking at, if the villagers would let us in. The gates in the wall were open and we drove in. There was nobody to be seen. There were low mud built dwellings all around but none seemed to have any windows. I got out of the car and walked ahead and got a glimpse of a couple of little girls who laughed at me and then disappeared somewhere. I looked up at the watch towers and realized that they were obviously disused. My guide had come up to me and got my attention by tapping me on the shoulder and then pointing down a short narrow lane to where about a dozen youngsters were congregated. I walked towards them, but they didn't run away and waited for me to get right up to them. Then there appeared a chubby man, about 50 years old, dressed in western garb.

My guide had a short conversation with him. He then told me that the old man was suspicious of us and wanted to know what we wanted. Told all I wanted was to take a few photographs, the man indicated that I could shoot as many buildings as I wished and that it was alright for me to photograph the children, but not him. I got the group of happy looking kids arranged while the man, probably the chief man of the village, stood off to one side. When I looked through my lens I could see all the children and, because I was using a wide angle lens, also the man standing where he thought he wouldn't be in camera range. I took a couple of shots and walked over to the man and shook hands with him. The guide informed me that we were just a few minutes away from the caravanserai; and that the villager was insisting that he go along with us. Apparently, the villagers kept some animals at the caravanserai and he thought it would be a good opportunity to check on them. I was agreeable and the fellow got into the back of the car.

Soon after departing the village, in the distance I saw a long low-lying building standing all alone in the desert. It was my caravanserai. I stood before the two huge gates guarding the entrance and, looking up, noticed that the archway was just like the entrance to the mosques I had visited. There were the remains of stalactite tilework and, very important, a small panel with a painting of a peacock's feathers. This sign indicated to Moslems that it was in order for them to say their five-times-a-day prayers inside the caravanserai. While the villager unlocked the gates, I walked along the massive walls built with beautifully dressed granite. The place was tremendous; and when I finally walked into the courtyard, I was prepared for its vastness.

In the center was a covered well while two sides of the courtyard were constructed with brick alcoves for the travelers to live in. I could see the sootiness left by innumerable fires used for cooking and warmth during several centuries. At the far end I could see the entrance to storerooms and the camel stalls. These, of course, were fully enclosed because it was more important that the goods and animals be better protected than the drivers. I followed the others into the animal stalls where the man from the village was pitching some kind of fodder to half a dozen cows. The place was very dimly lit, since the only light was that which came through the doorway. I told my guide and the driver to leave me alone in the courtyard. Perching myself in one of the alcoves I closed my eyes and tried to recreate the arrival of a caravan with the snortings of camels and the shouting of the drivers as they unloaded the bales of silk and sacks of exotic spices from their beasts of burden and drove them towards the well. So, there I was imagining myself in the same spot 500 years previously until I was brought back to this century by the guide telling me it was time to return to Isfahan where there was more to be seen.

On the way back to Isfahan we stopped at a large stone tomb in the shape of a two story building. The place had been the home of a very holy man to whom people, two hundred years earlier, had traveled hundreds of miles just to hear him read and expound on the Koran. When he died he was buried under the building which was then sealed up. We passed a little mosque with two small minarets decorated with blue tiles. This place of worship, I learned, was dedicated to the memory of one of the descendants of Mohammed's son-in-law, and successor, Ali.

My guide and I talked about a number of things as we drove along. I told him, to his undisguised pleasure, that as a child I had read many stories about Rustem who was one of Persia's greatest heroes. At one point I asked him why there were so many students at the Isfahan seminaries. His answer was not to the credit of the Iranian clergy. He said that men who didn't want to do any real labor would spend just a few subsidized years studying to become mullahs. When they had completed their course, they would find a small village that only had one mullah, or none at all, and announce his arrival. It was the duty of all good Moslems to provide food, clothing and shelter to any mullah who settled in their midst. As to my guide's ambitions, they were to become a good English teacher and, someday, visit the United States for which he had great affection. The driver turned around, at that point, and said those were his aims, too. (Remember, this was less than a year before the Iranian students were shown marching through the streets shouting, "Death to the Great Satan.")

Our next stop was the famous Masjid Jameh Mosque, the oldest in Isfahan, which dated back to the 11th century. It is familiarly known as "The Friday Mosque." Each place in the Middle East has its "Friday Mosque," Friday being the Moslem sabbath; but although this particular mosque was no longer used, because of its age it retained the title. In Isfahan there is also a Wednesday mosque to which barren women go to pray to be blessed with children. It was just outside the entrance to the Friday Mosque that I saw my first veiled woman in Isfahan. In fact, I saw half a dozen. The mosque is situated in the oldest part of the city, and it seemed that the most religious Moslems wanted to live close to the old mosque. Before entering the courtyard, we stopped at a stall, run by an Armenian, to get a glass of nice cool lemonade. From the proprietor I learned that no matter which religion a person followed everyone had to pay a tax to pay for the upkeep of the old place of worship.

The courtyard was immense (196 by 230 feet) and could easily have held a couple of thousand people. Let into the wall, just inside the entrance, were a number of inscribed stone tablets. These were hundreds of years old and were various official decrees which were put where everybody would see them when they went to the mosque. A pair of young brothers stood in front of some of these tablets while I took a photograph. In the center of the place was a square platform mounted upon a five foot base. My guide posed beside it as he explained its purpose. It is the duty of every Moslem to, at least once during his lifetime, make a pilgrimage to the holy city of Mecca. Of course not all of them can afford to obey the injunction to go to Mecca. Those who can afford it have to be instructed, before they leave on their pilgrimage, on what to do when they get there. They were told about the Kaaba, the holy shrine around which they had to walk several times and the "Black Rock", set into the side of the Kaaba, which they had to kiss as they came to it. The platform represented the Kaaba.

The mosque has four entrances with the largest and most elaborate leading into a spacious sanctuary which was built around 1072. The dome of this sanctuary, although 50 feet in diameter, is outdone by another dome which is 65 feet high and 35 feet in diameter and is often referred to as the most perfect dome known. The complex is a maze of vaulted corridors and rooms with brickwork displayed in many patterns. In the lowest part of the mosque, which was chilly despite the heat outside, there is one vaulted ceiling with brick laid in six different bonds. I saw a wall that appeared to have been burned and asked if the place had ever been put to flame. The answer given was that it was believed that the Zoroastrians, who venerated fire, had occupied the building at one time.

We entered a large basement storeroom where I found two large pulpits once used by the mullahs. They were platforms reached by going up about a dozen steps with the front of the pulpit and the sides of the stairs decorated with Arabic calligraphy executed in gesso. I didn't feel like preaching but I rested, for a few minutes, on the bottom step of one of the pulpits and had my guide take my photograph in that position.

I spent a great deal of time photographing the various brick walls and vaulting and took one shot in the bowels of the building which showed the daylight coming in from way up at the top through a specially built hole in the brickwork. It was so chilly down there that I was glad to get back up and out into the late afternoon warmth.

I went to the car rental office and paid my bill and gave nice tips to both the guide and the driver. I thanked them for doing an excellent job and promised to send them some of the photographs I had taken of them.

The next day found me at the airport at Shiraz, another old city further south, arguing with some taxi drivers about a decent rate to drive me out to the remains of Persepolis, and back. Naturally, the man I selected was driving a car with brand new tires.

Persepolis is Iran's most famous historical city and was the spiritual capital under the Archaemanians under Darius the First. Here are to be found the ruins of the palaces of Darius, Xerxes and other later kings. The city, with its defenses, was built on an immense limestone platform built from materials taken from an adjacent mountain. This was the place where the late Shah spent 20 million dollars on his "Founder's Celebration."

There were staircases carved from single blocks of stone with carvings alongside the steps that were much more delicate than later Assyrian carvings. According to my guide book there are still 550 columns still standing, but I didn't try to count them. I saw pillars that used to have a fascinating assortment of capitals. Examples of these; a lion, a griffon and a bull's forequarters, are now resting on the ground. Dominating the whole complex was the Apadana, a reception room of Xerxes. The Apadana had once been a hall with 36 slender fluted columns 60 feet high (a few were still standing for me to photograph) and able to hold ten thousand people. It had pavements of black and white and once had bronze and iron doors decorated with heraldic animals. One of the most imposing sights was the "Gate of All Nations" with its two massive carved stone human-headed winged bulls. There were reliefs all over the place with each figure clearly outlined and lifelike. Across the court from the Apadana stood the remains of the "Hall of a Hundred Columns" said to have been the meeting place of the Imperial Guard.

With my little guide book to help, I was able to locate the remains of the Palaces of Darius, Xerxes and Ataxerxes. Beyond the old walls of the city were the ruins of the palaces of Cyrus and Darius which used to be surrounded by great gardens. I knew that the old palace walls had been built with sundried mud brick which had long since collapsed and disappeared. I found not even one.

After spending three hours roaming around Persepolis, there was little doubt in my mind that I had been visiting Iran's greatest archaeological site. I had kept a close watch on the time because the commuter type plane on which I was to go back to Isfahan wouldn't wait for me, and I didn't want to spend the night in Shiraz. I found my driver asleep in his car, woke him up and got back to Shiraz airport with plenty of time to spare.

I returned to the hotel in Isfahan in time to get dinner, after which I spent an hour dictating about my day at Persepolis. Then, again, I left the hotel and wandered down the city's main street and saw the Shah Abbas mosque dome beautifully illuminated against the night sky.

I checked out early the next morning, said "goodbye" to the two pretty receptionists and walked out to find transportation to the airport. To my surprise, waiting for me were my guide and driver of previous days. They let me know that they wanted to personally see me off since they had enjoyed being with me on our tours and, when we got to the airport, they refused to take any money for the ride.

Two hours later, I checked back into the Inter-Continental in Tehran where I spent a day finding my own way around the city center and going down every little street I came across. An amusing incident occurred when I got a taxi to stop to take me to my hotel. Already sitting in the back was a Sikh in all the glory of his turban and jet black beard. We chatted about Tehran and I asked him if there was a large number of Indians in the place. He said, "There are some excellent Sikhs here and that is all that matters."

That was all for Iran, for me. I left hoping that the archaeologist I had met at the museum would get his appointment from the Shah and that our museum, in turn, would get some specimens of glazed brick. As is well known, there could be no future for my hope.

CHAPTER 9

INDIAN KNOTTED RED TAPE

The Indian continent is well represented in the GENERAL SHALE MUSEUM of ANCIENT BRICK; however, I received an invitation from the Dean of Indian Archaeologists, Professor H.D. Sankalia, to visit him at Deccan College in the historic city of Poona (Pune). He indicated that there was an interesting ruined Hindu temple in the vicinity from which a couple of 18th century brick could be obtained. Such an invitation couldn't be turned down!

I visited the Indian embassy in Washington and got the ear of one of the ministers who secured my visa for me and who put me in touch with the U.S. representative of the Indian Tourist Bureau. Arrangements were made for a car and guide to be made available to me in New Delhi, and my seat was booked on Air India.

So I found myself at J.F.K. Airport ready to board my plane only to be informed that although I could board immediately the take-off was going to be delayed a few hours. (It turned out to be a four-and-a half hour wait!) Not relishing just sitting in a stationary plane for an extended period, I asked if I could go to the Maharaja Lounge. Told that this was reserved for first class passengers, I produced the calling card of the minister from the embassy and was quickly given a card with which I gained entry to the sumptuous lounge. Knowing better than to drink alcoholic beverages before flying, I spent the time drinking orange juice. There were no seats with backs in the place and I had to sit on a very soft ottoman, getting up and walking every now and then to make room for more orange juice.

I arrived in New Delhi at 3 a.m. after having to wait in London and Rome for equipment changes. According to the pilot, on the last leg because of a tail wind our airspeed was 690 miles per hour. The airport was a madhouse. Apparently four large jets had arrived within minutes of one another. Going through immigration was easy but the capacity-filled Customs' hall was different. There were three lines which were barely moving. I tagged onto one of them and put my bags on the ground and tried to get to the money changer's. Here again the line was long,and barely moving. The man in the office was screaming at each customer who, in turn screamed back. I kept going back to the customs' line and moving my bags a couple of feet and then returning to my place in the money changing line. There were actually two windows with two men inside the office. However, only one man was working. The other was just sitting reading a newspaper.

After a chat with an English woman in the line we both barged up to the second window and together berated the "loafer" until he got on his feet and came to attend to us. Having got my rupees (about nine per dollar), I returned to the Customs line and impatiently waited and watched as the officer gave all the Indian nationals' luggage a thorough rummaging. In one case, a young woman with a child in her arms, he simply opened her two suitcases and dumped

156

everything into one large pile. This action produced a chorus of invective upon the officer's head from some of the Indians in the area. Interestingly enough they were all speaking English, not their native Hindi.

It took me two hours to get out of the hall, find a boy to help me carry my bags and camera case and get into a taxi. There was a second man sitting next to the driver, and as we drove out of the airport the taxi stopped at a checkpoint and each of them had to produce an identification card whose details were duly entered in a log book. This, I learned later, was to protect travelers from being robbed.

At 5:50 a.m. I was in my room at the Ranjit hotel. At first, the clerk told me I couldn't have my room until noon. However, twenty rupees ($2.20) changed his mind very quickly. It even produced a nice cup of tea. The clerk said, "Where are you from, sir?' To which I replied, "America." "He said "I had a man here from California. Have you heard of it?" Replying in the affirmative I then asked about getting something to eat. So a few minutes after getting to my air conditioned (a ceiling fan) room, a waiter brought me a tray with curried eggs and a pot of tea. Truly a divine meal. I then dictated all that had happened, had a shower and turned in and slept soundly on a lumpy mattress.

I slept until 1 p.m. and then went down to have my lunch. After this, twice, I telephoned the Tourist Bureau trying to reach the person whom I had been told would be handling my driver and guide arrangements. Nothing doing. She wasn't in the office. So I decided to go down to the Bureau. First, though, I wanted to go to The Archaeological Survey of India where I was supposed to meet with Shri M.N. Deshpande, the Director-General. According to the hotel clerk, this was in walking distance from the hotel so I set off and walked, and walked and walked. Eventually, I arrived at Cavendish Place, the hub of New Delhi. This was a nice shaded wide street with offices on both sides and several streets leading out of it to the old city. I asked the way to Janpath, the avenue along which the Archaeological survey was located. Apparently, I was close to it. Just before I turned the corner at the end of Cavendish, a young Indian man neatly dressed in western clothes addressed me. "Sir," said he," I have leprosy and if you don't give me some money I'll touch you and give the disease to you." I looked at his clear skin and reached for his hand. As I shook it, I said, "I am sorry for your problem but I think you have been cured." With that I walked on. At the corner I turned back and saw him bewilderingly looking at his hand and shaking his head.

At the Archaeological survey I got the usual story-"The very busy Director-General is on tour." Here we were again, running into the red tape morass. I was interviewed by an assistant to the Director-Generalwho passed me on to his boss who, in turn, passed me on to the Deputy Director. Along the way I was presented with an autographed monograph written by one of the assistants who was, himself, an archaeologist. Eventually, I was handed a very compli-cated form to fill out, in duplicate. This was partially done by the Deputy Director. He had entered that I would be permitted to arrange for export of a brick but that it might not be one I excavated but one from the same period. I was promised a five-minute meeting with the Director if I presented myself at his office the next day at ten-thirty.

157

Apparently, his "tour" was finished.

I asked permission to use the telephone and, again, called the Tourist Bureau. My supposed coordinator was still out. So I shook hands with all the friendly faces in sight and walked back to Cavendish to find their offices. I dawdled my way down the sidewalk, taking in all I could see.

The various peoples in a variety of dress. Many wearing western clothes; some wearing dhotis--the long loincloth worn by Hindus; and turbans, mostly white, with a sprinkling of the more colorful worn by bearded Sikhs. Noticeably almost absent were women. Those I saw were very poorly clothed. Unlike the Moslem religion founded by Mohammed in the 6th century, and Sikhism founded by the first Guru in the early 16th century, Hinduism has no known founder but started to develop some five thousand years ago. It was a Sikh, a big muscular fellow, who stopped me a few yards before I reached the Tourist Bureau.

He greeted me and asked if I was looking for a guide and driver. I admitted that I was trying to secure them from the official agency. With a wave of his hand, he dismissed that idea and remarked that the official guides would only take me on a set route. He offered me his services plus a car and driver at the same rate as the Bureau without any restrictions. I was very impressed by him and thought, if necessary, he would be a nice bulwark in a tight situation. The Tourist Bureau's lack of organization had already just about turned me off from dealing with them. So I engaged the Sikh and his driver on very nice terms. I told him to pick me up at the Ranjit at 8:30 a.m. the following day. He asked me where I was going after leaving Cavendish Place; and learning I was planning on returning to my hotel, shouted something in Hindi and out of the shadows emerged a man who apparently was to be our driver. In a few seconds I was in the car which took me to the Ranjit where I had supper, showered, did some dictation, and turned in early for a full night's sleep.

It was the sound of the muezzins calling the faithful to early morning prayer than woke me up the next morning. As I have mentioned previously, the call to prayer comes from the mosque minarets although the muezzins no longer climb the steep steps and usually stay at ground level and use P.A. systems to carry their voices.

When I went down for breakfast, I found my guide sitting in the small lobby. I invited him to eat with me. He said that he'd already eaten but would take tea with me. After my meal I collected my cameras and recorder and went out to the car. The guide said that since I had told him of my 10:30 appointment at the offices of the Archaeological Survey, we would be visiting just one great sight that morning.

I was taken to a park which seemed to contain several oddly shaped buildings of imposing brick and stuccoed bricks. The most prominent feature, a vast brick triangle whose apex seemed to be reaching for the sky, reminded me of the gnomom (pointer) of a sundial. That's what it was! I was at the famous Jai Singh observatory designed by the Maharajah Jai Singh, on the orders of the Emperor Muhammed Shah, and completed in 1710. The observatory boasted six buildings of which the fifty-foot gnomom of the sundial was just a part. The observatory can measure the time of day, correct to half a second, and the declination of the sun and the other heavenly bodies. Here, also, the composite instrument indicates the noon meridian at two places in Europe and one each in Japan and the Pacific ocean.

My cameras were put to work capturing the various components of the observatory and a couple of brightly-turbanned teen-aged Sikhs who, obligingly, stood by the historic marker at the entrance. (Several of these pictures later appeared in the Kingsport Times of Tennessee.) As usual, I got the name and address of one of the lads and later sent him two prints of him and his pal. My guide who, incidentally knew the full detailed history of the observatory, told me it was time for me to keep my appointment. So, off we went.

The Director-General of the Archaeological Survey, Shri M.N. Despande, was a very pleasant, friendly chap. After I had introduced myself he apologized for all the red tape I was encountering. Laughingly, he remarked, "You British left us with an excellent Civil Service organization complete with a million yards of red tape and we are still, ourselves, tied up with it." Remembering that I was scheduled for only five minutes, I had started the stopwatch on my wrist.

I was with the cordial gentleman for one hour and seven minutes during which time we had some tea and talked about many things connected with our mutually favorite subject, archaeology. We both had the same thoughts about certain antiquities being returned from world wide museums to their original countries. As an example, we agreed that if the Louvre, in Paris, were to return all its Egyptian and Grecian statuary to their original homes, there wouldn't be much left there other than paintings. Of course, this idea isn't at all popular with the world's museum directors.

Before I parted company with Shri Despande, he signed the form given to me on the previous day. This, apparently, gave me permission to collect and export one ancient or historic brick. He told me that there was one thing left for me to do, murmuring "Just a little more red tape." He escorted me into another office and gave some instructions, in Hindi, to his assistant whom I had met the day before. This worthy gentleman told me that it was necessary for me to dictate to his secretary a pre-dated letter of request for a brick. This being done, I waited for the resulting draft. It was handed to me a few minutes later. There was some resemblance between what I had said and the draft, but parts made no sense at all. So I asked for a piece of paper and wrote the letter. This was accepted by the secretary with a rueful expression. I signed the finished letter and, again, shaking hands with all in sight walked out to my car and guide.

It was time for lunch and I asked the guide to take me to a good restaurant. We drove back into Cavendish Place where he had the driver stop in front of a nice looking place. I invited the guide to join me for lunch. He declined and said he wasn't hungry. I insisted and told him that if he didn't join me I, also, would go without eating. Reluctantly, he led the way inside the place where we seated ourselves at an empty table. The restaurant was very busy but I noticed that nearly all the customers had stopped their eating to stare at me and my Sikh guide. I asked my companion why the great interest in us. "Surely," I said "khaki-clad westerners are not a rarity in Delhi." To which he answered, "They are staring at me, not you. These are all Moslems and not used to having Sikhs intruding into their 'haunts'." I told him to ignore them and order his meal. I understood, then, his reluctance to join me at the restaurant. There is no love lost between the Moslems and the Sikhs and other Hindus. We ate a leisurely lunch and then set out to see some of sights of that ancient city.

I was taken to a deserted mosque inside of which there was the lovely, but lonely, decorated white marble tomb of some long-departed highly respected Moslem. I wandered around in the small garden and then, despite a warning from my guide that it wasn't the safest thing to do, I fulfilled a longtime ambition and climbed to the top of one of the minarets. The narrow steps were filled with rubble but I managed to scramble along. It was worth the trouble for the fine bird's-eye view I got of the mosque and the surrounding area.

Our next stop was at the Rajghat, the place where Mahatma Ghandi's funeral pyre had been. From a vendor, I purchased some flowers which I took with me into the garden. There was a black marble low platform with a perpetual flame and decorated with fine flower arrangements, to which I added my small tribute. Several people were standing at the foot of the platform, quite a few with tears streaming down their cheeks. Not too surprising was the fact that although most of them were Hindus, there were a few Moslems there, too.

Just outside the Rajghat was a large bronze statue of Pandit Nehru, father of prime minister Indira Ghandi. Then, close by was a Sikh temple. This turned out to be one of the most fascinating sights I saw on my India trip. The temple stood in a small garden and everywhere I looked I could see decorations using reversed swastikas. The swastika was an ancient Aryan symbol and predated Hitler by thousand of years. Before entering the temple, I looked over to the old city gateway and saw what appeared to be the Star of David on two ancient portals. The star is also known as Solomon's Seal and was not adopted as the symbol of Judaism until the Middle Ages. Then it was in to the temple where my guide proudly showed me the several effigies of gods and goddesses to whom he prayed. Everything was brightly colored and surrounded by mirrors. The guide's favorite goddess was that of an elaborately dressed woman playing a flute.

Naturally, I took a photograph of her which, when developed, turned out to be the most amazing picture I had ever taken. The center showed a front view of myself taking a picture, while the subject appeared in a long line of mirrors which seemed to stretch into infinity. At the guide's request, I photographed several of the other figures and ornaments so I would be able to send him copies to carry with him.

Among the other places I visited in New Delhi was a cluttered complex of towers and foundations which was also the home of the famous non-rusting ancient iron pillar. Erich Von Daniken has a picture of this pillar in his book "Chariots of the Gods?". He infers that this was erected by aliens from outer space. Actually, it was a victory symbol erected by a 14th century conqueror of Northern India. As for the non-rusting, well, although the pillar is jet black I couldn't help thinking that it was regularly coated with a black substance to prevent rusting. This thought was prompted by some rough patches that show through underneath the coating. In the same place I saw a five story tile-covered victory tower, called Qatabminar, built in 1384 by another Moslem invader. It is 395 feet high and has 580 steps inside. At one time, people were allowed to climb to the top. However, it became a popular place for lovers' suicide pacts and, today, one can only get as far as the first story. There is an outside balcony but this is surrounded by barbed wire. Some time later, another Moslem conqueror decided to build a higher victory tower just across from the Qatabminar, as well as a fine mosque. Unfortunately for him, he was killed before the tower was more than about two stories high. The mosque was never built, although the foundations may still be seen.

An interesting and amusing incident occurred just outside this complex. Two turbanned gentlemen were squatting there, one of whom had a wicker basket of the type used by snake charmers. When he saw me, he flipped open the lid and started to tootle on his flute. Nothing happened, so his companion put his hand inside the basket and pulled out the smallest cobra I have ever seen. Then, from a small box he produced a large lazy scorpion. Nothing moved. The first fellow started waving his cobra around his head upon which the little blighter bit him on a finger. This didn't concern him at all. He simply sucked his finger and spat on the ground. Meanwhile the scorpion decided to move. It flipped itself over on its back and just laid there. I gave one of the men a couple of rupees and moved on. I had seen a snake charmer years before in Ceylon and had actually allowed the man to drape a very large cold cobra over my outstretched arms.

Before I left New Delhi, I located a firm of shippers and arranged for them to keep in contact with the Archaeological Survey and, eventually, ship my brick to the General Shale Museum. I also visited a spacious compound where I saw some fine craftsmen at work. In one building I saw a painter at work. In the next, metal workers; whilst in a third there were craftsmen working with wood and ivory and mother-of-pearl, turning out the sandalwood tables and screens for which India and Pakistan are noted. There was a shop in which I was invited to purchase unset gems at a quite reasonable price, and set stones at fantastically high cost. I entered a room devoted to the sale of gorgeous carpets. The only purchase I made was of a small 2-ft.x 4-ft. very tightly woven rug. The place was government controlled and I was given a receipt which showed exactly how many loops there were to the inch. This was to be sent to me by surface mail.

My plans were to spend a night and a day in Agra, home of the famed Taj Mahal, return to New Delhi and fly straight to Bombay for a couple of days' stay and then fly to Poona in time for my appointment with Dr. H.D. Sankalia. My guide and driver got me out to the airport with a lot of time to spare. I paid and thanked them and checked in for the flight to Agra.

I was fortunate in being able to find an empty seat in the New Delhi airport and sat down prepared for a 90 minute wait. The place was like a market with crowds hustling and bustling with complaints on all sides about the lack of seats. Every now and then some panhandler would approach me, without success. A small boy came up, flipped over some pages, and tried to sell me an illustrated copy of the Kama Sutra. I told him to go away. A couple of minutes later he was back wanting to sell me a book of photographs of erotic Hindu carvings, for which India is famous. This time I told him, very forcefully in Hindi, to disappear quickly. He went and didn't return. I decided to stretch my legs and found a small snack bar just around the corner from where I had been sitting. There was just time for me to get a cup of tea when my flight was called. So I boarded the plane and headed towards Agra which was home not only to the Taj but also a number of other fascinating sights and places.

I arrived at Agra in the early evening; and, as I started to look for a taxi to take me to the Clark Shiraz hotel, a slender young man approached me and addressed me by name. He introduced himself as a brother of my New Delhi guide. It seamed that his brother had called ahead and arranged for his sibling to meet me and look after me during my stay in Agra. The family ran a travel bureau! The young man was bareheaded and so slightly built that I couldn't believe that he was related to my sturdy muscular Sikh of New Delhi. Before he took me to the hotel, he had his driver take us to the Taj so I could see it in the moonlight. I couldn't get a full view of the mausoleum because the gates leading to it were closed. However, I saw the wonderful sight of the great dome and the four much smaller domes and the tops of the four minarets gleaming in the light from the full moon. It was really breath-taking. My hotel was quite luxurious. I quickly checked in, asked for a 5:30 a.m. wake-up call, with a Continental Breakfast delivered to my room at six. A short dictation session and then bed.

My new guide, and the car, were waiting for me at the hotel entrance. The first thing I had to do was find out about the relationship between the guide and his big brother, so I asked him if he was a Sikh. He answered in the negative and said that his brother was the only Sikh in the family. That matter having been cleared up, off we went.My guide told me it was too early to get into the Taj Mahal and that we would, first, go a place called Sikandra to visit the tomb of Akbar the Great, the grandfather of Shah Jahan who had the Taj built. Akbar, who became Shah at age twelve, got the title Great, not because of his fine generalship and kindly rule but from possessing great wisdom.

At the four-story mausoleum I found Akbar's burial chamber on the first level. His plain white marble tomb was covered and so I was permitted to take a photograph (a significant matter to be noted later in this chapter). Noticing that the base of the tomb was badly cracked with a hole in it, I asked the mullah in charge, "Why the damage?" He told me that a couple of centuries earlier Hindu robbers had broken into the Fort and got hold of Akbar's corpse, had stolen whatever jewelry he had been buried with and had torn the body apart and strewn the pieces over the countryside. The local Moslems managed to find all the parts which were returned to the damaged tomb.

After a short while we returned to Agra and went to the Taj. At the entrance we paid a fee and then I saw the whole complex...the mausoleum, the reflecting pool, and side buildings one of which was a still-used red sandstone mosque able to accommodate about 200 worshipers. The beautifully laid out gardens were in immaculate condition with lawns that would rival those of the famous English manor houses.

Many books have been written about the Taj Mahal and the fact that it took 17 years to build at a cost of 15 million dollars and is 220 feet high. What most people are led to believe is that it is the tomb of a righteous woman, Mumtaz, the favorite wife of the harem (that's what taj mahal means..the head wife of the harem) and her devoted husband, Shah Jahan. Well, Mumtaz WAS Jahan's favorite out of 2000 wives, during the last 19 years of her life bearing him nine children. She died giving birth to the last. What gets lost is the fact that she was a really vicious woman whose idea of entertainment was having two or three hundred people strangled in front of her. This was her favorite birthday celebration. She was said to have been the power behind the throne.

Regardless of all this, the Taj Mahal is glorious. Its typical onion shaped Moghul dome, slightly off-white, stands out majestically against the blue sky. If one stands and regards the building and the minarets for a few minutes it appears as though the minarets are leaning, slightly, away from the mausoleum. Actually they were built that way in case they collapsed during an earthquake, in which event they would fall away from the main structure. Shah Jahan visited the site every day during the construction. The white marble walls were cunningly decorated with inlaid semi-precious stones making a colorful floral pattern. Everything had to be symmetrical and when completed was just that. On the center of the vast marble first floor was erected an octagonal screen of fretworked marble, and Mumtaz' body was dug up from her temporary grave and put inside a beautiful white marble tomb, florally decorated like the outer walls. This was placed right in the center of the marble chamber. After Shah Jahan died his eldest son, Aurangzeb, didn't want to spend the money for a fine tomb for his father, to which he was entitled, and had the Shah's tomb erected beside that of Mumtaz which destroyed the symmetry. But all the foregoing was rendered meaningless because the tombs in the upper level of the building are false tombs, designed to mislead possible tomb robbers. The real tombs are in a small brick-walled chamber at ground level with the corpses, supposedly, buried seven feet beneath.

I say, "supposedly" because I believe that those two bodies were removed and robbed a long time ago! When I got into the real burial chamber, I was permitted to take a photograph of the two tombs, which were not covered in any way. There was the usual mullah in attendance, and I managed to corner him and asked him, "Excuse me, where are the Shah and Mumtaz really buried?" He puffed up and angrily said "You can see the tombs, can't you? The bodies are buried underneath." To this I answered, "If the bodies are still in their original places, why aren't the tombs covered like those of Jahan's father Jehangir, in Lahore, Pakistan, his grandfather Akbar's tomb just a few miles away, and that of the famous Mahmoud the Great at Ghazni in Afghanistan?" The mullah didn't answer; he just turned his back on me and walked to a corner of the chamber where he stood watching me in silence. I walked over to him and gave him some money. This mollified him and he produced a small flower which he crushed over my head as he muttered what I guess was a prayer. He handed me the crushed yellow blossom, which had a strong lemon-like smell. I still have this shriveled souvenir.

Of interest is the fact that it was Lord Curzon, the Viceroy of India at the turn of this century, who rescued the Taj Mahal from its badly deteriorated state using his own (and some government) funds. There is a fine hanging lamp casting light upon the upper chamber which, according to a sign, was provided by Curzon.

After leaving the Taj Mahal, we drove to what I was told was called the Baby Taj. On the outside were two mosque buildings, only one of which was truly a mosque, but I could see how it got the name Baby Taj. It was much smaller than the big Taj, but had one large and two smaller white marble domes. The doorway was a designer's delight. To obtain entry, I had to dish out the usual fee. I had been spending a small fortune on entrance fees, donations to mullahs and little children, and even thirty rupees to a man at the Taj Mahal for special services rendered. These consisted of covering my shoes with covers so I didn't have to take my shoes off when I went inside, fifteen rupees, and the same amount for removing them when I came out.

The mausoleum had several rooms with delicately painted panels on the walls. Most of them were floral and geometric patterns; however, above the doorway inside one there was a panel with a painting of five fish, two wine cups, and several pieces of fruit. The guide for the building said the Arabic script at the bottom of the panel said, "Eat, drink, and be merry." One room was devoted to the sarcophogi of the parents of Mumtaz.

Up one of the many staircases I was shown into the room with the tombs of her grandparents. These were not as attractive as those of her parents' which were of white marble but carved out of dull yellow marble which had been brought in from Persia (Iran) where they were born. This building, too, had lattice worked marble screens and ivory panels with gem inlays. So much for Mumtaz' family, but we weren't finished with her, yet.

We drove across the river to the Great Red Fort built by Akbar. This place was tremendous. The colonnaded courtyard was the biggest I had seen in any of the many forts I had visited during my travels. I imagined that that's where the public executions had taken place. In the center, surrounded by an iron fence, was a black and white marble monument in the shape of a sarcophagus. The inscription, in raised marble lettering, indicated that this was in memory of John Russell Galvin, the last Lieutenant-Governor of India's western provinces who had died in the fort in 1857.

Around the courtyard were small rooms which, in the past, had been used as shops tended by the local populace. There was a very large mosque in the fort. I learned that it had the largest capacity of any mosque on the continent. One thing that stood out was the fact that the interior construction was quite eclectic with Persian and Mogul designs side by side. Also there were columns with Greek acanthus-leaved capitals. The entire interior of the Red Fort, named after the red sandstone construction (this material had been brought from Jaipur, 140 kilometers away), was all brick, either exposed or with a plastered facing. There were steps leading to the Harem and other living quarters. I climbed several of them only to find the top blocked. I was looking for a very special room.

Shah Jahan had three sons (to speak of) and, as mentioned earlier, the eldest, Aurangzeb, had succeeded his father. Aurangzeb arranged for his other two brothers to come to an untimely end. When Jahan was getting on in years, Aurangzeb decided that his father was spending too much of the family fortune and it was time for him to be retired. This "devoted" son had his father imprisoned in a room in the Red Fort. His sole companion, and cook, (and whatever else you may desire to think of) was one of Jahan's daughters. They lived in this room for several years. Shah Jahan was fortunate enough to have been able to select the room in which he was to live out the rest of his days, giving him a fine view of the Taj Mahal, across the river. He spent his days staring out of the window looking at the last resting place of his beloved Mumtaz. Eventually, he became bedridden and unable to stay at the window. His cot was placed at right angles to the window and a mirror was hung on the wall so he could see the reflected image of the Taj. It sounds very romanticized, but it's true. Before he closed his eyes forever, the last thing he saw was the tomb of his adored wife.

Late that afternoon, I flew back to New Delhi where I caught another plane to Bombay. Bombay, built on an island separated from the Indian mainland by the Bassein Straits, is India's largest metropolis. It has a population of over ten million and is the largest deep-water port on the Indian west coast. I had a reservation at the Centaur Hotel which is opposite the airport so I just walked over there and right into a madhouse. The lobby was almost overflowing with some 200 Japanese gentlemen all of whom were trying to check in. The poor desk clerks were really being harassed by these people who were constantly told that there were no vacant rooms. I battled my way to the front and was immediately told the same thing. I protested and showed the clerk my reservation confirmation. This brought a smile to his face and he produced a registration form. The sight of what I was doing brought a chorus of complaints from those milling around me. I asked the clerk why they had such an influx of Japanese. He told me that they were passengers on a jumbo jet which had been taken out of service for repairs and that another plane would not be brought in for them until the following afternoon. Naturally, I felt sorry for these unfortunate travelers but that didn't help them.

A bellhop took my baggage and took me up to my room. After I had settled in, I went down to the lobby and found an assistant manager sitting at a desk. I arranged for a car and driver to pick me up at eight-o-clock the next morning. (I had been in Bombay a number of times before and knew exactly what I wanted to see and didn't need a guide). Then, since I hadn't had a morsel to eat since my breakfast, I went into the main dining room and had a meal fit for a Maharajah. After my dinner I went to the cashier and changed some paper money into coins worth about ten cents each. With about twenty of these in my pockets I went for a stroll in the area. The night was warm but a nice zephyr kept me comfortable. I had just gone a few yards away from the hotel when out of a row of shrubbery appeared a group of about half a dozen urchins. I had seen them playing around outside the building when I walked over from the airport and suspected that they were almost residents of the shrubs and shadows. They ran up to me with outstretched palms saying, "Some money, please, Sahib." I gave each of them a coin which I suspected was more than they expected and went on my way. I returned to the hotel after just 30 minutes. The youngsters were still in evidence but, recognizing me, they simply waved to me and didn't ask for more money. (They waited until the next day.)

My appointment with Professor Sankalia, at Poona, was a couple of days away so that gave me a day and a half to see what I wanted in Bombay. When I met my driver the next morning I told him to take me, first of all, to the Gateway to India. This is a ceremonial arch built by the British on the sea front and through which royalty and other dignitaries used to walk on landing. Arriving there, I found the place surrounded by hundreds of Hindus among which were TV cameras photographing, what I learned, was an annual festival of honoring a sea deity. Garlands were being thrown into the sea. Nobody bothered about me as I went right down to the front of the crowd and got a good view of the activities. Then we went to a district called Byculla. I had a very special reason for going there. Years ago, before Partition, I had seen a Moslem cemetery adjoining a Hindu burning ghat..where the dead were ceremoniously burned on pyres. I wanted to see if the place had been desecrated during the time the Hindus were chasing and slaying Moslems who were balking at leaving India and going to the new country of Pakistan. I walked into the ghat and looked over the wall. I was pleasantly surprised to find the cemetery in good condition, with most markers still upright, others slightly leaning. The grass needed mowing, though.

I had given the two keepers of the ghat some money, so they let me wander around and climb over a low wall from behind which I was able to take pictures of a pyre lighting and of an old woman bedecked with garlands of flowers, lying forgotten on a stretcher awaiting her pyre and release into her next life. There was a smell of sandalwood in the air, and I found out that was used for only wealthy families who could afford it. Also learned was that children under three are buried in a plot away from the ghat. After 18 months in the ground they are given a regular Hindu pyre, with their ashes scattered over the river Ganges.

Byculla used to be a nice residential section, with large apartment buildings with such names as "Picadilly." Today it is like a slum. There are streets of prostitutes who live in one-roomed cages..iron bars in the front. The local inhabitants gathered around me as I strolled along. I joked with a barber and a fortune-teller, and accepted a glass of freshly squeezed sugar cane juice from a vendor. What impressed me was the fact that, despite the dirty streets and the dilapidated buildings, the young boys and many of the men wore shirts that were laundry white. I got one of the young men to take my photo surrounded by half a dozen of the people. Before I left Byculla there were about thirty people surrounding me. My driver wasn't too happy about this and urged me to leave whispering, "You have three cameras, very valuable." However, at no time did I feel uneasy among these smiling people.

Among other sights seen during the rest of that day and the next were Malabar Park and a very colorful Jain temple. Malabar Park is on the top of Malabar Hill and was constructed over a great reservoir. In it are a number of fine shade trees and some fine displays of the topiarist's art: privet bushes in the form of an elephant and a pair with a sign "Cow and Calf" representing just that. Adjoining the park are two Towers of Silence, each about twenty feet high. On my previous visits these had been completely visible. This time I could barely make out the tops because of the trees that had grown up around them. The Towers of Silence are where the Parsees take their dead. Their religion, practicing Zoroastrianism, forbids the contaminating of fire, earth and water so bodies are placed on iron grilles in the towers and the vultures do the rest. I found the park a nice place to relax and do some dictating.

The Jain temple was impressive. Just outside there was a life-size figure of a one-legged mendicant. By the doorway was a large plaster elephant with a pink and gold cover on its back, and golden coils around each ankle. Atop the elephant was the figure of a mahout (driver). There was a prominently placed sign at the foot of the stairs which read, "Women experiencing their monthly period are forbidden to enter." The whole exterior was surrounded by pillars supporting scalloped arches. Here and there were three-foot high figures of religious figures from the Jaina pantheon. It was whilst I was standing in the gateway of this temple that I saw a strange figure approaching. He was dressed in white, with a piece of muslin covering his nose and mouth, and bent double sweeping the sidewalk in front of him, with a small hand broom, as he walked along. He was a Jain. In their belief of reincarnation, they make certain that they do not destroy any living creature, animal or insect, by any means. That includes swallowing a bug or treading on an insect. Although there are many Jains in Bombay, this was the only one I saw acting in this manner.

Crossing the various bridges between the mainland, where my hotel was, and Bombay proper I saw a sad sight. People living in makeshift tents on the sidewalks against the walls of the bridges. At one point I stopped and took a photograph of the scene beneath a bridge. There were communal open air laundries with hundreds of women at work washing their family clothes.

I flew from Bombay to Poona the day I was scheduled to meet with Professor Sankalia and checked into the Blue Diamond hotel. Modest, but comfortable.

I got directions and made my way to Deccan College and found my man in a large room, examining a five-thousand year-old brick kiln which had been excavated. The good professor was a pleasant, grandfatherly gentleman who introduced me to two of his field archaeologists who had just arrived. One of them showed me a small gold ingot, about two inches long and half an inch wide, he had discovered in some ruins that very morning. I chatted with the professor and told him of my visit to the offices of the Archaeological Survey of India in New Delhi. He commented that was just the beginning of the red tape I would have to cut to get my brick out of the country. Pictures were taken of my host and the ancient kiln and I was invited to the professor's home to meet his wife and partake of a little refreshment.

Mrs Sankalia was a lovely, friendly lady who produced some tea, fruit, and some English biscuits. I eyed the fruit rather suspiciously. Apart from the sugar cane juice, in Bombay I had kept to my rule of not eating any vegetables or fruit that hadn't been well cooked. Even my tea had to have boiled milk. The professor insisted that I eat the fruit which came from his wife's little fruit orchard. On the plate were an orange, a plantain, and two fresh figs! I was encouraged to try the figs first. They certainly tasted delicious. Then I had a cup of tea and a couple of biscuits. Protesting that was all I needed, I was urged to take the rest of the fruit back to the hotel. Her husband then showed me their garden and proudly indicated the extensive use of bricks for decoration. He gave me an author's copy of his autobiography called, "Born to Archaeology", with my name inscribed.

I returned to the hotel after arranging to meet the Professor at the College, the next morning. Naturally I was all agog about getting out into the field and retrieving a brick under such a famous archaeologist, who had, he told me, trained nearly every archaeologist in the country, including the Director-General. After dinner I began to feel some stomach discomfort. The figs were working. I went to the hotel manager and asked where I could find some Lomotil, or other medication. Somehow, my traveling kit was minus this needed substance. This was, probably, because I had never had a similar problem on previous trips. The manager told me that the malady was common in his area and that the local remedy was to eat an apple, one of which, minus the skin, was produced for my immediate consumption.

By the time I went down to breakfast, the next morning, all was well. I ate outside and made the acquaintance of a young man dressed in a saffron colored robe which just reached below his knees. I had heard him talking to his wife and realized that he was an Australian. He joined me at my table. I asked him several questions, all of which he answered, although he told me the way to attain true knowledge would be for him to give me half answers and let me work out the rest for myself. I gathered that he was a swami and, with his wife, came every year to Poona to study under his Guru. He would stay in Poona for five or six months and then, just before the monsoons came, go to England where he would work as a cabinet maker for six months to accumulate enough money to return to the aura of his guru for another five or six months. On being asked how long this would continue, he replied, "Until my guru tells me I am a wise man." There are several gurus in Poona and they are a welcome tourist industry there.

At the appointed hour I was back at the College with Professor Sankalia, ready to go out into the field. Imagine my surprise, and partial dismay, when he handed me two large 14 x 14 inches bricks. They were two inches thick, were identical and weighed many pounds. No inscription or design could be seen on them. The good professor said, "I thought I'd save you the difficult climb to the ruined temple and had one of my assistants go out very early this morning and retrieve these 400 year-old brick for you." I thanked him for his thoughtfulness and asked him what the next step was in order to get the necessary export permit. "Ah" he said, "Yes, the red tape with which I'm sure you are familiar, since you were born in England. Take these brick to the airline office and have them get the brick packed and flown to Sri Deshpande in New Delhi. I'm sure you have already made arrangements for shipment from there."

With the two heavy clay bricks under my arms, I found a motor cycle taxi which took me to the airline office. There I found a helpful employee who said he had a young friend whom he used for packing and who would even take them out to the airport for me. He left me alone and returned just about five minutes later with a barefooted youth. The boy spoke English and I explained how fragile the brick were. (Even though solid, a brick can break if dropped and the larger the brick the more pieces you end up with). I arranged to meet him at the airline office in an hour.

Meanwhile, I found a place to have a cup of tea and then wandered around the city center. Outside the railroad station there was a fine bronze statue of a striding Mahatma Ghandi, complete with his walking staff. This was a busy bustling city with a giant banner displayed near the station which read, "PAY YOUR TAXES-IT'S THE LAW." In the city center, the streets are nice and wide with plenty of room for automobile and bicycle traffic. The small two-passenger pedal cabs were plentiful, as were those built around motor cycles. There were several street vendors of sweetmeats and fruit pushing, or standing by, their light four-wheeled carts. Eventually, I returned to the airline office and examined the packing and sacking covered package containing my bricks. All was well. The boy had done a sterling job. The airline agent weighed the package and filled out the necessary form. As I paid for the freight, I asked if there was any possibility of it being addressed and shipped out of the country to the U.S. It wasn't possible. "Red Tape", the agent said.

I got my receipt and then asked where I had to go to send a telegram to New Delhi. I didn't have far to walk. In fact, the agent did it for me over the phone and wouldn't accept payment. The wire was addressed to Shri Despande and informed him of the dispatch of the brick and the name of the shipping firm awaiting his pleasure. I escorted the boy who did the packing for me outside and hailed a motorcycle driven conveyance. I paid the driver enough to get the boy out to the airport and back, and gave my messenger a nice sum for his work and time, plus a very fair tip.

I went out to the suburbs of this city which had been the most important British military center for over a hundred years. An old English characterization, popular over a fifty year period, was of a red-cheeked much "curried," pompous retired Indian Army officer sitting in his London club exclaiming, "Now, when I was in Poona etc." England was to be seen in the nice old homes which I found on several shady avenues I strolled down, that afternoon. These had been the residences of the families of military "brass hats" and high ranking civilian administrators before the 1947 partition. Several of these, with their extensive gardens, are now used as ashrams (meeting places where the gurus hold court). I found Koragoan Park Road where Shree Rajneesh and another lesser guru held forth to their swamis and other, as yet far from initiated, followers from literally all corners of the earth. I was permitted to enter Shree Rajneesh's ashram on condition that the lens caps would be on all three of my cameras. Being inside the ashram was a revelation! The "students" came in all ages, from infants to septuagenarians. The infants were part of entire families, some of which had traveled many thousands of miles to listen to the teaching of the swamis and, very occasionally, to hear a word at the feet of the guru himself.

There were scantily dressed groups dancing gracefully on lawns, or singing together. The bookstore, whose prices were highly inflated, was mobbed. From inside open-windowed meeting rooms could be heard voices, in a dozen accents, raised in heated debate. I had to sidestep quickly, a number of times, to avoid being bumped into by some reeling students who, apparently, were quite "high" and "walking on air." Leaving a men's toilet there seemed to be a stream of "high" men and youths the front of whose robes were quite wet, obviously, with urine.

When I emerged from the ashram into the road, I found it swarming with police, each man with a lathi, a long strong stick used in India to control crowds by beating the unruly ones. I went up to an officer and asked him what they were there for. "To control the idiots when they come out of the ashrams and start fighting members of the other ashram over there." (Over there was several yards down the road where the other ashram was situated.) "But," I said, "I thought these people believed in peaceful co-existence. Why would they fight?" "Peaceful co-existence!" exclaimed the officer, "If we are late getting here there would be stabbings and knife slashings galore."

Before I got to the end of the road I passed groups outside the other ashram. I was interested in the mix of races and the smell of hashish in the air. One fellow wearing a sarong started to walk over to another group, and I saw a knife fall from his waist onto the ground. My first thought was to pick it up and give it to him. However, I had a second thought and just walked on.

I walked down a dirt road and came to a large building site where I saw three young men chatting. I went over to them. One was a brickmason, one was a metal worker installing reinforcing rods in the walls, and the third was carrying an animal water skin over his shoulder. His job, was to see that the workers didn't become dehydrated. I told this fellow that I would call him "Gunga Din", after the character in Kipling's story of that name. All three were familiar with Kipling having read his stories in school and thought it a great idea. They decided that from then on he would be called "Gunga Din."

There was nothing left for me in Poona. After another pleasant night at the hotel I got its courtesy car to drive me to the railroad station in time to catch the "Deccan Queen", a train which travels between Bombay and Poona. It was worth the extra time going by train, because I saw some gorgeous scenery as we sped 120 miles through the craggy hills with several old Marathi forts crowning the peaks.

On arrival in Bombay I telephoned the Centaur Hotel. They had room for me and that's where I spent the night before catching a morning flight to England, for a couple of days' rest, and thence back to Tennessee.

The bricks? They are still in New Delhi wrapped in red tape.

CHAPTER 10

SERENDIPITY IN SERENDIP

"Embassy of Sri Lanka, good morning."

"May I speak to the Cultural Attache, please?"

"Certainly. One moment."

"This is the Cultural Minister, who are you, please?"

"Minister, I am the curator of the world's only museum devoted to showing the history of the brickmaker's art and I would appreciate your assistance as I plan my visit to your lovely isle to obtain one of its ancient brick."

"What is your name, and where do you think you will find your brick?"

"My name is Saffer, and I know that Sri Lanka has 99 ruined dagobas many of which were built with brick."

The voice then sharply asked me if I knew what a dagoba was. I said I did, whereupon the minister asked me to describe one. I told him that it was a Buddhist tomb containing the ashes of a departed person of note, plus some relic of Gautama Buddha.

"Yes" came the reply, "You are absolutely correct, but let me tell you that I am a Buddhist; and every part of a Dagoba, whole or ruined, is sacred to me. I do not like the idea of people standing and gawking at something I revere."

"But minister" I said, "It is not a question of just gawking at a brick but of people looking respectfully at a very old brick which shows how advanced your forebears were in brickmaking techniques."

"I am sorry mister, whatever your name is, but I will not help you. Of course you can visit Sri Lanka as a tourist, but I will see to it that you are not permitted to touch any of our ancient bricks."

"Well" I said, "I will go to Sri Lanka anyway. I have been there twice before and on one occasion played rugby for the Columbo Rugby Club and still have the scars to prove it."

There was a distinct change in his tone of voice. "You play rugger? This is very fine and I must do everything I can to help a rugby player."

I told him that I no longer played but was still a rugby referee and that I had written to Dr. De Silva at the Sri Lankan Department of Archaeology, in Colombo, but hadn't received a reply. After getting me to spell my name for him, the Cultural Minister said, "Mr. Saffer, we must discuss this matter very soon. When can you come to Washington?"

Four days later I was in his office where he told me that the reason for not getting a reply from Dr. De Silva was because there were several people with that surname in the Department of Archaeology and the letter must have gone astray. He informed me that immediately after my phone call he had sent a signal to the department asking the Director, Dr. Roland Silva, to extend every courtesy to me when I arrived in Colombo. I was handed a nice booklet dealing with all facets of Sri Lanka, from its ancient history to the places of interest visited by visitors to the island.

I gathered from the minister that rugby players were highly esteemed in his country and that the matches drew large crowds from the elite. I showed him a newspaper clipping I had saved from the Colombo Times which listed my name in a report of a match against the Royal Air Force.

Sri Lanka is a tear-drop shape isle just a few miles off the south east tip of India and has been inhabited since about 10,000 B.C. An advanced civilization started a massive irrigation system in the 5th century B.C.- a people which was quite thriving until its decline which started in the 13th century.

The original name of the isle was Sri Lanka. Arab invaders changed the name to Serendip. In 1505, along came the Portuguese who changed the name to Ceilan who, in turn, were turfed out by the Dutch in 1658. After 138 years, came the British who sent the Dutch packing. The name Ceilan does not come easy for an Englishman to mouth so its name was changed to Ceylon. A British colony, Ceylon got its independence in 1948 remaining as a member of the British Commonwealth. In 1972 the island was renamed Sri Lanka which means Resplendent Isle. This name change created quite a problem for the tea growers because they started exporting their product as "Sri Lankan Tea." Very little of this fine tea was sold. Few people knew of Sri Lanka and thousands of crates of tea were returned to the island. Nowadays, the tea is labeled "Ceylon Tea from Sri Lanka."

To get to Sri Lanka, I first had to fly to Bombay and then catch a Ceylon Air plane to Colombo where I landed in the late afternoon. I had a confirmed reservation at The Orient Pearl, a small hotel having just 30 rooms. I called them from the airport and within a few minutes a small car arrived to pick me up. On my arrival at the hotel, the fun started.

The assistant manager was a young man, tall and pleasant. However, when he looked for my name in the reservation book it wasn't there! He said there had been a mistake and that I had come to the wrong hotel. I showed him my reservation confirmation slip which didn't help one bit. The fellow told me that the place was filled and I should go elsewhere.

I asked him if I could use the telephone. I gave him a number and told him that it was the home of a member of the government (I gave him his name) whom I had been told to contact if I ran into any problems on my trip. The information had been given to me by my excellent contact at the University of California, in Berkeley, the late Dr. George Dales in whose Asian footsteps I had been following. The assistant manager was quite disturbed by this turn of events and begged me not to make the call.

"Either you find me a room, yours if necessary, or you will have to answer to a government agency," said I. "Please don't get us in trouble or we'll lose our license. I'll find a room for you," was his response. He gave me a room number and a key. When I went in I found two Japanese gentlemen taking a nap! Back I went to the desk and got another key. This time the room was, obviously, also still occupied because there were several suitcases on one bed and clothes strewn over the other. The next room I was given contained two hotel staff members taking a rest. I asked them to leave. They said it was their permanent room. Back to the desk, and another room. This one was vacant. I undressed and stepped into the shower which had a very large aluminum shower head. I turned on the water and looked for the soap. It was lying on the floor. As I bent down to pick it up, the shower head fell off and beaned me! Talk about being disturbed. If the assistant manager had been there I might have beaned him!

However, the nice shower relaxed me and I was feeling quite good as I walked out and stood, stark naked, in my room. Just as I reached for a towel, the door opened and in came two more Japanese gentlemen! I grabbed the towel believing that the world was full of traveling Japanese. They spoke English and assured me that I was in their room. To prove it, one of them opened a couple of drawers and showed me that they were full of his clothes. Out they went so I could get dressed and get out and back to the reception desk in the tiny foyer where I reached for the telephone.

"No! No!" cried the assistant manager. "Please go in to dinner and I will certainly, myself, move someone out of a room. We have a few of the hotel staff members who stay here rather than travel into Colombo to their homes. I will have the car take two of them home and bring them back in the morning. Tomorrow, some persons are going to leave."

So I went in to the restaurant and ordered my dinner. It was most satisfying and relaxing the only problem being the fact that I had to pay the waiter for the food before it was served, and not having any Sri Lankan rupees had to find the assistant manager and cash some travelers' checks before I could eat. Incidentally, the next morning they discovered my reservation form stuck inside the registration book!

After breakfast the courtesy car drove me into Colombo to the Department of Archaeology, on Edinburgh Crescent. I was expected and was greeted by Dr. Roland Silva, an archaeological architect who had attended a design school in London. I was shown into a large room where several other archaeologists came to meet me. The warmth of the reception was overwhelming. They queried me about the Museum of Ancient Brick and applauded our efforts to preserve the history of brick. One fellow asked me where I was staying and was surprised I had chosen a small hotel outside the city. I explained that I had selected it because it was on the road to Anuradhapura, the ancient capital of Sri Lanka, with its many dagobas and other archaeological sites. The decision had to be made as to where I would get my brick. The island was crowded with ancient ruins such as temples, ritual baths and pleasure gardens. I mentioned that I hoped to be able to see the Bo tree at Anuradhapura. They all laughed saying that I wouldn't be allowed close enough to see it.

The Bo tree needs some explanation. Without going into all the details of Gautama Buddha's life, I will just state that he gave up his life as a prince, left his wife and son and set out to solve the riddle of human misery. After six years as a hermit and wanderer he sat under a Bo tree (a Pipal tree) in southern India until, on the 49th day, he received "Enlightenment" and was then called "Buddha, The Enlightened One." A slip from this tree was smuggled into Sri Lanka about 245 B.C. and planted in a garden at Anuradhapura, where it grew to full size and is said to be the world's oldest living tree. It is very sacred to Sri Lankan Buddhists.

Back to the discussion as to where I was to get my brick. Some site maps were produced and there was no unanimity as to which of ten places the brick was to come. Then it was suggested that I get ten bricks, one from each site! I demurred, saying that just a single brick was all I had come and hoped for. The outcome was unanimous. I was to be given a brick from all ten sites! The very thought stopped me in my tracks. How on earth was I going to handle them all. I knew that each brick probably weighed between ten and fifteen pounds. My gentle objection was over-ruled. They felt that ten bricks was the least they could give me since I had traveled so far to get to Sri Lanka. My new friends told me to see the places of interest on the island and then return in a couple of days. Meanwhile, I had been handed a note asking me to visit the sports editor at the Colombo Times.

I was offered a lift downtown, which I accepted, and decided to have some lunch before going to the newspaper office. My offer to the man who gave me the lift to join me for lunch was politely declined because he had another appointment. I found a nice restaurant and was so impressed by the array of beautiful foods on the dishes put before me that I couldn't resist taking a photograph. My picture shows the surprised expression on the faces of some of the Sri Lankans who saw what I was doing.

After lunch I found my way to the newspaper office and met the sports editor. He said he had been apprised of my coming to Colombo and wanted to talk to me about the state of rugby in America. We talked about our favorite sport for about an hour and I surprised him by bringing out the clipping about my game in Colombo, many years earlier.

He asked me to keep in touch, and to keep him informed as to the growth of the sport of rugby back home. We parted company and I started to roam around the streets of downtown Colombo.

It had been several years since I had been there but somehow it seemed unchanged, despite the large hotels that had sprung up. In the center of the city was a clock tower with the hands showing the wrong time. I soon realized that it had stopped. Later I learned that one man had maintained the clock, at his own expense, for many years. Then he got tired of the job and asked the city to do it. The authorities declined, citing lack of funds, so the clock just stopped. It had been that way for years. From a vantage point I got a good look at the harbor, one of the largest natural harbors in the world, with several merchant ships tied up along the wharves. I felt some nostalgia since on my earlier visits I had come in on a merchant vessel.

On the last occasion, I had met a very interesting gentleman, a native of Belgium, who had settled in Colombo. He had a jewelry shop but was also a philosopher and had written thirteen books on the subject. His name was Menashi, and I had spent several fascinating hours with him. Wondering if he was still alive, I stopped at a curio shop and asked the proprietor about Mr. Menashi. He said he had been a close friend of his but that he had died just a few years earlier. This merchant tried to sell me an intricately carved piece of wood in the form of a three-foot handle ending in a ladle. He told me that it was a 400 year-old antique and had been used for ritual washing of the feet of the old kings of the island. I didn't even ask the price but did purchase three tiny

174

sandalwood elephants from him. Because of its cloying scent, this is my favorite wood. The merchant said that so many sandalwood trees had been cut down to make carved figurines and boxes, for tourists, that there were few trees left and that those were protected by law from being cut. I took a photograph of the man holding the ladle and continued my walk.

Sri Lanka has an interesting population of seventeen-and-a-half million. The Sinhalese, most of whom are Buddhists, account for 74%. They have their own language, an Indo-European tongue spoken only in Sri Lanka. The Tamils, mostly Hindus, account for another 12%. Then there are the Moors, descendants of the old Arab traders. These represent about 7% of the population and are Tamil-speaking Moslems. The Tamils are to be found mostly in the north of the island and have been demanding their own state and government. With encouragement from the Tamils in southeast India, this group has been resorting to violence in support of their cause.

During my tour of the streets, I saw many different peoples from white complexion to light brown to dark brown. I was able to pick out a couple of Burghers, descendants of the Dutch and Portuguese settlers, once a major business force, most of whom had left Sri Lanka since the end of World War 2. Nearly all the people were dressed in nice colored shirts with neat pants. Others wore western business suits. I saw an occasional woman wearing a sari and men dressed in white Indian garb, but no turban. There is a nice park and promenade called Galle Face right on the sea front. I meandered over there and enjoyed looking out at the vast Indian the ocean. Eventually, I got a taxi which took me back to my hotel where I had dinner and an early turn-in. Before I went to my room, however, the assistant manager approached me and invited me to his home for a New Year's Eve celebration a few days later. He told me that I would see something that few visitors to Sri Lanka had seen. He described what would happen.

Shortly before midnight the whole family would wail and moan at the departure of the old year, similar to a funeral service. Then, at the stroke of midnight, the home would be a place of happiness and joy at the arrival of the new year. It was a generous offer and I accepted, to his great joy. He said his sisters and mother would be making "many sweetmeats" for the occasion. I asked about hiring the car and the driver, a pleasant knowledgeable chap, for a couple of days to take me to Anuradhapura and Kandy, with an overnight stay in Kandy. This was arranged and departure set for 8 a.m. the next day.

The road to the north was nicely paved and smooth. Shortly after leaving the hotel, I had the driver stop at a place by the road where there was a group of young men dressed in dark sarongs. They were standing by some palm trees, each of which had cloth and rope strips encircling the trunk at some two-foot intervals. Half a dozen empty oil drums were in evidence and seeing that two of the young men had knives with curved blades in their hands I asked what was going on. With a wide grin, an older man came over and told me that they were collecting coconut milk to make arrack. I had tasted this local drink, once. Once was enough! Right after having just a jigger of it, in Colombo, I went to the cinema to see Walt Disney's "Fantasia" and saw it in psychedelic colors! To demonstrate how they got the green unripened coconuts down, one of the lads scaled a tree in less than five seconds and severed a clump of fruit which plopped onto the ground. Then, using a machete, each coconut was split and the milk poured into one of the oil drums. The man-in-charge offered me a taste of some fermented milk he had in a jar. I thanked him but declined. It seemed to me that climbing palm trees several times an hour could be very dangerous. It was, I was told. Every now and then one of the climbers would lose his footing and grasp and have a fall. When this happened, in many cases the boys fell on their knives and bled to death before help was found! I took my photographs, thanked them, and away we went.

We stopped again a few miles further on when I saw some young girls sitting on a fallen log by the roadside. Behind them was a flimsy home with a thatched roof and walls with a two-foot opening all the way around, some two feet down from the palm-thatched roof. After some cajoling, they gave me big smiles and let me take their picture. Off we went, again. I stopped to photograph a sandalwood tree which was growing sturdily by the road.

It was 130 miles to Anuradhapura, a very interesting drive during which we passed through several villages and small towns. Each place had a figure of Buddha in a small garden by the road. We stopped at every one where I put some money into a niche and took a handful of rose petals which I placed at the feet of the figure.

I noticed that there were pharmacies, galore, in the little towns. I remarked about this to my driver. He told me that they were not merely pharmacies but places that sold love philters and herbal remedies which would cure any known disease. Just to see what kind of places they were I went inside one. There was a well-fed Chinese sitting behind a cash register by the door. Now, although on this trip I had a supply of tummy medicine, I addressed the man and asked him if he had any"Lomotil." I didn't think he'd have heard of it so I was very surprised when he called out, in Chinese, to someone in the back of the shop. I only understood one word he said, "Lomotil." He smiled and nodded his head. I looked around his stock. The place was like a warehouse with shelves filled with a hundred bottles of different colored liquids, and fancy boxes stacked on the floor. The boxes emitted some strange aromas. There was no sign of any pharmaceuticals. Out of the back came a younger version of the cashier, carrying a small box which he proceeded to open. "How many?" he asked. "Twenty-four," I replied. Twenty-four little tablets were extracted from a jar inside the box and placed in a small envelope which was then handed to me. "How much?" I asked. "Five rupees, please." was the surprising answer. At the exchange rate at that time, that translated into about 40 cents!In the States the price would have been about three dollars. To make sure they were reasonably fresh, I looked at the box and found a date showing they were only a few months old.

Back on the road, we were at the Anuradhapura limits four hours after we set out. I asked the driver to stop just before the blue signpost and I took off my shoes. He looked at me wonderingly and said that it wasn't necessary for me to go around in my stockinged feet. My reply was to the effect that it was a holy city and to be sure I had my shoes off at the right spots I would just leave them off. I didn't know it, of course, but this was where serendipity commenced.

Anuradhapura was a royal city of Sinhalese kings for over a thousand years. In the 5th century B.C. it became one of the major centers of Buddhism in Asia, remaining so until it was destroyed in 992 A.D. by an army from southern India. The first thing that drew my attention, as we drove in, was the imposing top of one of the dagobas with a dome and spire that appeared to be covered with an aluminum paint. There was a walkway from the top of this building over to another dagoba. Before going to see more, we stopped so I could take some pictures of a ruined palace of which only several granite columns remained, some still standing and others lying on the ground, with a horde of monkeys climbing all over the place. As they chattered, they just ignored me no matter how close I went to them.

I asked the driver to park the car so I could proceed on foot. The path was of hard clay and the moment I stepped onto it I felt the great heat coming through my socks, searing my feet. I hopped around and made a dash for the sparse grass growing out of the clay alongside. Even this was hot under the strong sun. Still, I made my way to the entrance to the dagoba with the painted top and I went inside. The place was cavernous with dim light coming from an electric light bulb hung many feet off the floor. My eyes first saw a lovely figure of a reclining Buddha whose robes were mostly orange in color. The beautiful restful face had a feminine appearance, which is a feature of many statues of Buddha. There was a saffron robed priest in attendance, standing in front of a cloth covered table upon which was a figure of a contemplating Buddha. No words passed between us, and I took my picture and left. My driver was outside and walked with me into another dagoba. There, too, was a large figure of Buddha. This one was an imposing sitting figure. My next stop was at a wire fence that prevented further passage. It was erected at the foot of what appeared to be a grass covered dagoba until I looked a little more intently and found that it was made of bricks which was partially covered by grass. Over the centuries, earth had covered parts of the brick and grass had sprouted on it. I tried to calculate how many hundreds of thousand bricks had been used for the covering of this hemispherical dagoba and its spire. It was a masterpiece of masonry construction. (I was later given a copy of a drawing showing the details of the brickwork. Each brick had to have been individually cut so as to fit its neighbor as they formed a circle.)

As I stared at the mound, I looked down at the foot of the fence close to my feet where I saw a couple of bricks which had fallen from the dagoba. It would have been simple for me to take got one out but I didn't even reach in and touch either of them. This dagoba reminded me of the stupa mound at Mohenjo-daro in Pakistan. Incidentally, the words stupa and dagoba mean exactly the same thing. Stupa is used throughout Asia, except for Sri Lanka where they use the Sinhalese word, dagoba.

I retraced my footsteps, still very much aware of my burning feet, and came to a spot where there were six miniature dagobas, built of masonry which had been painted white, and which really gleamed in the sunlight. They were all in a row and were uniform in design and about four feet high. My driver said he thought these tombs contained the ashes of some ancient priests.

177

Sri Lanka has some lush growing areas but, also, some very arid parts. The wet zone is the mountainous center and the south west corner. There they have an annual rainfall of 146 inches. In the dry zone, the northern and eastern areas, they just have rain during three months amounting to up to 60 inches. Throughout the centuries, the Sri Lankans have built more than a thousand artificial lakes and reservoirs to aid irrigation where it is needed. Recently, they have diverted the waters of the Mahaweli, its longest river to the dry zone. The result has been an increase in rice and hydro-electric power generation. I found myself at the foot of a very steep hill with a long flight of concrete steps leading to the top. I tried running up the concrete but it was much too painful. So I got onto the grass and scrambled my way to the summit. The view was worth all the effort. I found myself standing on the shores of a vast artificial lake whose opposite shore appeared to be a mile away. There was a slight breeze blowing up there and I just sat and cooled off for a while.

Going back down the hill, sliding on the grass, I found an amused priest smiling at my undignified descent. There was a surprise! The priest, in a saffron robe seemed to be just a child! I pointed to my cameras and then to him. He smiled, giving assent, so he was recorded on my film. I asked my driver if he knew about the young priest. He did. When the boy was born, as is the custom there, his horoscope was cast and it showed that he would become a priest at age twelve. So it was ordained; and so he had to be admitted into the tremendous Sri Lankan Buddhist priesthood. At the department of archaeology they told me that thousands of Buddhist priests live in caves on the island. The archaeologists expressed their wish that they could get the priests to move out so they could examine the caves. A vain desire, they said.

The driver left me to my wanderings. I looked at everything, including a large mass of granite to which I seemed to be strangely attracted. I climbed onto a ledge around which I came across a couple of ancient rock carvings. One of them I recognized immediately. I had seen reproductions of this in Colombo, as well as pictures in books on ancient art. About two feet square and not an erotic carving, it depicted two lovers in an embrace. That was a thrilling moment. I climbed down and got to a large granite ritual pool into which a priest was dipping one foot to test the heat of the water, I guessed.

Then I started to look for the Bo tree. I knew it was in an elevated garden and so my eyes were turned upwards. Soon I could see such a garden above a small open air place of worship. I had to go up a few steps and found myself facing another shrine. There were three people, two men and a woman, standing in front of a table behind which were two little statues of Buddha. Just as I got there, one of the men, not a robed priest, started chanting in a very deep rasping tone that didn't sound at all musical. For a couple of minutes I watched until I realized that the other man and the woman were crying. It was politic that I not intrude and walked around the side of the little shrine and looked up at the garden which seemed to be full of verdant trees. There were two iron fences, one at ground level and the other around the garden, both festooned with bright pieces of cloth on which were painted, I imagine, prayers. Because of these, it was impossible for me to see anything in the garden clearly and the gate leading to the stairs to the garden was padlocked. So all I could do was take a lot of photographs in the hope that when my slides were projected onto a screen I would see more than I could with my naked eye.

Just as I turned to leave, I became aware of a tall bespectacled saffron-robed priest standing just behind me. I said, "Good afternoon." "Good afternoon" he answered. Then came the big surprise. The priest said "Your driver is a friend of mine and he told me that you did a very nice thing, taking off your shoes before coming into Anuradhapura. It wasn't necessary, you know." "Well," I replied, "it seemed the respectful thing to do." The priest told me that such reverence from someone who was not a Buddhist deserved recognition and that he was the "Bo Priest" and that he was going to take me up to the tree. He produced some keys, unlocked the gate at the bottom of the stairway and another at the top. I was in the garden which had a set of fancy golden railings around. He led me to one spot and said, "Here is the Bo tree." I looked and saw the bole of a tree which had been cut off, at about four feet, and capped with metal. From two feet below the cap emerged a healthy leafy bough, several feet long, which was supported near its top by a forked metal stand. Not taking anything for granted, I asked the "Bo Priest" if I might photograph the sacred tree. He had no objection. I then photographed the priest, holding onto the golden railing, and the figures of elephants which were placed as though supporting the garden. That was serendipity. The amazing pleasant experience caused by an unplanned series of actions.

Surprisingly, the priest refused to accept some proffered money from me. I say "surprisingly," because Buddhist priests are mendicants; and although not permitted to verbally ask for alms, and need money or food for subsistence, they are allowed to accept them when offered. I shook hands and parted with the priest, after getting his parents' address so I could send him some photographs, and sought out my driver. When I told him that I badly wanted the kind "Bo Priest" to have some money he told me to give it to him and he would get him to take it. This was done and the priest appeared, once more, to thank me for the gift which, he said, would pay for some stronger eyeglasses.

That was all for me at Anuradhapura, after a great spiritually uplifting day, and we set off on the drive to the mountain city of Kandy which, after Anuradhapura, became the capital of Sri Lanka. It was also the last to fall to the British. This city of 130 thousand is situated at an elevation of 1,600 feet on the banks of the Mahaweli river. This, too, is a holy place because it is the home of Dalada Maligawa, "The Temple of the Tooth." The tooth being a relic of the Buddha and said to have been smuggled into Sri Lanka, from India, in the hair of a princess. When we got there, I was taken to a restaurant where I filled the void left by having not eaten since early morning. There were some hotels (Kandy is a much-visited tourist city); but after a suggestion from my companion, I elected to spend the night out in the open air with just a thatched palm leaf roof for cover, for a charge the equivalent of two dollars. The next day I spent visiting the "Temple of the Tooth," walking around the University of Sri Lanka grounds, and paying a visit to the National Academy of Dance. At the Academy, thanks to my driver, I was fortunate enough to see some of the classes in action. The Kandy Dancers are world famous. After some lunch I went to the lovely Royal

Botanical Gardens and then, in the middle of the afternoon, I watched as dozens of elephants came for their daily bath in the river.

After that we high-tailed it back to Colombo and the Orient Pearl where I was warmly welcomed by the young assistant manager who told me his family was very excited about my proposed visit to their home for the new year celebration.

I went back to the Department of Archaeology the next morning to see about making arrangements for shipment of the promised bricks. Dr. Silva greeted me and asked how I had fared on my visit to Anuradhapura. He looked at me with some disbelief when I told him I had been right up to the Bo tree. I thought he felt I was pulling his leg. To test me, he asked me if I could describe the railings around the garden there. My description was accurate, and he then believed I had really managed the impossible and been permitted to see and photograph the tree. Then he told me his story. A few years earlier, he had been approached by some priests and invited to meet them in Anuradhapura. As mentioned earlier, Dr. Silva, a Buddhist, is an architectural archaeologist and had studied design in England and what the priests wanted was for him to see the layout of the Bo tree garden and design some decorative railings to replace some centuries-old iron ones. He said that, for the first time, he got to see the Bo tree, a sight he'd never believed possible. He had submitted his design, which was accepted, but was not invited back to see them after they had been cast and erected!

I met with four of the people at the department and was told that I didn't have to wait for the ancient bricks to be brought in but that they would ship them by air to the museum in Tennessee. One of the archaeologists, named Siran Deraniyagala, brought me the copy of the brick detailing of the mountainous dagoba I had seen. He also gave me his address and invited me to spend the new year's eve at his home! That was embarrassing, to say the least. I told him I would have to check on the flights and would get back to him. I was in a pretty pickle. Here I had promised to attend another celebration and now I was faced with turning down "the hand that had fed me." Fortunately, the matter was resolved for me.

I was invited to walk over to visit the museum just across the way from the Department of Archaeology. It had just been started in that location and it didn't have a very large display. The first thing that caught my attention was a fabulous large alabaster figure of Buddha. It sat there with its hands in the lap exuding peace and relaxation. The photo I took of it is one of my favorites. There was an ancient throne, a carved wooden figure of an ancient king and, ("what's that?") hanging on a wall was a carved wooden piece with a ladle exactly like the one I had been offered, for a price, in the curio shop in the city. There was enough on show to give a visitor an overview of the island's history. Returning to the department I was immediately surrounded by half a dozen staff members who excitedly told me that the news had just been announced that Ceylon Air, my carrier to Bombay, had gone bankrupt and their offices were closed. My seat had been booked on a flight leaving three days later. As far as I knew there was no other way of getting back to Bombay for a flight home. Someone mentioned that he thought that Swissair stopped in Bombay on its flight to Zurich and that they might accept my Air India/Ceylon Air ticket and either fly me to Zurich or, at least, get me to Bombay.

I made a dash to the Swissair office and explained my predicament. The agent told me that they had a flight leaving early the next evening for Bombay and Zurich and that they would contact Air India and get permission to accept my tickets. A visit to Zurich would be very nice, I told them. If this could be worked out, I'd spend a couple of days there before catching a plane to the States. They told me to get back to them the first thing the next morning. So I left, had another fine lunch, which was also photographed for the record, and then returned to Edinburgh Crescent where I thanked all the fine archaeologists who had been so helpful. Everything there had been so positive and lacking red tape; quite the opposite of the Indian authorities. I was disappointed that I would miss the new year eve celebration; however, this way nobody's feelings would be hurt, since failure to attend was not of my doing.

The next morning I telephoned Swissair who told me that Air India refused to permit the transfer of all my ticket. All they would agree to was a seat on Swissair as far as Bombay. That was somewhat of a relief, though I had already begun thinking about my first visit to Zurich. I left the Orient Pearl that afternoon and went to the Swissair office where I got a boarding pass for the evening flight. At my request, the agent called Air India in Bombay and, again, tried to get permission to take me all the way to Switzerland. I thought if they contacted a different person they might be successful. No Luck.

I arrived at Bombay airport at midnight and immediately tried to check in at Air India. There was only one, very surly, agent at the counter. He pompously told me that the seats were all reserved and my name was not listed. Again, I tried to get transferred to Swissair whose plane wasn't due to leave for another thirty minutes. Again, no dice. The Air India agent wrote my name up on a blackboard and told me I would be the first one on standby. I looked for a place to sit from where I could keep an eye on the Air India agent and his board.

The place was so crowded there wasn't a seat to be found anywhere. Dozens of people were sitting or lying on the floor! From a vantage point I stood with my eyes glued on the door leading to the plane. From time to time, one or two pretty young Indian girls, obviously stewardesses, smiled at the agent, waved a pass at him, and went through the door. After about an hour, I walked over to chat with the agent for British Airways. Hearing my complaint he said if I had come to him even as recently as fifteen minutes earlier he would have put me on a B.A. plane which had just left for London. He said he would have accepted the Air India ticket. It was too late and all he could do was commiserate. Back at my vantage point, my feet aching from so much standing, I watched about a dozen more pretty young ladies pass through to the plane without having a ticket. Looking at the standby board I saw that mine was the only name there. After four hours, during which I approached the agent several times to no avail, I went back to him and said the time had come for a decision to be made. His response was that his decision was that I would have to wait until the following afternoon to get on a plane. Then I had a little forceful conversation with him.

"I have seen enough stewardesses board the plane to serve three planes. Obviously they are going to London for a holiday and have no right to be occupying seats when you have paying passengers on standby."

"That is none of your business."

"It certainly is my business! Give me your Black Book."

"I haven't got a Black Book and even if I had one that, too, is none of your business."

"Of course you have a Black Book and I shall give you two options. Either you get one of the girls off the plane, she must have family here, or I get your Book. If you don't give me the Book, I'll bring one of the police officers over and let him decide. They know you cannot refuse to let me write in it."

After this exchange, angrily he picked up a phone which was connected to the plane and shouted into it. A minute later a girl with tears on her cheeks came off the plane. I felt a little sorry for her but knew it would be much easier for her to stay the night in Bombay than me. The agent scowled at me, waved me on, and I boarded the crowded plane where a hostess showed me to a seat next to a young lady who turned to me and said, "You mustn't feel sorry for the girl who just left. Her home is here in Bombay and she can go on holiday tomorrow."

Because of the stops and delays for aircraft changes, it took me 34 hours to get back to Tennessee! The bricks were flown over, as promised; however instead of ten they sent us eighteen...one from each of eighteen centuries. These were later driven to the Sri Lankan embassy, in Washington, where the ambassador, His Excellency Dr. W.S. Karunaratne, made a formal presentation of the artifacts to the C.E.O of the General Shale Museum of Ancient Brick.

CHAPTER 11

OTHER SUCCESSES

A number of the specimens in the Museum of Ancient Brick have come very easily as the result of a lot of letter writing and telephoning, often overseas. Some have been obtained within a matter of months and others as a result of many years of persistent prodding.

Take Greece, for instance. For almost three decades I tried to get permission to visit that classical country in order to take just one brick from any ancient site. I approached every new Greek ambassador and each time was abruptly turned down. Then, in 1990, after a twenty-seven year wait I received a document authorizing me to remove one piece from each of two sites. This firman was signed by the Minister of Culture, Melina Mercouri the famous actress. ("Never on Sunday.") One of the sites was the well known city of Mycenae. The other was Gla, a prehistoric acropolis apparently only know to Greek Archaeologists, located near the town of Thiva (Thebes). I spent a week in Athens during which I visited the Parthenon and other area historic buildings and places, while waiting for the Director of Antiquities to return to the city for a meeting with me. He was most helpful and made phone calls to a couple of museums in the country requesting their personnel to give me all the help they could, as well as presenting me with beautifully illustrated guidebooks to two Athens' museums. I traveled to the sites, got my brick at each place, secured my export license and flew back home with my trophies in a well-constructed case.

Then there is a brick from The Great Wall of China. For nineteen years I wrote flowery letters to several people whose names had been given to me as good leads. For nineteen years I received not a single reply. Then, one day while visiting my daughter in Northern Virginia, I got a message from my secretary telling me to contact a Mr. Wang at the Embassy of the Peoples Republic of China. I telephoned there immediately and asked for Mr. Wang. "Which one?" asked the receptionist, "We have ten Mr. Wangs."

At my request she started to call each office. The fourth one found the correct gentleman whose name was Wang Zi Ping who amazed me by telling me that there was a brick from the Wall awaiting formal presentation. I went into D.C. and met Mr. Wang who showed me the "treasure." It was inside a box, which was covered with a brown textured cloth, with lid held down by a series of loops and ivory pegs. I opened the box and found that it was lined with padded blue silk upon which rested the brick. It bore an inscription which Mr. Wang said showed it was from a portion of the wall, at Beijing, which had been rebuilt in 1584 during the 11th year of the reign of the Ming emperor Wan Li. The formal presentation by the ambassador to General Shale's George C. Sells took place in the embassy's Great Hall, with lip-smacking Chinese wines, canapes, and a couple of speeches.

Some years ago, when we still had diplomatic relations with Iraq, I got a letter from the Deputy Director of Antiquities, in Baghdad, inviting me to visit that country and select some specimens of ancient brick. The writer's name was spelled the same as mine, except for the omission of an "f." Previously, at his government's request I had sent a set of slides with a taped commentary on U.S. brickmaking over there and Dr. Safer thanked me for that gesture and said, when I arrived in his country, he would act as a personal guide and take me around the major archaeological sites. That was great until I tried to get a visa for Iraq. I had made the acquaintance of the Cultural Attache at their D.C. embassy and I told him I would fly to Baghdad after leaving Pakistan. He said, "Wonderful, Basil. I'll send you a visa application form which I shall see is expedited." This gentleman with whom I became very close friends, and who had entertained me with dinner at his home, knew I was Jewish; but that had made no difference to our relationship even though his government was virulently anti-Zionist.

I had just finished re-arranging my schedule so as to include Iraq when I got a call from my friend (for his possible safety, I shall not name him) telling me that there was a problem with my visa application and that I should go to his embassy as soon as possible. We met in his office where he told me that since I had stated my religion as Jewish on the application, his Ambassador couldn't issue the visa. Visas for Jewish visitors had to be issued out of Baghdad. We visited the Ambassador who hinted that I should fill out a new application and think of something else to list as my religion. I asked His Excellency if he would deny his faith. He said not and that he shouldn't have even suggested it. I told them I had booked a seat on a flight to Baghdad and would chance trying to get in the country by just landing and announcing, "Here I am and I have an appointment at the Department of Antiquities." Both the ambassador and my friend begged me not to try that. Instead, they suggested that I give the Cultural Attache a list of the places from where I would like to have brick for our museum and they would see I got them. I wrote down the sites in my friend's office and we went out to lunch at a kosher restaurant.

When I arrived back from my successful expedition to Pakistan, I found a large crate from Iraq waiting for me. Inside were three fine specimens. They were: a brick from Nebuchadnezzar's Babylon (c.540 B.C.) with that king's name and titles stamped on: one from Nimrud (c.500 B.C.) completely covered with a cuneiform inscription: and one from Ur-of-the-Chaldees (c.3,000 B.C.), birth-place of Abraham. This was a nice gift from a not-so-nice country.

Ever since the partition of India into India and Pakistan, the two countries have had many squabbles, and two wars over   beautiful Kashmir. After some correspondence with the Indian Department of Antiquities, I managed to have them send me a 5,000 year-old brick from the Indus valley city of Kalibangan. The fired bricks there are the oldest fired brick ever discovered and a formal presentation was set up at the Indian Embassy. Mr. George C. Sells, C.E.O. of the General shale museum showed up to receive this great treasure. There was fighting in progress on the Indian continent and the ambassador was surrounded by a dozen reporters trying to get some comments about the war from the ambassador. However, when Mr. Sells stepped into the audience room, the ambassador, in a loud voice, said, "Here is Mr. Sells. Please leave us since we have something more important to talk about. We are going to discuss ancient bricks and drink some tea." So it was ordered; and so it was done.

Another, but more unusual, ambassadorial presentation was that made at the Yugoslavian embassy. I had learned of the discovery of a 2,000 year-old Roman brick yard at a place called Ptuj (pronounced, Tooee). After getting the brick aboard a Jug Air plane several of us showed up for the ceremony. Champagne was flowing all over the ambassador's office whilst the usual speeches were made. As we left the Embassy, the Yugoslavian Press Officer shouted. "I have the perfect publicity headline for the newspapers. "COMMU-NISTS PRESENT CAPITALISTS WITH IMPERIAL BRICK." Needless to say this was not used by the press but we then possessed a very unusual brick which had holes carved out to allow water pipes to be run through.

After a couple of years work we managed to secure a brick from the first Governor's Mansion, built in Australia at Parramatta. This was built in 1790 and the brick were made by a transported felon by the name of James Bloodworth. This rare brick, too, was the object of an ambassadorial presentation in D.C. The ambassador stated that this was the first, and the last, brick from that structure to leave Australia.

Another fine brick was sent to the museum by the government of Israel. It weighs 64 pounds and came from an Israelite fortification dating back to King Solomon (c.995 B.C.).

The Danish embassy was the scene of another presentation. The brick came from the first brick structure built in Denmark, at Soborg, in the late 12th century. I amazed the ambassador by addressing him in Danish. When I was in High School I paid two visits to that country and before making the second trip studied the language and learned enough to travel for several days without speaking a word of English.

To me, the prize specimen in the museum is a sundried mud brick (c.2,500 B.C.) which came from the remains of the ziggurat at Ur, which many biblical archaeologists believe was Tower of Babel. A very close look reveals the visual impression of a fingertip. If one lays his hand across the top of the brick, the fingers fall into grooves, while the thumbs automatically slide underneath to thumb depressions. By doing this you get the strange feeling that you are in touch with the hands that made and lifted the brick so many years ago.

So the hunt goes on. Whenever I see the word brick in a report of an archaeological discovery I immediately try to establish contact with the head of the expedition and see if a specimen can be spared for us from a demolished wall, providing we don't have a brick from that country and period already.